Parties, Elections, and
in the State o'

Daughtering and mothering

Sisterhood used to be the most powerful metaphor for relationships between women. Now there is a new interest in the mother–daughter relationship, which in all its complexity often acts as a better symbol of the diversity and difference inherent in women's relations in general. However, while recent theorizing has focused on the role of mothers and mothering, far less attention has been given to the active role taken by women as daughters. With this focus on daughtering, the book offers new conceptualizations to extend the normal boundaries of psychoanalytical theory.

Daughtering and Mothering develops its discussion from viewpoints in psychoanalysis and psychology, as well as cultural anthropology. The contributors take up three main themes, firstly on the sexual dimension of female subjectivity, challenging the notion that the father is necessarily the first sexual object. They also discuss contextual issues, examining women's roles in therapy, management and education, and in external relations in general. Finally they argue that the concept of 'good-enough-mothering' is an idealized version of the mother–daughter relationship, and one which can only enhance existing patterns of dominance by class, race or culture.

Challenging many ideas on motherhood and sexuality, this book will be of great interest to Gender and Women's Studies Departments and all psychologists and analysts interested in gender issues in their work.

Janneke van Mens-Verhulst, Karlein Schreurs and **Liesbeth Woertman** lecture at the University of Utrecht and have worked extensively on female identity development, feminist therapy and health care innovation.

mothers see daughters as doubles

daughters can find selves repeating mothers' lives
→ to break out, must be active

removal of mother prevents passage of traditional "womanhood" from moth to daughter - other women try to impress their ideas on daughter

Daughtering and mothering

Female subjectivity reanalysed

Edited by Janneke van Mens-Verhulst,
Karlein Schreurs and Liesbeth Woertman

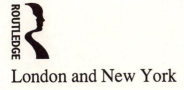

London and New York

First published 1993
by Routledge
11 New Fetter Lane, London EC4P 4EE

Simultaneously published in the USA and Canada
by Routledge
29 West 35th Street, New York, NY 10001

© 1993 Janneke van Mens-Verhulst, Karlein Schreurs and
Liesbeth Woertman

Typeset in 10 on 12 point Times by
NWL Editorial Services, Langport, Somerset

Printed and bound in Great Britain by
TJ Press (Padstow) Ltd, Padstow, Cornwall

British Library Cataloguing in Publication Data
A catalogue record for this book is available from the British Library.

Library of Congress Cataloging in Publication Data
Janneke van Mens-Verhulst
   Daughtering and mothering: Female subjectivity reanalysed / edited by
   Janneke van Mens-Verhulst, Karlein Schreurs, and
   Liesbeth Woertman
   p. cm.
   Includes bibliographical references and index
   1. Mothers and daughters.   2. Mothers and daughters – Psychology.
   3. Identity (Psychology)   I. Mens-Verhulst, Janneke van.   II. Schreurs,
   Karlein.   III. Woertman, Liesbeth, 1954–
   HQ755.85.D379   1993   93–14821
   306.874'3 – dc20   CIP

ISBN 0–415–08649–3 (hbk)
ISBN 0–415–08650–7 (pbk)

Contents

Contributors

Harriet Bjerrum Nielsen (Norway) is a linguist and is senior lecturer at the Institute of Educational Research, University of Oslo. Her research is gender socialization of children and young people at school and in their leisure time. She has published several articles and books. The most recent is *The story of boys and girls. Gender socialization in the perspective of developmental psychology.*

Luise Eichenbaum (USA) is a practising psychotherapist and supervisor. With Susie Orbach, she co-founded the Women's Therapy Centre in London in 1976, and with Susie Orbach and Carol Bloom she co-founded the Women's Therapy Center Institute in New York in 1981. She lectures throughout the UK, Europe and the United States on women's psychology, the difficulties between women and men today, and technical issues in psychotherapy. Luise lives in New York and Susie Orbach in London, but they try to work together on both continents as often as possible. They have published several articles and books, including *Understanding women: a feminist psychoanalytic approach* and *What do women want?*

Karin Flaake (Germany) is a sociologist and an instructor at the Department of Feminist Research of the Institute of Psychology, University in Berlin. She researches both gender-relationships in career development and psychoanalytic aspects of female identity.

Jane Flax (USA) is associate professor of Political Science at Howard University, Washington DC, and a psychotherapist in private practice. She is the author of many papers on political theory, philosophy, psychoanalysis and feminist theory which have appeared in a variety of journals and books including *Thinking fragments: Psychoanalysis, feminism and postmodernism in the contemporary west.*

Carol Gilligan (USA) is professor of education at the Human Development and Psychology Faculty at the Harvard Graduate School of Education. She began writing about women's development and psychological theory in 1977, when her article 'In a different voice: Women's conceptions of self and morality' was published in the *Harvard Educational Review*. Her most recent publication, co-authored with Lyn Mikel Brown, is *Meeting at the crossroads: women's psychology and girls' development*.

Martine Groen (the Netherlands) is a social scientist and a feminist psychotherapist. She co-founded the Moon Foundation, the first Dutch Women's Therapy Centre, and worked with prostitutes. She has published on prostitution, longterm relationships and feminist therapy.

Judith Jordan (USA) is director of Women's Studies and assistant director of Training in Psychology at McLean Hospital, Belmont, Massachusetts; instructor of Psychology at Harvard Medical School; and visiting scholar at the Stone Center, Wellesley College. She is the author of several of the Stone Center's publications.

Ruth de Kanter (the Netherlands) is a psychologist at the Department of Developmental Psychology at Utrecht University. She has been a feminist therapist for several years, and specializes in the development of gender identity in children in different family arrangements; lesbian mothering, donor insemination and fathering, and has published several articles on these topics.

Madelien Krips (the Netherlands) studied social work. She was a co-founder of the Moon Foundation, the first Dutch Women's Therapy Centre, and is involved in projects aimed at the introduction of feminist mental health care in regular mental health care institutions. She lectures at the Institute for Courses on Women's Mental Health Care in Utrecht, and has published several articles in Dutch.

Halldis Leira (Norway) is a psychologist and lecturer at the Psychology Department, University of Oslo. She also works as a psychotherapist at a child and youth psychological polyclinic. She has written several articles, including the essay: 'Can conception of the impossible become recognition of the possible?', which was awarded the best article of the year prize by the Journal of the Norwegian Psychological Association.

Nina Lykke (Denmark) is a linguist and associate professor and director of the Department of Feminist Studies, Odense University. She has published several articles and two books on feminism and psychoanalysis; *Rødhatte og Ødipus* ('Little Red Riding Hood and Oedipus') was published in Danish in 1989. She is also engaged in research on the semiotics of gender, nature and technology.

Janneke van Mens-Verhulst (the Netherlands) initiated the Loosdrecht Conference on 'Daughtering and Mothering'. She is a social scientist lecturing at both the Department of Clinical and Health Psychology and the Department of

Women's Studies of Utrecht University. Her areas of interest are innovations in Mental Health Care using recent insights from second order cybernetics and chaos theory. She is involved in many research projects on theory development in support of mental health care for women. Her publications are mainly in Dutch.

Susie Orbach (UK) co-founded the Women's Therapy Centre in London in 1976, and The Women's Therapy Center Institute in New York 1981. She is a practising psychotherapist and supervisor and lectures throughout the UK, Europe and the United States on women's psychology, the difficulties between women and men today, and technical issues in psychotherapy. She is the author of *Fat is a feminist issue* and has published several articles and books with Luise Eichenbaum including *Understanding women: a feminist psychoanalytic approach* and *What do women want?*

Annie Rogers (USA) is assistant professor in the Human Development and Psychology Program at the Harvard Graduate School of Education, a founding member of the Harvard Project on Women's Psychology and Girls' Development, and a psychology tutor at Adams House at Harvard. She is currently finishing her book *Two playing: a feminist poetics of psychotherapy.*

Monica Rudberg (Norway) is a psychologist and senior lecturer at the Institute of Educational Research, University of Oslo. In the past decade, she has conducted research projects on the history of childhood and on gender socialization in youth culture. She has published several articles and books, the latest being *The story of boys and girls. Gender socialization in the perspective of developmental psychology.*

Janet Sayers (UK) teaches psychology, social work, and women's studies at the University of Kent. She is also a psychoanalytic psychotherapist with a small private practice. Previous books include *Biological politics, sexual contradictions* and *Mothering psychoanalysis*. She is currently writing a collection of feminist psychoanalytic case histories – *The man who never was* (working title).

Karlein Schreurs (the Netherlands) is a psychologist. She lectures at the Department of Clinical and Health Psychology at the University of Utrecht. She has carried out research on lesbian identity development, sexuality and intimate relationships. She has published several articles and a number of books in Dutch.

Janet Surrey (USA) is a research associate at the Stone Center, Wellesley College. She is also instructor in Psychiatry, Harvard Medical School and director of Psychological Services of the outpatient clinic, McLean Hospital, Belmont Massachusetts. She has written several articles for the *Stone Center Working Papers collection.*

Mieke de Waal (the Netherlands) is a cultural anthropologist. She is interested in research on sexuality, cultural minorities, non-verbal communication and photography. Her Ph.D. research was awarded the '1990 J.C. Ruigrok' prize of the Dutch Scientific Society.

Liesbeth Woertman (the Netherlands) is a psychologist. She lectures at the Department of Clinical and Health Psychology at the University of Utrecht on both the socialization of gender and sexuality in addition to research on body and self-image of women. She is also a therapist working with women victims of incest or rape.

Acknowledgements

The history of this volume begins during preparations for Utrecht University's 355th anniversary. As part of the celebrations, Janneke van Mens-Verhulst proposed a major international conference on Daughtering and Mothering. The idea won the support of the Department of Clinical and Health Psychology at the university, and the organizers are extremely grateful to Professors Cohen and Dijkhuis for their enthusiastic support for this women's endeavour.

The actual realization of the conference is due in part to the guarantee subsidy provided by the National Fund for Mental Health, financial contributions from the Institute for Courses on Women's Health Care, and the co-operation of the De Maan Women's Mental Health Care Project.

The so-called Loosdrecht Conference was held in September 1991 and was attended by twenty-nine participants from eight countries: Rosi Braidotti, Kathy Davis, Luise Eichenbaum, Mary Fischer, Karin Flaake, Jane Flax, Ingrid Foeken, Helmi Goudswaard, Martine Groen, Judith Jordan, Thea Heddes, Ruth de Kanter, Myra de Keizer, Patricia Klein Frithiof, Madelien Krips, Halldis Leira, Nina Lykke, Janneke van Mens-Verhulst, Anja Meulenbelt, Susie Orbach, Georgie Oudemans-MacLean, Ine van Oijen, Renée Römkens, Monica Rudberg, Janet Sayers, Karlein Schreurs, Selma Sevenhuijsen, Janet Surrey and Mieke de Waal.

It turned out to be an inspiring event. The insights which came together there in the form of essays and papers have been used to form the basis of the book.

Of the participants, sixteen agreed to participate in the realization of this volume. If we take the debunking of the motherhood myth as example, we find the theoretical background to the practical work of Madelien Krips from Holland expanded by Halldis Leira of Norway. We are also fortunate in that Harriet Bjerrum Nielsen, Carol Gilligan, Annie Rogers and Liesbeth Woertman later agreed to contribute.

We would like to express our thanks to Kathy Davis for her advice, and to Springer Verlag for permission to include a shortened version of an article Judith Jordan had published with them.

Editing an English-language publication with twenty authors from six different language areas is a hopeless task for non-native speakers. The fact that the whole project came together is in part due to the efforts of Anne Lavelle. This book would not have been possible without her careful translations, integral language revisions and journalistic advice. Marjolein Kok of Logitekst took the piles of paper and using DTP transformed them into a manuscript.

The editors

Introduction

Janneke van Mens-Verhulst

In the seventies, the most powerful metaphor for relationships between women was that of sisterhood. This obtained not only in the women's liberation movement, but also in the contexts of educational organizations and therapy centres. Real mothers were rare animals, or had to pretend to be, if they wanted to be part of the scene. The role of mothers was primarily symbolic, limited to psychotherapists' couches or therapy groups for women.

In the nineties, there is a revival of interest in the metaphor of the mother–daughter relationship. This revival is undoubtedly linked to a growing consciousness that differences between women are part of everyday reality at work, if not at home; especially differences in age and power. The female pioneers of then are now confronted with a new generation of women who, biologically speaking, could be their daughters. The older, professional women find younger women looking to them for advice, attention and empathy. Women teachers, therapists and bosses see themselves treated as symbolic mothers, supposed to offer the same, or even more, care and protection than real mothers ever could. Frequently, the 'nominal' mothers do not know how to turn dependence into in(ter)dependence, and often cannot cope with the emotions that charge these processes. If they do not offer the desired support, they will be blamed for it. If they do offer it, they sometimes find themselves blaming or persecuting the clients, students or employees involved for not being grateful enough. The other side of the coin is that the younger women are not always conscious of their positions as symbolic daughters, and are equally unable to unravel the emotional and social bind in which they are caught. The end may even be a situation of merged depression; of mutual powerlessness, reproach and criticism. Or, in another scenario, a situation wherein both parties are hurt by prevalent insensitivity and numbness, caused perhaps by mutual efforts to avoid conflicts.

A better understanding of the dynamics between mothers and daughters could be helpful in understanding the dynamics between women in general, not only in the family, but also in the context of management, education and therapy. The relationship between mothers and daughters is seen as an archetype of real and symbolic generation differences between women. However, the usefulness of the mother–daughter metaphor for acquiring insights and dealing with the emotional problems involved is restricted by a number of severe theoretical limitations and gaps. Until recently, relationships between women were usually described from a 'male' perspective. This implies a great emphasis on heterosexuality, a lot of attention for the mediative function of the father, and an almost unconditional belief in the necessity of autonomy as a state of adulthood. All this happened at the expense of understanding lesbianism, the mediative function of the mother, the inevitability of human interdependence, and the joy of connection. The theories are also biased towards stressing the active, intervening side of motherhood, and the passive, submissive side of daughterhood – thus adhering to the image of an adult and a juvenile; perhaps even offender and victim. In general, the problems of the daughter are met with much more compassion than the problem of the mother.

This book provides analyses of many aspects of mother–daughter relationships that were hitherto neglected or ignored. It starts from the premise that daughters and mothers both take an active part in shaping their relationship. That is why the term 'daughtering' is put forward, along with the term 'mothering'. If mothering can be defined as actions and activities related to the role of mothers (usually conceived of as daily care of the young – looking after them, raising them in an intense and emotional relationship), daughtering must be understood as all the actions and activities inherent to the role of daughters. Therefore, daughtering implies being involved in an originally dependent relationship involving being cared for by older or more powerful people. However, the concept does not define how this care is received: whether the recipient wallows in it, welcomes it, tries to reciprocate, or resist it. This emphasis on the active, intervening side of daughterhood facilitates the articulation of the problems of mothers from a 'motherly' point of view. An underlying theme in daughtering and mothering is also exposed: the spontaneous development of female subjectivity as opposed to intervening practices managed more or less consciously, arranged more or less intentionally and professionally by 'established' female subjects. Finally, the psychological paradigm behind theorizing on female subjectivity is reanalysed and revalued, and connections are made to the general psychological theorizing on becoming a subject, in particular by Jordan.

The following sections offer a multidisciplinary collection of essays on daughtering and mothering introduced by extensive examinations of current theory and the role of these new insights, by Schreurs, Woertman and van Mens-Verhulst. The contributions stem from clinical, developmental, social and cultural psychology, and from cultural anthropology. They refer to family, therapy and teaching practices, involving a total of three debates on the development of female subjectivity.

One debate concerns the sexual dimension of female subjectivity and the role of mother therein. The assumption that sexuality in girls awakens during the Oedipal period and that father is the first sexual object is challenged. Lykke argues that the mother is the first object of their daughter's sexual feelings. This neglect of erotic feeling in girls for their mothers stems from a taboo on homosexuality.

Moreover, mothers play an important role in the experiences of the body and sexuality during adolescence and adulthood, as is illuminated by Flaake and Sayers. Flax stresses the development of sexual identity as a continuous, lifelong process.

A second debate centres on contextual influences on mothering and daughtering. A major issue here is which people or events are deemed indispensable in intervention in the assumed symbiosis of mothers and daughters if a daughterly connection with the 'external' or 'real' world is to be established. Should it be an outsider, a male, a critical moment of discovering 'the' sex difference; or do women themselves fulfil this function, as mothers, (girl)friends, teachers and therapists? Inspiring analyses are offered by de Kanter, de Waal, Bjerrum Nielsen and Rudberg, Gilligan and Rogers, Orbach and Eichenbaum, and Surrey.

A third debate challenges dominant ideas on motherhood and female adulthood. It questions notions on the one and only 'good' way of mothering, and even the idea of 'good-enough-mothering'. The argument posed here is that the mothering ideal should actually be mistrusted because it keeps alive infantile fantasies, and supports relations of dominance between classes, races and cultures. The contributions of Sayers, Leira, Krips, Groen, and also Gilligan, Surrey and Flax offer an insight into some of these previously hidden functions of mothering.

Against the backdrop of these three debates, questions are raised on the inadequacy of the language available to support thinking about daughters and mothers. New concepts and distinctions are proposed, sometimes explicitly, sometimes implicitly.

In several chapters (Leira and Krips, Groen, and also Flax) endeavours are made to reflect upon attributions made too easily and too obviously from a white, North-European and Anglo-American point of view. These contributions attempt to combat an unrealistic geographical and cultural centrism in the theorizing on daughtering and mothering. However, the presented texts here will unavoidably be 'coloured' by the social backgrounds of the twenty authors and editors. Actually, we are all white, professional women, ranging from thirty to fifty-two years old. Among us are at least thirteen 'real' mothers, biological and non-biological ones, hetero- and homosexual-oriented, and we are mothering nine daughters, aged between two and twenty, alongside an unknown number of sons.

Part I

Daughtering

Chapter 1

Daughtering
The development of female subjectivity

Karlein Schreurs

Many students in social sciences (about two-thirds are women) appear to have an aversion to an explicit feminist view of science and therapy. They argue that the process of women's emancipation has been completed, that everyone has the same opportunities, and that discrimination against women has disappeared. Unfortunately, this is wishful thinking. Female students hope they will not be confronted with difficult choices and ambivalences stemming from their womanhood. Nowadays, women certainly have more options in deciding how they want to shape their lives. However, this does not mean that more subtle mechanisms have lost their impact.

If we look at education, then we find that girls have caught up with boys, and approximately the same number of girls and boys now get a college education. Boys, however, are overrepresented in the sciences, and girls in the humanities. When choosing a profession, boys tend to take into account market principles, whereas girls decide more on the basis of a caring perspective. In short, at first sight things seem to have changed fundamentally, but careful examination shows that changes filter through at a slow pace. In other words, apparent changes are often no more than that; gender roles are changing faster than the psychological make-up of women and men. So, if we want to understand female subjectivity, we will have to theorize both on constant aspects in women's lives and on the changes which certainly exist.

Object relations theory, as elaborated by Chodorow (1978), offers explanations for the constancy in the inner world of women. Some main points of this theory will be summarized here. Chodorow claims that mothering is reproduced by women and passed on to the next generation of women. The first human bond of both girls and boys is usually that with their mother. Because gender is an important aspect of individuals in our culture, difference becomes especially salient for boys and men. In contrast, sameness is important in the lives of girls and women. In order to achieve a male identity, boys have to separate from their mother and identify with their father, who is usually absent for much of the time. This leads to rigid ego boundaries in boys, and to a negatively-formulated identity, i.e. male equates with 'not-female'. As this paper is concerned with daughtering, the development of boys will not be considered here.

Girls do not have to draw such strict boundaries between themselves and their mothers; they do not have to separate as radically from their mothers, nor do they have to repress this bond. Instead of rigid ego boundaries, they develop permeable ego boundaries. Fundamentally, women feel connected to the world around them; female identity is mainly a relational identity. These aspects of female identity lead girls to accept the greatest share of mothering, and make attractive those professions in which relational and nursing capacities are required.

As stated above, Chodorow's theory can explain many of the constancies in women's lives. However, if this was the only scenario, we cannot explain changes and shifts. If we apply this theory rigidly, it predicts chains of mothering mothers. Moreover, women themselves would not be able to break these chains. Change would only be possible by intervention from outside, for instance through changed educational practices.

Changes in constancy or constancies in changes are the leitmotif running through the contributions in the first part of this book. In some articles the object relations paradigm is supplemented and differentiated. Other contributions offer alternatives to object relations theories.

One limitation of object relations theories is their neglect of the body in mother–daughter relationships. As a consequence, important aspects of physical experience, sexuality and eroticism in women's lives cannot be understood. Object relations distinguish the pre-Oedipal from the Oedipal phase. In the pre-Oedipal phase, the bond with the mother is central. The bond with the father develops in the Oedipal phase. The oral, anal and phallic phases, which are distinguished in drive theories, are seen as paralleling these object relational phases (Tyson and Tyson, 1990). The first experiences of genital lust are placed in the Oedipal phase, and the role of the father is supposed to be of central importance. However, observations of female babies and toddlers show that they discover their genitals much earlier than in the Oedipal period, and that they masturbate at an earlier age (cf. Galenson, 1990). Let us consider the care of (female) babies which is usually done by their mothers. Babies are usually suckled by their mothers, the body against which they normally nestle is their mother's, mothers touch their babies' genitals and buttocks when changing nappies. Even if fathers participate in the caring, exclusive care by fathers is almost nonexistent. So it is difficult to imagine how mothers could avoid 'awakening' genital sensations in girls. As a consequence, mother must be the girl's first object of genital lust. This line of reasoning is elaborated by Lykke. She proposes distinguishing a new 'Antigone' phase in the development of girls. In this phase, the girl's awakening sexual feelings are directed at the mother.

If we accept that mothers play a role in eroticism and the lust experience of their daughters, does this mean that they validate their daughters in this respect? Fathers make tender utterances, such as 'What a little flirt my best girl is'. However, mothers would rarely use similar approaches with their daughters because of the taboo on homosexuality. But there is more at stake here, as Flaake's contribution shows. In our culture, the beauty, attraction and desirability of the female body is defined by way of an object position in male lust experience. On the other hand, those bodily processes linked to reproduction, e.g. menstruation, have negative connotations. Therefore, most women will not feel as though they 'inhabit' their own bodies, and will develop a negative body image. Based on object relations theories, Flaake states that mothers pass on this negative body image to their daughters, and this chain can only be broken when mothers themselves develop positive body images and experience sexuality in a positive way. Generally, therapy will be necessary to accomplish this goal. In Flaake's contribution, one sees again the power of object relation theories as tools to explain constancies in women's lives. However, change can only be brought about through outside intervention. Is therapy really the only way? Or are we blind to other ways because our thinking is restricted by the straitjacket of object relations theories?

A second way of integrating change and constancy is by contextualizing both the position of the mother and that of the daughter. Daughters separate from their mothers. De Kanter criticizes the vision on the mother–daughter relationship as a universal bond independent of social context. She argues that this relationship is always imbedded in a cultural and social environment. This author sees separation as a task for daughters in their process of becoming women in their own specific social context. Therefore, they must perceive their mothers as women in all their different roles, positions and contexts. In short, daughters become 'situated' women and mothers are 'situated' women.

A method of placing mother–daughter relationships in a social context can be found in De Waal's contribution. She emphasizes the arrangements in which interactions between mothers and daughters take place. Paralleling the general informalization of social relations, these interactions resemble more the negotiations between equals than the disciplining of behaviour by an authority. However, De Waal shows that even under these 'democratic' conditions, mothers seem to have the last word. Daughters respond to this with their own strategies.

De Waal picks up on some constancies and changes over generations of women. Bjerrum Nielsen and Rudberg elaborate this theme further. They distinguish gender identity from gendered subjectivity. Gendered subjectivity refers to a gender-specific way of relating to the world and oneself. Gender identity is the meaning girls and women attribute to being biologically female. Bjerrum Nielsen and Rudberg state that changes in gendered subjectivity are not paralleled by changes in gender identity. As a consequence, the different generations of women, i.e. grandmothers, mothers, daughters and granddaughters, have to deal with different conflicts. Using this distinction in gendered subjectivity and gender identity, these authors are able to place mothers and daughters in a chronological context.

To summarize, object relations theories are the main frame of reference in this first part of the book. These theories are dealt with in three different ways. Firstly, the importance of the body in the mother–daughter relationship and the role of the mother in the developing sexuality of the girl are emphasized in the contributions by Karin Flaake and Nina Lykke. Secondly, the necessity of contextualizing mother–daughter relationships is argued by Ruth de Kanter. Finally, alternatives to object relations theories for approaching the bond between mothers and their adolescent daughters are offered in the articles by Mieke De Waal and by Harriet Bjerrum Nielsen and Monica Rudberg. In this first section we concentrate on the side of the daughter in the relationship. The usefulness of object relations theories in understanding the mother's side in different contexts will be dealt with in part two.

REFERENCES

Chodorow, N. (1978) *The reproduction of mothering. Psychoanalysis and the sociology of gender*. Berkeley: University of California Press.
Galenson, E. (1990) 'Observation of early infantile sexual and erotic development'. In M.E. Perry (ed.), *Handbook of sexology, VII*. New York: Elsevier.
Tyson, Ph. and Tyson, R.L. (1990) *Psychoanalytic theories of development: an integration*. New Haven: Yale University Press.

Chapter 2

A body of one's own

Sexual development and the female body in the mother–daughter relationship

Karin Flaake

This article concentrates on a special aspect of the mother–daughter relationship, which has not been analysed as yet from a feminist perspective: the sexual development of girls and the relevance of the female body within the context of the mother–daughter relationship.

In psychoanalytic literature, it is the father who confirms and acknowledges the value of the daughter's femininity. Most authors legitimize the daughter's need to turn to the father by emphasizing a 'deficit' in the mother. Freud and other theorists who argue in this tradition presuppose a characterization of the mother in terms of an organic deficit. She lacks the only valuable genital, a penis, so the daughter turns away from her in disappointment. During the Oedipal phase the little girl turns to the father and only by this transfer can she achieve a femininity of any value (Freud, 1920; 1925; 1931). The fundamental notion in this construction is that neither mother nor daughter are able to value the female body.

Similarly, the French psychoanalyst Christiane Olivier (1984) argues that it is impossible for mothers to see their daughters' bodies as erotic, thereby precluding a positive image of the daughter's own female body. According to Olivier a positive evaluation of the female body can only be bestowed by men. A positive evaluation of the female body by women is unthinkable, and hence women's dependency on men is inevitable.[1]

There are other psychoanalytic approaches, for example Chodorow's (1978), which differ from the traditional approaches mentioned so far. These approaches are based on a feminist viewpoint linked to the object relations theory. They do not see the mother–daughter relationship as being based on a deficiency, but as highly valuable in emotional terms, and the relationship to the father as secondary. But these approaches hardly mention the body and sexuality. Their main interests are social and intrapsychic relational situations.[2] These theories thereby avoid a confrontation with an especially problematic dimension of female development: the relationship of women to their own body, and to their own sexuality, and the meaning of the mother–daughter relationship in this context.

Thus far, traditional psychoanalytic approaches to the mother–daughter bond, which are based on the idea of a deficiency as motive for orientation and dependency on men, can be understood as a mirror of a problematic reality. It is a reality in which women cannot enjoy their own bodies. The social reality is that the female body is a male-defined and occupied territory. Often women cannot see their sexuality as a genuine source of power, creativity and enjoyment, but remain oriented towards a male definition of female sexuality.[3] Under these social circumstances, the mother–daughter relationship precludes both the possibility of valuing the female body and the granting of space for female desire. Femininity therefore, is not based on one's own self worth, in which the mother shares her pride about the body and its pleasure, but rather its dependence on men for acknowledgement and value; the task falls on the father to acknowledge his daughter's femininity. It is only with the sense of otherness, the perception of the opposite sex, that bestows meaning on femininity.

These structures are not inevitable. They are the result of a social reality based on male dominance. To overcome this reality, it is important to understand the mechanisms by which devaluation of femininity is transferred from one generation to the next. In this context, I want to discuss the conditions under which women are able to appreciate their own bodies without depending on male acknowledgement, and thus provide confirmation of their daughters' sexuality in a positive way.

DAUGHTERS, MOTHERS AND SEXUALITY

Contemporary studies of developmental psychology show that children develop a sense of their own body, including genitals, during their second year (Chehrazi, 1988; Galenson and Roiphe, 1977; Glover and Mendell, 1982; Heigl-Evers and Weidenhammer, 1988; Kleeman, 1977). Starting at the age of 15 to 16 months old, girls discover their visible genitals and their vaginas. They discover their clitoris as a sensual organ, enjoying the pleasure of stimulation. These first experiences with their own sexuality become the foundation of a positive sense of their own bodies which is important for their later sexual development. Often the daughter's early discoveries of her own body are not welcomed by their mothers. Mothers prevent their daughters' bodily pleasures and sexual activities, and thus daughters are unable to develop a positive attitude toward it; they inhibit their daughters' development of a positive self image of their genitals. Observations of children – for example by Stern (1986) – have shown that the pleasurable discoveries of little girls irritate their mothers. For example, mothers ignored such activities and even prevented them. Harriet E. Lerner (1977) describes mothers' silence in naming the female genitals. This silence conveys the unconscious message that the daughter is not allowed to have sexual desires as well as ignoring or preventing autoerotic activities of the daughter.[4]

In her psychoanalytically-oriented study on groups of children Schmauch (1987) describes how problematic the development of girls can be for their mothers during the separation and individuation phase which starts at the age of two. The mother–daughter relationship appears to be relatively harmonious and unimpaired during the first two years. The relationship becomes conflictive as the girl develops her own identity as a sexual being, enjoying her growing autonomy and the erotic charm of her body. Many mothers cannot celebrate this development; they turn away temporarily from their daughters instead. With great insight Schmauch describes how a young girl's belief that her search for physical identity includes her movement, nakedness, erotic charm and the exploration of sexual pleasures causes her mother to turn away, and thus she loses the ability to enjoy these aspects of herself. She can no longer enjoy autonomy, nakedness and sexual activities, and therefore she loses her erotic charm. The girl returns to a presexual phase of development; her overt sexuality, the possibility of becoming an active, erotic object, and rival for the father disappears temporarily. Thus, Schmauch claims the mother's behaviour is influenced by her unconscious aspirations. She assumes that mothers unconsciously envy their daughters' sexual desire and autonomy because they themselves cannot fulfil their own desires and autonomy. The daughters remain dependent on their mothers, and thereby open to their mothers' needs.

In later developmental phases, the sexuality aspect of the mother–daughter relationship is similarly problematic. In adolescence, the girls' bodies develop to the state of womanhood, making it possible for them to discover their sexual desires in an adult way. Sociological and psychological studies show that mothers and daughters rarely discuss the full range of the daughters' sexual development, thus reducing it to a technical problem. At best, the mother informs her daughter about bodily functions, hygienic necessities and birth control. Discussions on these topics are primarily factual. Mothers and daughters do not speak about emotions, or the sensations accompanying the daughter's development; about desires or fantasies, about shame or pride concerning the body, about inner sensations during menstruation, or about the desire to explore the changing body or sexual preferences (Apter, 1990; Burger and Seidenspinner, 1988; Haase, 1992; Waldeck, 1988; 1992).

In her study on the societal conventions concerning menstruation, Waldeck (1988) has shown that mothers pass on their own limitations to their daughters by defining menstruation as 'dirty' – in accordance with the predominant view in our culture. The bleeding body has to be made invisible. Menstruation in another cultural setting can be a reason for celebration, something to be proud of, because it can mean that the girl has become a woman, and now has procreative powers. But in our culture, the mother's envy of her daughter, including the wide range of options available to her as a young woman today can be linked to the predominant views on menstruation which leave the daughter with the message: 'Your life is before you. You are young and beautiful, but that which makes you a woman is dirty and has to be hidden' (Waldeck, 1988: 342–3). This makes it difficult for the girl to be proud of her body, and to let her body become a centre for her female identity.

From the mother's perspective the bodily development of her daughter confronts her with the upcoming separation and her own aging process. It can remind the mother of her own unsatisfied sexuality, her own unfulfilled desire for autonomy, and her own problems with femininity. The daughter's growth into womanhood and the fact that her adult life lies before her can cause the mother to reflect on her own life; previous hopes and disappointments, gratification as well as her sense of limitations. What will happen when this balance is removed, how the mother perceives her future life, how she values her own physical womanhood and sexuality – all determine the nature of her relationship with her adolescent daughter.

A POSSIBLE WAY OUT

The Swiss psychoanalyst Hettlage-Varjas (1987) points to a possible way out of these mother–daughter bonds which pass on sacrifice, suffering and self-diminishment from one generation to the next. She stresses how necessary it is for the mother to separate from the daughter. This separation presupposes the mother's separation from her own mother. Such an inner separation prevents women from using their daughters to compensate for their own sufferings and oppressions (cf. the contribution of Orbach and Eichenbaum in this volume). As Hettlage-Varjas puts it:

> If we are able to realize that we are separate, we will be able to mourn our own dependencies to the point where we are today. We will be able to confront ourselves with our own sufferings, instead of filling the deficits by keeping our daughters dependent on us.
>
> (Hettlage-Varjas, 1987: 25)

Part of this process of inner separation from the mother is the ability to develop a sense of one's own body, including sexuality. This process is ongoing for many women throughout their entire lives. In their case histories, Torok (1974) and Laufer and Laufer (1984) have demonstrated that woman's inability to touch her own body joyfully is due to fantasies about her own body and her mother being an unseparated entity.[5] Torok sees the development of a sense of one's own body by overcoming the mother's prohibitions of autonomy and sexual desire as an important goal of psychoanalytic therapy. 'It is as if you had given me power' is what a patient said to Torok when she was able, for the first time, to touch herself sexually (Torok, 1974: 207). This patient felt a new power linked to 'confidence in her own abilities and her own future' (Torok, 1974: 207). This is the foundation on which it is possible to develop physically-based female consciousness, removing the exclusive power that men have had in defining the value of femininity. Mothers can also confirm their daughters' sexuality. In such a situation, mothers can teach their daughters a positive value of the female body; they are able to allow their daughters a sense of their own body as a primary source of satisfaction.

A prerequisite here is that the mother establishes a balance between devotion and establishing limitations, closeness with and distance from her daughter. This balance is important for both the acknowledgement of the daughter's autoerotic activities, and the mother's continuing approval for all of her other endeavours, providing her with a basis to separate from the mother.[6] Both are essential in the mother–daughter relationship; connectedness and inner separation, commonality and the recognition of differences.[7] The mother can then send this message to the daughter: your body, like mine, is female, it is good and valuable, and you can experience physical enjoyment and sexuality with your own body, independent of me. With this message, the girl can experience her own femininity as an autonomous source of enjoyment and creativity, and with this fundamental self-confidence, she is no longer exclusively dependent on the opposite sex for the acknowledgement of her femininity.

Today, only a few women will have had the chance to be brought up by mothers with such qualities. Female therapists could provide women with a second opportunity for socialization by offering an opportunity to develop a positive sense of their own body. Bell (1991) gives examples, drawn from her practical experience of patients wishing to be acknowledged by their mothers. This acknowledgement includes an erotic sense of their own body, and their need for an introduction to sexuality by their mothers. A desire to be acknowledged by the mother often plays a role in transference; these desires are described by Karin Bell as 'necessary steps in the direction of female identity' (Bell, 1991: 122). These desires often present themselves as homosexual fantasies. The patient, in her role as daughter, wants the therapist, as a representative of her mother, to play the part of a female companion. She longs for a relationship in which she can see herself as independent, but also feel secure, because the mother's sexuality is her point of reference for her own sexuality. In order to give patients the possibility of a new experience of sexual acknowledgement as an erotic being, therapists have to deal with their own homosexual wishes and anxieties. They have to transgress their homophobia.[8]

Women can make this positive experience of being acknowledged as erotic and autonomous entities in contexts other than the therapeutic. Opportunities exist wherever women deal with women, and are able to overcome the traditional pattern of the mother–daughter bond, which often influences relationships among women. In spite of their deficiencies and differences, it is essential that women can share their female-defined, positive attributes. This implies mutual support in developing a positive sense of one's own body, and in the discovery of one's desires.

NOTES

1 More differentiated, though similar in meaning, Heigl-Evers and Weidenhammer (1988) argue in favour of the necessity of men in the developmental unfolding of female sexuality and the acknowledgement of female physicality in their attempt to reconsider the basis of Freudian theory as it affects femininity.
2 According to Chodorow, erotic preoccupation appears to occur more frequently in the father–daughter relationship than in the mother–daughter relationship. She describes the female Oedipus complex: 'If there is an absolute component to the change of object, it is at most a concentration on her father of a girl's genital, or erotic, cathexis. But a girl never gives up her mother as an internal or external love object even if she does become heterosexual' (Chodorow, 1978: 127).

3   Lawrenz and Orzegowski (1988) outline how widespread such an orientation on male desire is among women, even today. They conducted interviews with women ranging in age from 21 to 32 about their sexual fantasies.

4   Simone de Beauvoir graphically describes how sexual desire was ignored by her mother in her book entitled *Memoirs of a dutiful daughter*. When she was 7 or 8 years old, she told her mother about a 'special sensation between her legs' and told her what she 'felt'. Her mother reacted 'with an indifferent look, spoke about something else and I believed that I had made an uncalled-for comment that didn't require an answer' (p. 39). So the discovered sensation of desire remained unacknowledged; 'I was not explorative enough to try it again, to relive the enjoyment once more' (p. 56).

5   Laufer and Laufer (1984: 75) describe two aspects of this phenomenon: 'One's own hand pleasurably touching one's own body is experienced as the mother's hand. The girl fears her only option for satisfaction is to passively relinquish herself to the mother. When her own genitals are unconsciously indistinguishable from the mother's, the girl's aggression for the mother becomes directed at herself. Both problems make clear how important it is for the girl to internally separate from the mother'. Torok (1974: 205) states, 'The effect of forbidding masturbation . . . the child chains her body to the mother and within this bondage, she lays out her own vital plans'. Pleasurable self-stimulation is understood by the girl as separation from the mother, as a step away from her dependent relationship with her.

6   Within the context of Winnicott's description of the ability to be alone, Hettlage-Varjas (1987) stresses that self-actualization can only occur in a protective environment. Benjamin (1988) views the tension between asserting oneself and recognition, autonomy and independence as detrimental components of the structural principles in the socialization process.

7   Benjamin (1988) emphasizes that mothers can only maintain this tension when they perceive themselves not only as mothers but also as women, as sexual beings with needs and interests apart from their relationship with their child.

8   A productive approach to homosexual seduction in a therapeutic setting is clearly described by Schmidt-Honsberg (1989).

REFERENCES

Apter, T. (1990) *Altered loves. Mothers and daughters during adolescence*. New York: St Martin's Press.

Beauvoir, S. de (1990) *Memoirs of a dutiful daughter*. Harmondsworth: Penguin.

Bell, K. (1991) 'Aspekte weiblicher Entwicklung'. *Forum der Psychoanalyse*, 7, 111–26.

Benjamin, J. (1988) *The bonds of love. Psychoanalysis, feminism and the problem of domination*. New York: Pantheon.

Brückner, M. (1990) 'Zwischen Kühnheit und Selbstbeschränkung. Von der Schwierigkeit weiblichen Begehrens'. *Zeitschrift für Sexualforschung*, 3, 195–217.

Burger, A. and Seidenspinner, G. (1988) *Töchter und Mütter. Ablösung als Konflikt und Chance*. Opladen: Leske & Budrich.

Chehrazi, S. (1988) 'Zur Psychologie der Weiblichkeit'. *Psyche*, 42, 307–27.

Chodorow, N. (1978) *The reproduction of mothering. Psychoanalysis and the sociology of gender*. Berkeley: University of California Press.

Dinnerstein, D. (1979) *The mermaid and the minotaur: Sexual arrangements and human malaise*. New York: Harper & and Row.

Flaake, K. (1990a) 'Erst der männliche Blick macht attraktiv'. *Psychologie Heute*, 1, 48–53.

Flaake, K. (1990b) 'Geschlechterverhältnisse, geschlechtsspezifische Identität und Adoleszenz'. *Zeitschrift für Sozialisationsforschung und Erziehungssoziologie*, 1, 2–13.

Freud, S. (1920) 'The psychogenesis of a case of homosexuality in a woman'. In *Standard edition of the collected works of Sigmund Freud. 18*. London: Hogarth.

Freud, S. (1925) 'Some psychical consequences of the anatomical distinction between the sexes'. In *Standard edition of the collected works of Sigmund Freud. 19*. London: Hogarth.

Freud, S. (1931) 'Female sexuality'. In *Standard edition of the collected works of Sigmund Freud. 21*. London: Hogarth.

Galenson, E. and Roiphe, H. (1977) 'Some suggested revisions concerning early female development'. In H.P. Blum (ed.), *Female psychology. Contemporary psychoanalytic views*. New York: International Universities Press.

Glover, L. and Mendell, D. (1982) 'A suggested developmental sequence for a pre-Oedipal genital phase'. In D. Mendell (ed.), *Early female development*. Lancaster: MTP.

Haase, H. (1992) 'Die Preisgabe. Überlegungen zur Bedeutung der Menstruation in der Mutter-Tochter-Beziehung'. In K. Flaake and V. King (eds), *Weibliche Adoleszenz. Beiträge zur Sozialisation junger Frauen*. Frankfurt am Main/New York: Campus.

Heigl-Evers, A. and Weidenhammer, B. (1988) *Der Körper als Bedeutungslandschaft. Die unbewußte Organisation der weiblichen Geschlechtsidentität*. Bern/Stuttgart/Toronto: Hans Huber.

Hettlage-Varjas, A. (1987) 'Frauen zwischen Wunsch, Angst und Tröstungen. Neuere psychoanalytische Aspekte zur weiblichen Emanzipation und Sexualität'. In M. Simmel (ed.), *Weibliche Sexualität. Von den Grenzen der Aufklärung und der Suche nach weiblicher Identität*. Braunschweig: Gerd J. Holtzmeyer Verlag.

Kleemann, J.A. (1977) 'Freud's views on early female sexuality in the light of direct child observation'. In H.P. Blum (ed.), *Female psychology*. New York: International University Press.

Laufer, M. and Laufer, E.M. (1984) *Adolescence and developmental breakdown*. New Haven: Yale Universities Press.

Lawrenz, C. and Orzegowski, P. (1988) *Das kann Ich keinem erzählen. Gespräche mit Frauen über ihre sexuellen Phantasien*. Frankfurt am Main: Luchterhand.

Lerner, H.E. (1977) 'Parental mislabelling of female's genitals as a determinant of penis envy and learning inhibitions'. In H.P. Blum (ed.), *Female Psychology*. New York: International Universities Press.

Olivier, C. (1984) *Jokastes Kinder. Die Psyche der Frau im Schatten der Mutter*. Düsseldorf: Claassen.

Poluda-Korte, E.S. (1988) 'Brief an eine Freundin'. In C. Gehrke (ed.), *Mein heimliches Auge, III*. Berlin: Konkursbuch Verlag.

Rohde-Dachser, C. (1990) 'Das Geschlechterverhältnis in Theorie und Praxis der Psychoanalyse'. In H. Brandes and C. Franke, (eds), *Geschlechterverhältnisse in Gesellschaft und Therapie*. Münster: Literarischer Verlag.

Rohde-Dachser, C. (1991) *Expedition in den dunklen Kontinent. Weiblichkeit im Diskurs der Psychoanalyse*. Berlin: Springer.

Schmauch, U. (1987) *Anatomie und Schicksal. Zur Psychoanalyse der frühen Geschlechtersozialisation*. Frankfurt am Main: Fischer.

Schmidt-Honsberg, L. (1989) 'Gedanken zur weiblichen Homosexualität. *Psyche, 3*, 238–55.

Stern, D. (1986) *The interpersonal world of the infant*. New York: Basic Books.

Torok, M. (1974) 'Die Bedeutung des "Penisneides" bei der Frau'. In J. Chasseguet-Smirgel (ed.), *Psychoanalyse der weiblichen Sexualität*. Frankfurt am Main: Suhrkamp.

Waldeck, R. (1988) 'Der rote Fleck im dunklen Kontinent, *Zeitschrift für Sexualforschung*, *1*, 189–205; and *2*, 337–50.

Waldeck, R. (1992) 'Die Frau ohne Hände. Über Sexualität und Selbständigkeit'. In K. Flaake and V. King (eds), *Weibliche Adoleszenz. Beiträge zur Sozialisation junger Frauen*. Frankfurt am Main: Campus.

Chapter 3

Questing daughters
Little Red Riding Hood, Antigone and the Oedipus complex

Nina Lykke

Stories of mothers and daughters are popular in fairy tales. Many a tale may be read as a metaphorical account of the daughter's quest for the archaic mother, but also of the barriers thrown up against it by patriarchal society. Let us consider, for example, Little Red Riding Hood. She is an active or questing heroine whose project, to find flowers for Grandmother in the forest, is symbolically pervaded by erotic desires of the early mother–daughter relationship. But she is also a suffering heroine. Her quest is not brought to a successful end. Instead, she is devoured by the wolf, and thereby transformed from an active subject into a passive object.

Through this dual position – as both questing and suffering, both active and passive heroine – Little Red Riding Hood may symbolize the genesis of feminine subjectivity, as its story is told by classic psychoanalysis, i.e. as a story about the girl's development from a maternal space, in which she may pursue her sexual aims actively, into a paternal area characterized by the daughter's passive sexuality.

As such, this story is not very encouraging. Furthermore, the way it is told by classic psychoanalysis can also be described as misogynous. Nevertheless, like many other feminist researchers, I think it is a story that has something to tell us about the discourses of the mother–daughter–father relationship by which we are inscribed in patriarchal society. This was my reason for returning to the story in two recent books (Lykke, 1989; 1992), and for discussing it once again in this article.

Specifically, it is my purpose to draw attention to a certain aspect of the classic psychoanalytic account of femininity: its outline of a psychosexual space between the girl's pre-Oedipal attachment to the mother and her heterosexual attachment to the father, her so-called passive Oedipus complex.

This space was treated with much ambiguity and ambivalence by classic psychoanalysis. However, in contrast to so many other ambiguities in the Freudian theory of femininity, this one has not been explored by feminist psychoanalysis. Important trends within the feminist tradition have indeed welcomed the Freudian attribution of theoretical importance to the early mother–daughter relationship, and placed much emphasis on his statements about the pre-Oedipal phase in girls. At the same time, however, they have too easily assumed that Freud is right in contending that the girl remains longer in a pre-Oedipal, and thus infantile-symbiotic state, than the boy – without questioning the ambiguous premises on which this thesis is built.

In my view, it is important for feminism to discuss these Freudian ambiguities as well, and to question whether the term 'pre-Oedipal' adequately defines the girl's psychosexuality in the last part of what Freud – on uncertain grounds – decided to call her 'pre-Oedipus' phase. For Freud's way of defining this part of the girl's 'pre-Oedipality' is, I think, marked profoundly by his fear of recognizing fully the development in the girl of the same kind of dangerous non-infantile-symbiotic incestuous feelings for the mother he had celebrated in the little boy by giving them the famous name Oedipus complex. The conclusion I have drawn is to treat the last part of the girl's so-called pre-Oedipality as an independent space, which I have dubbed the Antigone phase (cf. Lykke, 1989; 1992).

In this article, I intend to show why an unambiguous focus on the specific, no longer pre-Oedipal qualities of this space, may contribute to a deeper understanding of the genesis of feminine subjectivity: its emergence through a stage in which we have begun to perceive and symbolize gender difference, but in which the significances of this difference are still not fixed into stable and oppressive symbolic meanings. The exploration of this stage may also throw light on important non-infantile-symbiotic aspects of the variety of erotic desires embodied in the mother–daughter relationship.

My argument takes its point of departure from the classic psychoanalytical story of the early 'pre-Oedipal' mother–daughter relationship. Through a subsequent description of the ambiguous Freudian treatment of the moment in the story from which I derive my concept of the Antigone phase, I will proceed to my own reinterpretation of the classic psychoanalytic story of femininity: i.e. to my definition of the Antigone phase[1] and to a discussion of its perspectives. In the last part of the article I will return briefly to the fairy tale of Little Red Riding Hood in order to further illustrate these perspectives.

THE 'PRE-OEDIPUS' PAST OF THE GIRL

My account of the Antigone phase takes its point of departure from Freud's famous statements on the pre-Oedipus past of the girl. This element in the Freudian theory of femininity emerged in his articles on that subject written in the early thirties (Freud, 1931; 1933). As I will demonstrate, Freud's way of defining these past sections of our life story is interwoven with certain ambiguities. But before I take up the discussion on these, let me first recapitulate the main points Freud made about the early mother–daughter relationship.

In these late works Freud fully acknowledged for the first time that, underlying a strong attachment to the father, is always a long phase of exclusive and intensive attachment to the mother.[2] This phase can last as long as four or five years after birth.

The discovery of this phase obviously came as a big surprise to Freud, especially because it includes certain sexual desires which he considered very unexpected in little girls. According to Freud's new insights, the girlchild becomes sexually attracted to her mother during this phase in exactly the same way as the boy, and develops cathexes of her based on a full range of differentiated libidinal wishes: 'the very surprising sexual activity of little girls in relation to their mother is manifested chronologically in oral, sadistic, and finally even in phallic trends directed towards her' (Freud, 1931: 237).

To Freud's unconcealed amazement, the girl's sexual fantasies about the mother may develop to the extent that when a little sister or brother is born she imagines she is the one who 'has given her mother the new baby' (Freud, 1931: 239). And last but not least, in this phase of the girl's life the father will appear on her fantasy stage as nothing more than 'a troublesome rival' (Freud, 1931: 226).

With these statements about the importance of the 'pre-Oedipus phase' in girls, Freud draws the early mother–daughter relationship into focus – and ascribes to it a theoretical significance, for the development of feminine subjectivity, which cannot be over-estimated. This is, of course, the chief reason why this 'pre-Oedipus phase' has attracted the interest of feminist psychoanalysis to such a great degree.[3]

THE FREUDIAN AMBIGUITY

The significant ambiguity in the Freudian account of the early mother–daughter relationship can clearly be traced in the dialogue, included in Freud's 1931 article, on the use of the terms 'pre-Oedipal' and 'Oedipal'. The dialogue was carried on with Jeanne Lampl-de Groot, one of the women analysts who by doing important research on the subject (cf. Lampl-de Groot, 1927) had inspired Freud to explore the long, important phase in the girl's life before she enters into the passive Oedipal attachment to the father by the age of four or five.

The Freudian ambiguity relates to the naming of the newly found space. Jeanne Lampl-de Groot's term for it is 'negative Oedipus complex', a term she clearly attaches to cathexis of the mother in the 'phallic phase'. In her opinion, this is a phase that represents a stage in which the girl has developed the capability to object-love, and is able to see her mother-object as an independent other who is in a position to choose or to be possessed by another suitor: the father. To the girl, he then takes on the guise of rival and enemy. In other words, Jeanne Lampl-de Groot relates her term specifically to the last phase before the girl enters into the passive father-attached Oedipus complex.

Freud's term is not negative Oedipus complex, but 'pre-Oedipus attachment to the mother'. As I described above, he does not relate it to the same kind of specific cathexis and libido organization as Jeanne Lampl-de Groot. In contrast, he extends the signified area to an undifferentiated cathexis of the mother that lasts more or less from birth until the age of four or five, and that is based successively on all the different early organizations of the libido (oral, anal-sadistic, phallic). But still, the Freudian concept does include the consideration of the father as nothing but a troublesome rival, i.e. a position that is usually taken up by the Oedipal father in Freudian theory.

Freud should, of course, have known that there is a distinct difference between what he is signifying with the term 'pre-Oedipus attachment to the mother', and the signified area of Jeanne Lampl-de Groot's term 'negative Oedipus complex'. However, he does not address this ambiguity, but instead insists on his own term, 'pre-Oedipus attachment to the mother', without indicating any basic difference between his definition and the one proposed by Jeanne Lampl-de Groot. In his summary of the points on which he agrees with Jeanne Lampl-de Groot, he explicitly mentions that she sums up her results 'in the formula that the girl goes through a phase of the "negative" Oedipus complex before she can enter the positive one' (Freud, 1931: 241).

In addition, Freud clouds this already ambiguous picture in yet another way. On the one hand, he explicitly agrees with Jeanne Lampl-de Groot that the little girl exhibits all the characteristics (cathexis of the mother in the phallic phase, rivalry with the father, etc.) that he would not hesitate to call Oedipal when found in the boy. On the other hand, he denies that the girl has any kind of Oedipus complex fully comparable to that of the boy: 'We have the impression here that what we have said about the Oedipus complex applies with complete strictness to the male child only . . .' (Freud, 1931: 228–9).

The unambiguous exposition in Jeanne Lampl-de Groot's work published in 1927 is thus obscured profoundly by Freud. Why? Perhaps because he unconsciously feared the space opened, at least in rough outlines, by Jeanne Lampl-de Groot's work. This is a space in which the daughter might in fact threaten to obliterate the father's privileged sexual position (and the position of the father analyst too) by showing a genuinely rivalrous 'Oedipal' desire for the mother; a desire which the father could neither dismiss as merely infantile-symbiotic, nor consider built upon a secondary identification with himself, which would allow him to feel secure in the belief that he (and his gender) was still the primary master and determinator of the relationship to the mother.

Freud was, of course, not merely another homophobe; in fact, he was a clever analyst of homosexual desire in males. But as the lengthy feminist and non-feminist discussions of Freud's famous failures in his analysis of Dora[4] show, he had problems in analysing homosexual desire in women. The Dora-text was written about 30 years before the article on femininity in 1931. However, the textual ambivalence and ambiguity that occur in the two texts as soon as the phenomenon referred to as negative female Oedipus complex by Jeanne Lampl-de Groot surfaces are too striking to be mere coincidence.

THE ANTIGONE PHASE

For a feminist psychoanalysis it is necessary to overcome the confusion Freud caused when he blurred the distinction between pre-Oedipus and Oedipus relationships in the case of the girl, i.e. the confusion that arose when he insisted on using the term 'pre-Oedipus' to describe both the 'genuinely' pre-Oedipal phase, defined by the dual infantile symbiosis between mother and daughter, as well as the triangular drama between the daughter and her mother–lover and father–rival during Jeanne Lampl-de Groot's negative Oedipus complex phase. Let me return to the Jeanne Lampl-de Groot account whose integration in the Freudian text produced the problems.

The logical consequence of Jeanne Lampl-de Groot's account of the 'negative feminine Oedipus complex' is not to conclude, as Freud did, that the girl remains longer in the pre-Oedipal phase than the boy. It would be to define a separate phase characterized by the daughter's object-love of the mother and the presence on her fantasy stage of an important third term: the father–rival. In other words, the logical conclusion is that we are dealing with a specific phase that developmentally has transgressed the dual relationship of the pre-Oedipal symbiosis between daughter and mother, and instead comprises the triangular drama of the ('negative') Oedipus complex. The implication of Jeanne Lampl-de Groot's account is that the mother figure appears to the daughter during her 'negative Oedipus phase' as a separate and independent other – separated from her in the both dangerous and attractive sense that she represents an object with the ability to act as an independent subject: i.e. as a figure who, independently of the girl, may choose (or let herself be chosen by) sexual partners (perhaps the girl rather than the father, or vice versa). The daughter's experience of Oedipal rivalry with the father, as described by Jeanne Lampl-de Groot, is not possible without these preconditions.

This phase – whose distinct and different outlines appear when the logical conclusions of Jeanne Lampl-de Groot's theoretical approach are drawn – is the one I chose as the point of departure for my story of the Antigone phase. Like classic Freudian psychoanalysis as a whole, Jeanne Lampl-de Groot's concepts are, however, caught up in what is sometimes called the phallic illusion – or what I prefer to describe as fetishism of the Phallus. My story of the Antigone phase aims to go beyond this kind of fetishism. So to develop my definition of the Antigone phase further, I will briefly comment on how I use this concept, fetishism of the Phallus, and how it changes the classic psychoanalytic conceptualization of the genesis of femininity, including that of Jeanne Lampl-de Groot.

FETISHISM OF THE PHALLUS

First, I must emphasize that fetishism of the Phallus here does not refer to the Freudian concept of sexual fetishism, but to a feminist and dialectical materialist framework I developed (with my colleague Mette Bryld) in order to determine the basic structures of capitalist patriarchy (cf. Bryld and Lykke, 1983) – and on which my reinterpretation of the Freudian theory of femininity is built.

A key methodological concept of this theoretical framework is patriarchal fetishism. This concept defines a common form of consciousness in patriarchal societies, and describes how patriarchal structures are perceived as natural (based on the different natures of woman and man), rather than as products of specific, historical, changeable societal conditions. It thus refers to how patriarchal societal structures have been fetishized, i.e. endowed with a universal validity and force that they do not in fact possess. The concept also points out the reasons for this form of consciousness: these societal structures (e.g. the patriarchal division of labour by gender) have an appearance of naturalness.

Fetishism of the Phallus is one of the expressions of patriarchal fetishism, and refers to the fetishization of the penis as Phallus, i.e. as the genital: the organ of sexual conquest and potency *par excellence*.

Following my dialectical materialist concept of fetishism I consider Phallus fetishism as having material reality under the present historical conditions; capitalist patriarchy ascribes a special value to the penis, and makes it appear as Phallus. At the same time, Phallus fetishism is also essentially and universally unreal. Nowhere in the penisbody of penis is there a specific male libido or anything else that would essentially dissociate men's sexual energies, potencies and possibilities to take a sexual object into possession from those of women. In my story of psychoanalysis – as in Freud's – there is only one libido, independent of sex.[5]

By the concept fetishism of the Phallus, I mean the specific historic unreal reality connected to the status of the penis in patriarchal society. The consequence of this position is that the psychoanalytic theory of femininity has to be defetishized: freed from the fetishist distortions of its concepts. The fetishism to which important categories in classic psychoanalytic theory of femininity refer has to be exposed in its unreal reality, instead of being guised as a universal trait of human development. Until this is done, I will not be able to integrate the undeniable insights of classic psychoanalysis into my interpretation of the psychosexual development of the feminine subject. For, from my point of view, what is wrong with the classic psychoanalytic theory of femininity, including Jeanne Lampl-de Groot's contribution, is that it is hopelessly caught up in fetishism of the Phallus – in the belief that the historical status of the penis as Phallus is a natural and universal condition of human life.

Clear objects for the process of defetishizing are the concepts 'phallic phase' and 'castration complex', which determine the development of femininity in classic psychoanalytic theory, including Jeanne Lampl-de Groot's version of it. Both concepts are closely related to my concept of the Antigone phase, derived as it is from Jeanne Lampl-de Groot's 'negative Oedipus complex' phase. The phallic phase is thus the space in which Jeanne Lampl-de Groot located her negative Oedipus complex. The castration complex is the psychic event which ends a girl's phallic phase and her object love of the mother – her negative Oedipus complex. Because of these close connections to the conceptualization of the Antigone phase, I shall briefly summarize the way I defetishized the concepts of the phallic phase and the castration complex.

In my reinterpretation of the Freudian theory of femininity, the establishment of the castration complex in the girl is the point in her development under patriarchal conditions when the unreal reality of society's fetishism of the phallus appears to her. Through its appearance, she is made to experience her penisless body as if it were castrated, i.e. cut off from the Phallus, and thereby apparently from sexual potency and the ability to possess a sexual object. This conception of castration illustrates quite well the tricky thing about fetishism. It throws light on the seriousness of the consequences when the products of certain historical and societal conditions appear as if they were nature incarnate.

In the developmental line, the phallic phase of Freudian theory precedes the castration complex. However, if the establishment of the castration complex is defined as above, then the phallicity of the 'phallic phase' logically becomes doubtful. When we look at the girl's development in a prospective perspective, the so-called 'phallic phase' precedes the point at which the fetishism of the Phallus is established as castration trauma in her. So we may reinterpret the girl's 'phallic phase' as pre-fetishist, which means that it is contradictory to call it 'phallic'. Consequently, it may be defined as a clitoral–genital phase. (The congruent phase of the little boy is similarly to be considered as penis–genital, but not phallic.) Given these preconditions, the term phallic phase can only refer to the retrospective perspective, i.e. to the perspective of the grown-up person looking back on her childhood. Here, however, I believe it is a valid description of our experience in patriarchal society. When the grown-up woman looks back on her childhood, she will, of course, have passed the inscription into the unreal reality of fetishism. This means that the phase which originally was clitoral–genital will now appear to her as phallic, because it was connected with feelings of potency and capability of possessing sexual objects – and fetishistically those are phallic qualities. While it is inconceivable that the girl should develop phallic body-images before the castration complex has inscribed her into the phallic discourse of patriarchal society, I find it more than likely that she will consider every potent bodily action as phallic (including her own former activities) after this inscription, which has made the qualities 'phallic' and 'sexually potent' appear to her as if they were amalgamated indissolubly.

Thus, in some ways, the Antigone phase is the same as Jeanne Lampl-de Groot's negative Oedipus phase – and principally coincides with what she and Freud theory have determined as the girl's phallic phase, i.e. a phase that is terminated by the castration complex.[6] But both 'phallic phase' and 'castration complex' are considered here in a radically different way. They are seen as products of the fetishism of the Phallus – of the specific unreal reality that transforms penis into Phallus in patriarchal society – and not of essential conditions.

THE MYTH OF ANTIGONE

But why choose Antigone to name this space in the feminine psyche that Jeanne Lampl-de Groot pointed out – and that Freud subsequently both denied and confirmed in a highly ambiguous way?

According to the old Greek myth, Antigone was the daughter of Oedipus and his mother–wife Jocasta. After Oedipus' death, Antigone's brothers, Eteocles and

Polyneices, fought each other to gain power over Thebes, their home city. The two brothers killed each other during a big battle. Creon, Jocasta's brother, and the new king of Thebes, forbade the burial of Polyneices. According to Creon's *raison d'état* Polyneices' fight against Eteocles was an act of treason against the state, Thebes, because Polyneices had been expelled from Thebes by his brother, who had then become the apparently legitimate king of the city. Antigone, however, buries Polyneices and is sentenced to death by Creon: she is going to be buried alive in a cave. Although her life has been threatened, Antigone does not submit to Creon's will. She opposes him to the end. Her final act of defiance is thus to hang herself in the cave instead of letting herself be suffocated by earth.

What has this story to do with the phase in between the girl's pre-Oedipal attachment to the mother and her passive heterosexual Oedipus complex? According to the interpretation of Antigone presented in the principal classic work on matriarchy (Bachofen, 1861), both her and her father–brother Oedipus' mythic dramas are struggles between systems of father and mother right, i.e. between the abstract patriarchal law of the father, represented by Creon and his *raison d'état*, and concrete matriarchal law, based upon the principle that origin from the same womb must be respected above everything else. That is why Antigone takes care of her brother. Like herself, Polyneices was borne by Jocasta.

Developing this interpretation further, you might say that what makes Antigone guilty in Creon's eyes is a too close relationship to her mother's womb. Another name for such a relationship is, however, incest. Antigone's crime is thus comparable to that of Oedipus when he made his incestuous marriage – and in a way, also to his other crime: patricide. Because if Creon's law is the father law, Antigone's defiance of it can be seen as a symbolic killing of the father. By burying Polyneices, she overrides the law of the father. As if mockingly playing on exactly these 'Oedipal' themes in Antigone's actions, Creon chooses to (re)establish the father law by having Antigone buried alive: i.e. suffocated by the mother: Earth. Symbolically, he demonstrates that a too close or incestuous relationship to the mother is fatal, and that it is he who decides what is an appropriate distance to the mother's womb. That both Antigone and the people of Thebes understood these symbolical connections in Sophocles' drama about her, is borne out by the use of metaphors, such as 'bridal chamber' and 'bridal couch' in connection with the cave in which Creon is going to let Antigone die.

Antigone's 'crimes' and punishment may thus be interpreted as congruent with the ones her father and brother, Oedipus, committed. This is exactly my reason for choosing the myth about her as the metaphorical name for the psychic space which Jeanne Lampl-de Groot described as the girl's negative Oedipus phase. In this way, the metaphor will in itself question the dogma I want to challenge – the dogma that the girl allegedly remains in a pre-Oedipal stage longer than the boy. Taking my point of departure in a defetishized version of Jeanne Lampl-de Groot's phase of the negative female Oedipus complex, I will contend that the development of girl and boy may be considered congruent up until the castration complex separates the psychosexuality of the sexes in patriarchal society.

UNFIXED GENDER SIGNIFICANCES

A basic consequence of this suggested congruence between the girl's and the boy's early development is that the girl – when she leaves the pregendered infantile universe of pre-Oedipality – does not immediately enter into a sphere defined by 'castration', i.e. by symbolically fixed gender significances, in which a male body signifies phallicity, and a female one castration.

During the Antigone phase, the symbolic significance of gender difference has begun to manifest itself in the girl's perception: the symbiotic pre-Oedipus relationship between mother and daughter has been broken up by a third term, the father – i.e. a figure that represents a different gender. But as long as the girl is not caught up in the fetishism of the Phallus, i.e. before the castration complex is established in her, gender difference can, logically, not yet signify symbolically fixed meanings. The signifiers, female and male body and genitals, have not yet come to signify the cultural meanings, castrated versus phallic, in the girl's perception.

In conclusion, I shall illustrate this perspective of the Antigone phase by returning to my point of departure: *Little Red Riding Hood*, and more specifically to the key scene of the fairy tale, the famous discussion between Little Red Riding Hood and the wolf in Grandmother's bed. This scene can be read as a struggle between signifiers. A struggle that may resemble the one which perhaps takes place in every growing individual in patriarchal culture. The question to be settled is: whose genital organs are going to represent potency and power? Those of the mother? Or those of the father? In the tale, this struggle takes place when Little Red Riding Hood and the wolf are discussing whether the person representing the aim of her quest and desired object, the ambiguous – both feminine and masculine – person occupying Grandmother's bed, has small or big organs. A discussion which, in a society based on fetishism of the Phallus, sadly enough ends up with a final symbolic institutionalization of the big visible organ as the signifier of sexual potency and power *par excellence*.

This struggle between signifiers may, as I said, be read as a metaphor for what happens in the triangular drama of the Antigone phase. But this does not imply that we are dealing with a drama about repression of a specifically female discourse by the phallic one that is established in the girl through fetishism of the Phallus. My thesis of congruency between the development of girl and boy until the castration complex implies that the meanings of female versus male genitalia in the Antigone phase are still totally open to a diversity of possible interpretations. In my opinion, it is this openness, and not an inherent femaleness, that is repressed.

There is, of course, one element in the development of the sexes up until the castration complex that cannot be considered congruent: the genital organs of girl and boy have a different form. However, I consider this difference unimportant as far as the question of psychosexual essence is concerned, because I agree with Freud's belief that there is only one libido, independent of sex, i.e. a libido that may express itself through a lot of different bodily organs, pregenital as well as genital, female as well as male – without thereby being essentially transformed into 'another' libido. The formal difference between female and male genitalia is, in my story of psychosexual development, made culturally important and significant through the discourses of society, not because of any inherent essence.

So one of the basic reasons why I have introduced the concept of the Antigone phase – in which the symbolic meanings of bodies, acknowledged as gendered, are open, negotiable and unfixed – is that it may represent a key to a better understanding of our original openness towards gender, and psychic traces that may remain in the grown-ups. These are traces that might remind us of our psychosexual possibilities: to play with a diversity of gendered identities, to revive, for example, the so violently interrupted game of Little Red Riding Hood and her wolfish Grandmother.

NOTES

1 Described in detail in Lykke, 1989.
2 Freud's first step towards a recognition of the girl's early mother attachment was, however, taken in Freud 1925.
3 The pre-Oedipal phase in girls has, for example, been explored by French feminists like Luce Irigaray, Hélène Cixous and Julia Kristeva – mothers of now widespread and popular theories of 'écriture feminine', a utopian feminine writing that takes its point of departure from the pre-Oedipal mother–daughter relationship. Or we may consider another very influential example: the feminist psychoanalytic theories developed by the American Nancy Chodorow, who emphasizes how the pre-Oedipal phase determines all further development for the girl so profoundly that she, under patriarchal conditions, will normally never be able fully to leave the pre-Oedipal symbiosis with her mother, and establish an autonomous self capable of relating to others in a non-symbiotic way.
4 Cf. Freud, 1905, and the discussions of the Dora case in Bernheimer and Kahane, 1985, and in Cixous and Clément, 1986.
5 Cf. 'There is only one libido, which serves both the masculine and the feminine sexual functions. To it itself we cannot assign any sex . . .' (Freud, 1933: 131).
6 See: Lykke, 1989. In this book I show that the Antigone phase is to be subdivided into two parts: the active and the passive. They are separated by what I call the first castration trauma, i.e. that part of the castration complex that is connected with the girl perceiving a symbolic transformation of her own body as a result of the Phallus fetishism. This initial experience of castration does not, however, end the phase. According to classic psychoanalytic theory, a second stage of the castration complex makes its appearance later than this first traumatic event. This second stage concerns the girl's 'discovery' of her mother's 'castration'. Or in other – defetishized – words: the transformation of her mother image in accordance with the historical laws of the Phallus fetishism making the female body as such signify 'castration'. This subdivision of the castration complex into two separate traumatic events makes it relevant to consider the Antigone phase as divided into two parts. On the one hand, the phase is not over until the castration complex has fully manifested itself, i.e. involved the girl's perception of both her own and her mother's body. On the other hand, the incipient inscription into the patriarchal–fetishistic universe of discourse, with which the girl's perception of her own 'castration' is associated, will clearly have significant effects on her psychosexuality as well as on her perceptions, not only of her own body, but also of the external world, including her mother's body. In the second part of the Antigone phase the girl's mother

image, for instance, will change. While the representation of the mother in the first part of the phase is clitoral and potent; in the second part of the phase, it is still potent but now phallic.

REFERENCES

Bachofen, J.J. (1861) *Das Mutterrecht*. Frankfurt am Main: Suhrkamp, 1975.

Bernheimer, Ch. and Kahane, C. (eds) (1985) *In Dora's case*. New York: Columbia University Press.

Bryld, M. and Lykke, N. (1983) 'Towards a feminist science: on science and patriarchy'. In A. Ravn, B. Slim and E. Langtved Larson (eds), *Capitalism and patriarchy*. Aalborg: Aalborg University Press.

Cixous, H. and Clément, C. (1986) *The newly born woman*. Minnesota: University of Minnesota Press.

Freud, S. (1905) 'Fragment of an analysis of a case of hysteria'. In *Standard edition of the collected works of Sigmund Freud. 7*. London: Hogarth.

Freud, S. (1925) 'Some psychical consequences of the anatomical distinction between the sexes'. In *Standard edition of the collected works of Sigmund Freud. 19*. London: Hogarth.

Freud, S. (1931) 'Female sexuality'. In *Standard edition of the collected works of Sigmund Freud. 21*. London: Hogarth.

Freud, S. (1933) 'Femininity'. In *Standard edition of the collected works of Sigmund Freud. 22*. London: Hogarth.

Mack Brunswick, R. (1940) 'The pre-Oedipal phase of the libido development'. *Psychoanalytic Quarterley, 9*, 293–319.

Lampl-de Groot, J. (1927) 'The evolution of the Oedipus complex in women'. In *The development of the mind. Psychoanalytical papers on clinical and theoretical problems*. London: Hogarth, 1966.

Lykke, N. (1989) *Rødhætte og Ødipus. Brikker til en feministisk psykoanalyse*. (Little Red Riding Hood and Oedipus. Towards a feminist psychoanalysis) Odense: Odense University Press, 1989. Forthcoming in German translation: *Rotkäppchen und Oedipus*. Wien: Passagen Verlag.

Lykke, N. (1992) *Til døden os skiller. Et fragment af den feministiske Freud-receptions historie* (Till death do us part. A fragment of the feminist reception of Freud). Odense: Odense University Press.

Chapter 4

Becoming a situated daughter

'Later, when I am big, I will be Daddy, so then we will also have a father in our house' – Hannah, four years old.

Ruth de Kanter

The early mother–child relationship forms the root of the process of becoming a human subject. Individuation and separation from the loving, caring, nurturing and powerful relationship with the mother are seen as necessary steps in the developmental process. Physical birth, in which mother and child are physically separated, is followed by a psychological birth in later years and decades. I will argue that the main developmental task of the daughter is to acknowledge the mother as a situated mother/woman, and the main developmental task of the mother is to acknowledge the daughter as a situated girl or 'woman-in-development'. This developmental process of mothers and daughters leads me to four different topics.

Firstly, I will discuss a case of gender-identity development in the daughter of a lesbian mother as an illustration of the interplay between lesbian family relationships, and the way a small daughter defines her identity using heterosexual symbols in the given language as signs of contextual gender-identity development. Secondly, I will raise the question of whether the early mother–daughter relationship, which is generally viewed as a dual relationship, should not be seen as a triangular relationship from the very moment of birth onwards. I will stress the fact that the dual relationship is always in a mother/woman–child relationship context. Thirdly, I will argue that within the individuation and separation processes between mother and daughter, we need to distinguish the mother/woman at three different levels. This also means that the social context intervenes at these three different levels, and that the developmental processes of individuation and separation take place at these three different levels. My assumption is that this is ongoing throughout the life-cycle. Finally, I will stress the particular importance of aggression as a necessary aspect for the formation of contextual female identity.

THE DEVELOPMENT OF GENDER IDENTITY IN A DAUGHTER OF A LESBIAN MOTHER

I see gender identity as the notion of being a girl/woman or boy/man, and the psychological and social meaning of this notion. This view is an extension of the more restricted psychological subjective meaning of gender identity as the awareness of being man or woman.

Gender identity changes not only during individual development, but also in different social contexts. For example, when my four-year-old daughter states: 'Ruth, later when I am big, I will be Daddy, so then we will also have a father in our house', she constructs a social and psychological meaning of gender identity within the framework of heterosexual notions. In her fantasy she fills the gap of difference: she will become other than mother. In her fantasy, she will become what is obviously not given: a father/man in the house as 'the other' parent, different from her lesbian mother and mather.[1] She knows that most, but not all, children have a father and mother in their home, so in her fantasy she uses this social reality and constructs a family position where she can play an important role. Her fantasies at that particular moment are formed around a subject position which is different but equal to the position of her mother. She constructs not only her own identity, but also those of the biological and social mother. Sometimes, the social mother has to fill the gap and the daughter makes her 'Daddy'. But when her biological mother is not at home, she calls the mather 'Mummy'. She situates herself and her parents in the heterosexual language of nuclear family relationships because signs referring to positions in lesbian families are lacking. She tries to find solutions in language to differentiate positions. On one occasion she invented the difference between 'Mummy' and 'Mother', referring to the difference between the biological and the social mother. Mummy is related to the semiotic, mother to the symbolic (Kristeva, 1975: 142). Hannah changes positions in the family structure, she takes different identities at different times as mother, father or baby. She uses accepted social categories, splits and makes unities between mother and child, or between mother and father, or between mother and father and child. She plays with the identities by filling in the gap between her and mother. When she is angry, she makes the social mother the Bad Mother. Or she makes mather the Good Mother and Mummy 'the Bad Mother' when the latter is cross, or does not give attention. In this repetitive process of becoming a subject, the daughter situates herself in the social context of a lesbian family, and she uses or rejects the reactions of Significant Others. She constructs notions of herself, of who she is and will become as a daughter of lesbian mothers. She is a woman-in-development, changing all the time but also staying the same Hannah.

IS THE MOTHER–CHILD RELATIONSHIP DUAL OR TRIANGULAR?

An example of the decontextualization of the mother–daughter relationship is the way the woman's position in motherhood is neglected in most theoretical accounts. I will argue that the third term is not external to the body, the feelings and the thoughts of the mother, but could be located in the womanness of the mother. However, only mothers seem to exist in the perspectives of Freudian or Lacanian theory. There is no differentiation between woman and mother; only the mother is part of the Symbolic Order. For the mother, the child is the phallus, the lust object, and the mother is the phallus for the child. The phallus, as paternal metaphor, neglects the woman's position. It is clear that in Lacanian theory there is no subject position for women, a point that is illustrated in the phrase 'la femme n'existe pas' (Lacan, 1966). The third term is represented by 'the father', or the 'Law of the Father'. The father's function is freeing the mother and child from each other's all embracing love. By doing so, a subject position (for the male child) becomes possible.

When interviewing women on their experience of early motherhood a mother told me:

> During pregnancy, I never felt the child that was growing inside me as part of myself. I always experienced the foetus was not 'me'; it did not belong to my own body, although obviously my body was growing. What was inside me has always been another person.

This woman is referring to the insider's view of a woman's experience of pregnancy as a process of split unity, as opposed to the outsider's view of the body of the mother as a whole. The question of whether the relationship between mother and child is a dyadic or triangular relationship is related to this dualism between the view of the experiencing female self and the predominantly male outsider's view.

We need to question who is the other, the outsider, who looks at the pregnant and suckling body of a woman? Male and female scholars, as outsiders, do not only have different perspectives of the mother–child relationship, but the insider's view of women as mothers or daughters also differs. They can easily change positions because a mother has always been a daughter herself, and can look at the relationship from both sides. As the mother is always seen from the viewpoint of those who make claims to her (Wright, 1989: 145), it is important to realize which perspective scholars, male or female, use to theorize about mothering. As feminist scholars, it is our task to strip scientific theory of its male perspectives, and to contextualize the theory of the mother–child relationship by stressing the importance of the woman's position as a third term in the mother–child relationship. The woman could be heterosexual or lesbian, married or unwed, white or black, in or out of the labour market. Her position as a woman situates the mother in the symbolic. If we acknowledge the mother is never completely fused with her child, her womanness can split the dyadic into a triangular relationship.

In our case, the little daughter of a lesbian couple contextualizes the mother–daughter relationship by using the sign of the father as a mark of difference, even if there is no father in the home. As I understand it, the word 'father' does not necessarily refer to a living person, or to a real position in the family, but it tells us how this little girl relates to signs in language. She uses dominant language on family relationships. At a certain point in her development, she identifies with the symbol of the father in order to be able to distinguish herself from the two mothers, and in order to distinguish the two women/mothers from each other. The use of this symbol is attractive because it is permeated with meanings of power and protection. So I think it is understandable that all children use this symbol in order to position themselves in culture and give themselves a respectable place. This girl helps to split the dyad by using the symbolic language of dominant family relationships.

Following Lacanian tradition, Kristeva introduces the notion of woman-effect, a special relationship to power and language. According to Kristeva, the identity of the woman has two sides – the woman-effect and the mother function. When, during the process of becoming heterosexual, the daughter is forever banned from the territory of the mother, one could see this as castration (Kristeva, 1975: 149). Kristeva refers to a male symbol to break through the mother–child relationship. At the same time she states, however, that the archaic relationship with the mother during the pre-Oedipal period is a creative and revolutionary force which must not be repressed or silenced. In this imaginary relationship with the archaic mother, there is no distinction between needs, questions and desire, there is no third term (Kristeva, 1975).

In our case, the little girl is banned from the territory of the mother, not only through the intervention of language and culture, but also through the intervention of a social reality where nuclear families dominate. But at the same time, the little girl is not necessarily exiled from the territory of women, because the other woman, the social mother, is not silenced or repressed. The other woman and her femininity continue to be present as important psychological positions for the girl to relate to. Even if castration means exile from the territory of the mother, the territory of women remains intact. The girl could turn towards the other woman to attain and maintain her female identity. The result could be that in the process of becoming a female subject, the female identity of daughters of lesbian women is not dependent on the reassurance of a father. The daughter not only fantasizes about becoming a father but also about being pregnant and carrying a baby. By doing so she unifies the mother and the father figure within herself, and she situates herself in both the lesbian and in the heterosexual world of family relationships.

According to the object relation theory of Chodorow, the mother initiates the difference between her and the male baby, and she continues the primary object relationship with her daughter through primary identification. The mother re-experiences her own daughterhood in the relationship with her daughter. It seems that the mother is able to regress to her former position as baby/little girl by giving the baby the sensitive attention she feels it needs (Chodorow, 1978). In my interpretation of Chodorow, it is not the mother, but mother's womanness which initiates or neglects the difference, be it a son or a daughter. Doesn't the (con)fusion of gender identity between mother and daughter in Chodorow's writings refer to patriarchal constructions where the mother swallows the womanness?

In our case, there is a constant fusion and taking distance between mother and daughter, initiated from both the mother's perspective and the daughter's. Being the same and being different creates a constant tension of fusion and autonomy. This switching gives developmental space to both mother and daughter. Although both are women in development, there is no equality in the relationship between mother and daughter; mother and daughter are differentiated by difference in generation and the changes in historical context. The daughter discovers the reality of the outside world through the interventions of the womanness in the mother.

In contrast to the idealized and unsituated mother–daughter relationship as the prototype of a harmonious connection between the two, I would suggest that from the mother's perspective interventions in the relationship between mother and baby take place at all moments in daily care and regulative practices. As illustrated above, in reality the mother is never imprisoned in a dyadic relationship with her child, be it male or female. Although she may have the illusion of being or desire to be 'one' with her baby, the social context intervenes in the private world of her thoughts, feelings and fantasies. Thus, in addition to the distance created by her womanness, this internalized social context whether conscious or unconscious creates distance in the so-called dyad. The norms, the expectations of the outside world and the pedagogic and psychological scientific knowledge on mothering intervene always in the relationship between mother and daughter (Urwin, 1985). The imaginary mother has to enter reality and the symbolic world of language and culture, otherwise she could not live as an adult woman. According to Walkerdine, mother and daughter cannot exist outside the confines of the social world. That world always redirects mother's attention away from the daughter (Walkerdine, 1989: 158).

My conclusion is that womanness and the social context are both factors in the splitting force between mother and woman, and make the mother–child relationship triangular rather than dyadic. According to the insider's view being a mother is one, although sometimes the main, aspect of a woman's identity. It is the outsider's dominant male fantasy and the insider's feminist illusion of close fusion, relatedness and empathy, as acquired feminine capacities and personality characteristics, that construct a dual mother–child relationship and close harmony between mother and daughter. This construction of duality of the mother–child relationship refers to the desire of men or women to return to paradise; it reduces women to eternal mothering.

THREE LEVELS OF SEPARATION AND DIFFERENTIATION

When daughters as women-in-development are confronted by problems of power and love in the outside world, their experiences with their own mother are often reactivated. Daughters could re-experience their youthful anxieties about losing their mother's love or their autonomy, or both. When we start with the idea that all children have to separate and individuate physically and psychologically from the mother as their first love object, we need to ask ourselves two questions. What are the different levels of the object 'mother' children have to separate from, and what represents the object 'mother'?

Children have to separate from three levels of the object 'mother'. This developmental process starts from the moment of birth and goes on throughout life: separation from the real living person, separation from the positions and separation from the symbol.

Separation from the person refers to the concrete living bodily presence of the mother. Every daughter identifies with the person of the mother, and must distance herself from this person in order to become a woman. Some women never separate sufficiently, their personal identity never becomes distinct from that of their mother, and it is thus impossible to distinguish between their own feelings and those of their mother. As a result, lack of individuality becomes the main psychological problem for these women.

Separation from the position of the mother refers to Walkerdine's question on how the mother represents the world outside the home, and the outside world of being a woman that the girls must grow up to enter (Walkerdine, 1989: 158). As a woman, the mother has positions in different structures:

- the economic structure – as a woman, the mother either has or has not a position in the paid labour market;
- ethnic structures – as a woman, the mother is more or less aware of and identifies with her ethnicity;
- the sexual structure – as a woman, the mother has a position in hetero and/or homosexual relationships;
- the emotional structure – as a woman, the mother feels more or less dependent on, autonomous of or connected to other people;
- the cognitive structure – as a woman, the mother is more or less able to express her own viewpoint or think for herself;
- the behavioural structure – as a woman, the mother is a free agent to a greater or lesser degree.

Some daughters never separate sufficiently from their mother's various positions, their social identities never become distinct from those of their mother.

Separation from the symbol Mother refers to the process of distancing from the symbol of Love and Power. Daughters have to learn to say goodbye to the imaginary position of being a helpless child, and to the all-powerful mother. They have to accept that mother's mirror image is a woman; daughters have to separate from the perfect, fantasized relationship with their mother in order to be able to become 'women'.

When daughters are able to separate from the person, the position and the symbol of the mother they can accept that mother is a situated woman with her own sense of subjectivity and gender identity different from their own subjectivity and gender identity. This means that daughters are able to place 'mother' in the social-historical, sexual, racial and ethnic, economic and political context of her life cycle. To gain their own subjectivity and feminine individuality, they need to acknowledge the subjectivity of the person out of whom they are born. As I have argued above, attaining subjectivity means acknowledging the social context of 'the womanness in the mother' as a third term, which places the mother–daughter relationship in a triangular rather than a dual relationship. We need to accept and acknowledge the Law of the Mother, that is to say the difference between mother and woman. Only then are we able not to blame the mother for the power-relations in which motherhood is organized.

In my view separation from mother at these three levels can have at least four possible outcomes for daughters:

- fear of losing love of mother/woman, but attaining a sense of relative autonomy as a person or position;
- fear of not attaining autonomy, but maintaining the sense of being nurtured by mother/woman;
- fear of losing both love of mother/woman and personal or positional autonomy;
- maintenance of the sense of being nurtured with the attainment of a sense of relative autonomy.

These conflicts between the sense of being nurtured by mother/woman and the sense of relative autonomy come into being on every occasion where a woman-in-development is confronted with power or powerlessness. But the difference between the adult and child position is that as a child, the daughter does not perceive the mother as a situated woman with power or powerlessness in the outside world.

I suggest that children of lesbian mothers can possibly separate and differentiate more easily between mother and woman than children in heterosexual families who have only 'one' mother. The former can split mother and woman from each other without losing 'mother' as female nurturant-object, or without losing a female love-object. Female nurturing and female sexual love-objects are not split. If the 'mother' is away, the other woman can become mother in the sense of nurturing and/or loving, and both women can represent the outside world.

AGGRESSION IS A NECESSARY ASPECT OF SEPARATION AND INDIVIDUATION IN THE MOTHER–CHILD RELATIONSHIP: WHY?

Separation from the mother as love-object is often accompanied by existential fear and aggression. Whereas Melanie Klein locates aggression as a drive within all children, and as a psychological effect of the separation from the violent love/hate relationship with the mother (Klein, 1957), I see it not as an effect of, but as a necessary condition for separation and individuation, directed at all three levels of separation – at the person, the position and the symbol of the mother. According to Klein, all children project their own aggressive feelings onto the mother-object in order to deal with their own aggression. Children split the mother-object into a Good and Bad mother, and believe that the mother is angry at them.

As I understand it, aggression is also related to the ambivalence of what the object 'mother' represents – love and protection, as well as power and control (Dinnerstein, 1976: 132; Walkerdine, 1989; Sayers, 1991). The mother represents the dirty goddess, both source of and threat to their existence. In children's pre-rational sense of self, the mother is the undifferentiated 'It'. She is not yet a 'You' because there is not yet a 'Me' or an 'I'. Fear of losing this 'It' could call into being the fear of death (Dinnerstein, 1976: 131). In my view, aggression could be a defence against this existential pain and fear. Moreover, in their love and care for children, mothers also regulate them. Not only by withholding care or caring too much, but the normal act of caring is simultaneously a disciplinary act, because the caring starts and stops at moments in time and space most often determined by the mother. This disciplinary power of the caring mother could easily come into conflict with the wish of small girls to understand the inner and outer world of mothers and women. Daughters also regulate their mothers, although in a different way, for example by aggression. So the daughter's aggression could also be a response to this link between her mother's care and discipline.

In object-relations theory, aggression emanates in the relationship between mother and child as an effect of mother's frustration. Perceived as the main need-fulfilling object, the mother is not sensitive enough and frustrates her daughter's need for love and protection. Not having received enough nurturing, mothers envy their daughter's position of being nurtured or being more independent than they were, and therefore they push away their little girl earlier than their little boy. The little girl, however, does not want to give up her little baby/little girl's position, but the mother no longer accepts this. As a result the mother–daughter relationship is characterized by more aggression.

In my view aggression could also refer to the frustration of the daughter's fantasy of continuing the harmonious attachment to the mother, and in which the mother is perceived as the only safe, nurturant and protective figure. But one could also see aggression in the mother–daughter relationship as an unconscious resistance to the ambivalent female image: the power of the mother as opposed to the powerless-ness of the 'woman' in the mother. So either the mother or the daughter or both are held responsible, and could be blamed for the aggression in the relationship.

In contrast to these views of locating aggression either as a drive in the child or as a response to the mother's frustration, I would like to stress the necessity of aggression in the developmental process of separation and individualization in both mother and daughter, in which each acknowledges the difference between daughter/woman-in-development and mother/situated woman. Aggression, pain, hurt, anger and grief are the main aspects of this loss of the illusion of being for ever connected. In the love and power relationship between mother and daughter both struggle for the acknowledgement of their own subjectivity. Daughter and mother could form mirrors for each other, representing the 'I' one would simultaneously like to be not like to become. A constant struggle between sameness and difference characterizes the mother–daughter relationship. Negative feelings are necessary expressions in this development of daughter's and mother's subjectivity. Often, these expressions of violent affect are directed towards the main love-object: mother or mother's mirror-image. The greater the daughter's denial of subjectivity in order to become different and not like mother, and the more the mother as a woman experiences her own dependency and needs her daughter for the confirmation of her femininity, the greater could be the aggression in the mother–daughter relationship. During female development as I understand it, there is a constant struggle for power and love between mother and daughter. Therefore, I assume that a harmonious connection without struggle could be the death of the subjectivity of mother or daughter or both. In my view, different ways of expressing aggression are structural elements of the waves in the mother–daughter relationship.

My conclusion is that aggression is a precondition in the process of becoming a subject of desire. Through fear of losing their love and through aggression as a defence against not being acknowledged as an individual human being with their own right to enter relationships with the outside world, daughters revolt against their mother's symbolic love, power and regulation practices. Daughters revolt not only for the acknowledgement of their own subjectivity, but simultaneously they resist accepting their mothers' subjectivity. The developmental task of accepting the 'womanness of the mother' goes hand in hand with fear and aggression as a defence against this fear.

SUMMARY

In order to become a situated daughter, the daughter cannot be mother's mirror. The social context always intervenes and acts as a dividing force. It is this third term which both situates daughters and mothers as women-in-development. To become a subject of desire, daughters have to separate from the object 'mother' at three different levels – as a person, as a position and as a symbol. Aggression is a necessary element of this process of gaining one's own subjectivity.

NOTES

1 I suggest the term mather to refer to the social mother in lesbian families. This term is etymologically related to mother, madre (It), mater (Lat), but different from the terms mother and father.

REFERENCES

Chodorow, N. (1978) *The reproduction of mothering: psychoanalysis and the sociology of gender*. Berkeley: University of California Press.
Dinnerstein, D. (1976) *The mermaid and the minotaur*. New York: Harper Colophon Books.
Klein, M. (1957) *Envy and gratitude*. London: Hogarth Press.
Kristeva, J. (1975) 'Une femme'. *Les cahiers du GRIF*, 7, 22–7, trans. Kristeva, J. (1980) 'Menige vrouwen'. In *Te elfder ure*, 25 (27), 141–50. Nijmegen: SUN.
Lacan, J. (1966) *Ecrits I*. Paris: Editions du Seuil.
Sayers, J. (1991) 'Beyond mothering psychoanalysis: power, fantasy and illusion'. Paper presented at the Conference on Daughtering and Mothering, September 1991, University of Utrecht.
Urwin, C. (1985) 'Constructing mother: the persuasion of normal development'. In C. Steedman, C. Urwin and V. Walkerdine (eds), *Language, gender and childhood*. London: Routledge & Kegan Paul.
Walkerdine, V. (1989) 'Growing up the hard way'. In V. Walkerdine, and H. Lucey (eds), *Democracy in the kitchen*. London: Virago Press.
Wright, E. (1989) 'Thoroughly postmodern feminist criticism'. In T. Brennan (ed.), *Between feminism and psychoanalysis*, 141–52. London: Routledge.

Chapter 5

Teenage daughters on their mothers

Mieke de Waal

Do qualitative research on teenage girls and you will find you cannot get away from their mothers. Literally, because before you can get to the daughter's room for your chat, you first have to spend the obligatory half-hour making small talk with mum over a cup of tea. And figuratively, because the mother is one of the most important people in teenage girls' world of experience. When I asked girls to place the names of people in their immediate surroundings in a series of concentric circles to show degrees of intimacy, mum was in the first or second place every time. However, conversations with and observations of girls have shown me how ambivalent this relationship with the mother usually is. When I got talking to girls about important matters in their life, such as falling in love and friendship, their bodies and sexuality, loneliness and popularity, they proved very reluctant to speak freely about these sensitive matters in front of their mothers. The girls spoke rebelliously about the ways their mothers (and fathers) attempted to limit their freedom if they knew too much.

In this article, I will describe the relationship between daughters and their mothers as sketched for me during lengthy and repeated meetings with a total of around fifty teenage girls over a period of three years.[1] Their stories and my observations are placed against a backdrop of the shift from a command to a negotiation household as analysed by Abram de Swaan (1988; 1989). The conclusion of this research appears to be that it has not become easier for teenage girls to develop an identity of their own, separate from their mothers, even though the contrary may seem to be the case.

THE CHANGING POWER BALANCE WITHIN FAMILIES

Relationships between daughters and mothers cannot be divorced from the wider social context in which they acquire form. De Swaan (1988) has expounded which changes have occurred in Northern European society over the past century. He shows how social relationships have become more equal in various sectors of social life. This applies, for example, to relations between employers and employees, between men and women, and between the old and the young. Through changes in the balance of power, a shift occurs from command to negotiation, to borrow de Swaan's terminology. Although relations between people are less stratified than before, the process in which people give shape to those relationships has become more stringently regulated. The emphasis has shifted from social control by others to learning to control oneself.

Relationships within the family have also become less hierarchical. This applies in the first place to relations between father and mother. Father's will is no longer law, and mother does not have to stay with her husband if she wants to leave. Although parents still hold primary authority over their children, children are no longer powerless in their relationships with parents. Many parents prefer discussion and negotiation with their children rather than giving orders. But if children still see parents as making unreasonable demands, more options to manage without their parents are now open through the institutions and organizations set up specially for them.

Changing family structures and relationships, therefore, have an effect on the shift from command to negotiation, and in its turn this shift is linked to the changing power balance and increased emotionalization and individualization within families. Brinkgreve and de Regt (1990) observe:

> Emotionalization means that relationships between family members are increasingly and more exclusively defined as emotional relationships and are only valid within that framework. If one or more of those involved no longer experiences the relationship as emotionally satisfactory, its raison d'être no longer exists and dissolution is the obvious course of action. In this sense, emotionalization also leads to individualization; only relationships which are perceived as 'good' by all parties, and meet individual desires and needs remain intact.
>
> (Brinkgreve and de Regt, 1990: 331)

According to these sociologists, emotionalization and individualization of family relationships have a great influence on children. On the one hand, children become more insecure; any argument raises the spectre of disintegration of the family. On the other hand, they believe the realization that family ties are not unbreakable also has advantages; from a very early age, children recognize that different options are open at all times, even to them.

NO TWO MOTHERS ARE THE SAME

Within modern families, every member has more space than previously to define personally their role as mother, father, daughter or son. No two mothers are the same. Some mothers pursue careers on the labour market, others devote all their energies to home and children, and other mothers combine work at home with a job outside the home. There are a lot of mothers who care for their children and their home single-handed, but there are also those who share these tasks with their partner.

Of the mothers of girls in my research, a minority had jobs outside the home.

Almost all of these mothers were divorced, and one was widowed. Of the married mothers, three worked on the family farm, and one had a non-commercial second-hand clothing 'business' in a bedroom at home. However, a number of the married women also did unpaid voluntary work. It is striking that although the daughters of divorced mothers often had great admiration for the academic and work achievements of their mothers, they still hoped the same kind of life wasn't in store for them. The fact that these mothers worked was the result of their disappointing love lives. In the age group I researched (twelve to sixteen-year-olds), almost all the girls appeared to see a good education as life insurance; you had to have it, but you hoped you wouldn't need it.

A quarter of 'my' girls were being raised in one-parent families. When I discussed this with them, they all agreed that, in spite of the sadness about the missing parent, growing up with one parent was not all bad.

Firstly, when mother and father are together, they discuss all kinds of adult subjects, and there is a major difference between what is and what is not intended for children's ears. A single parent, who has no adult confidant on hand every day, is usually on a more equal footing with the children. In the odd case, the balance tips and the daughter has to take on a parental role.

Secondly, girls who grow up alone with their mother often enjoy greater freedom than children whose parents live together. According to the girls I talked to, there are reasons enough for this: fathers have more difficulty than mothers in letting go of their daughters; mothers alone have less control options than a parental united front; mothers alone tend to compensate for the loss of the other parent and own absence at work by giving more freedom. One of the girls said: 'If your parents are divorced, or one of them is dead, then they quickly think: "Oh, everything's so awful for the kids, I'll give them as much as I can and let them do what they like" '.

A third, and final, difference mentioned by the girls is the territorial division which occurs with parent pairs, and does not exist in single-parent families. The girls who live with both parents tend to talk to their fathers primarily about 'business' matters – progress at school, house rules, plans for the future. 'Feelings' are usually reserved for mothers – falling in love, problems with friends, insecurities, things about their bodies, personal information about other people.

Differences between mothers are not only linked to participation or non-participation in the labour market, or to their relationship or cohabitation form, but also to the 'mother role' they adopt. If one mother opts for an authoritarian stance, another will use the 'friend' approach. Partly as a reaction to this, not all daughters are the same. There are daughters who boldly enter into conflicts with their unassailable mothers, whereas others accept without question everything mother says. And there are daughters who see their mother as their best friend and who want to spend as much time as they can with her, whereas others are scared witless by their mothers' want-to-know-everything and want-to-understand-everything attitude. Mothers have to adjust or maintain their mother role depending on how daughters respond.

In 'my' group of girls, there were some who had a friendly but rather impersonal relationship with their mothers. Anneke, for example, rarely had a serious conversation with her mother, partly because she was afraid of expressing all her criticisms of her sisters. Nor did she talk about other things which occupied her mind – a first bra, periods; such confidences were reserved for her best friend. In contrast, other girls did talk about their bodies with their mothers. They said they could discuss everything, except boys. And finally, there were girls who perceived no difference between their mothers and themselves. You could even see this in the literal sense; they looked like younger copies of their mothers. One of these girls said: 'My mum and I, well we're just the same. We think the same, we like the same things. We just have exactly the same character and understand each other without talking. I can tell her everything and she understands everything'.

'My' girls had not yet worked out which type of mother was the best – the more reserved authoritarian type, or a mother who is almost a friend. They enjoyed grumbling about more reserved, authoritarian mothers because they 'don't understand anything' and 'make up idiotic rules'. The advantage of such a mother, however, is that you can really get to grips with rebellion. The advantages of a 'friend-mother' are very different – you can borrow her clothes, go shopping with her and chat about everything. However, these things are only fun if you remain 'exactly the same' as your mother. When a daughter decides she wants something different, then these girls encounter problems.

No two mothers are the same, and no two mother–daughter relationships are the same. In spite of all these differences, however, there appears to be a great number of similarities in the ways mothers and daughter get along together. I would like to devote the rest of this article to these common patterns.

WHERE NO DAUGHTER SHOULD TREAD

The individualization and increasing multiformity of family relationships sketched above could imply that the situation in one's own family is barely comparable with that in others. But it is. Although behavioural rules are less stringently determined now and exhibit more interrelated variations, this does not mean that everyone is 'doing their own thing'. Conversations with 'my' girls indicated that in broad terms, all of them were being raised with the same limitations. What their parents expected from them may not always have been clear to daughters, but what they must not do was considerably less vague.

If there was one point of total consensus among 'my' girls, then it was the fact that girls have considerably less freedom of movement than boys. And they knew why: girls have to be protected more than boys. Parents have different strategies to guard their daughters from undesirable intimacies or imputations by others (Fox, 1977). The first line of defence is rigorous limitation of freedom of movement. This limitation can be removed by choosing suitable protection. By accepting chaperons, the girls can increase their freedom of movement. There are four areas in which 'my' girls experienced limitation by and protection from their parents.

First, there are geographic limitations: girls are not allowed to go where they like. This applies to specific neighbourhoods, to public places and to large shopping malls in the city where groups of more or less delinquent young people hang out. If girls go to these places, then they have to be accompanied by a trustworthy person.

A second limitation is time. The outside world is only accessible to most girls for part of the day. Going out after dark is allowed only when the girl is accompanied by an adult or big brother, and later by the acknowledged boyfriend. A further kind of time limitation reserves specific experiences for specific ages. Girls should not want to experience everything they can immediately; there are things that should be reserved for later.

A third limitation is in activities. Certain pursuits are still considered 'boyish', and adult activities such as smoking and drinking alcohol are also prohibited.

The final limitation is social contacts. A self-respecting girl doesn't mix with just anybody, or so the parents believe. To start with, she should behave modestly in the presence of boys – you never know, they may only be after 'that'. But parents aren't sexist – certain girls are out of bounds too; 'tarty types' could be a bad influence, and in any case would sully their daughter's reputation. Nor should girls go out with people who are a number of years older and do not belong to the parents' own circle of friends.

MOTHERS: PERSUASION RATHER THAN FORCE

In the traditional division between the sexes, which was common in the parental homes of the girls in my research, mothers were the primary educators. Fathers, if they were there at all, tended to remain in the background and only acted in conflicts between mother and daughter. So it was up to the mothers to persuade their daughters to be satisfied with only part of the cake. How do they do that?

The shift from external to self-control which de Swaan (1988) and others have observed in a historical context can also be seen in approaches to raising children. To an increasing extent, mothers appeal to their children's sense of personal responsibility. They no longer expect children to follow without question all kinds of stringent prescriptions imposed from above, but want the child to understand why he or she should do some things and should refrain from others. This new approach is aimed at encouraging girls to internalize norms and to develop a social character which will lead them to want and do the things they are supposed to want and do. If this self-control or normative restriction[2] is successful, then the strategies of limitation and protection discussed above become largely superfluous.

Mothers have various methods of inculcating attitudes in their daughters. First, they reason and rationalize: they make their daughters partners in their motives (whether real or not) for establishing certain rules. In doing so, they emphasize their good intentions and altruism; 'it is for your own good', they say. Second, they hold themselves up as an example. They tell daughters about their own teenage years and explain how they would react in specific situations. In reply to a question on how she knows what her parents expect from her, Alice said: 'I don't really know. . . . My mother tells me a story about when she was young and what she thought then . . . and then I think: "So that's what she wants, that's what she thinks is best" '.

A third method is telling stories about other people and using an approving or disapproving tone to indicate what is desirable behaviour.[3] And finally, mothers encourage specific activities and contacts while discouraging others. They control a powerful resource here – money. They will pay for some things, and not for others. If normative restriction is successful, the girl perceives no difference between her parents' way of bringing her up and her own desires; she has internalized their norms.

Alice expressed it as follows:

'Well, the things my parents would rather I didn't do are things I don't really want to do anyway, like drinking beer, doing all kinds of stuff with a boy, smoking, staying out late at a disco. . . . I do a lot of sports and all kinds of other things and I'm busy, and I've got my homework as well'.

When the approach chosen by mothers is unsuccessful, they usually try to change their daughters' minds by playing on their feelings and sense of duty. They say: 'We're not angry, but we are disappointed'. The girls I talked to experienced this kind of statement as much worse than when their mothers simply became angry. In the latter case, a verbal tussle will clear the air, but disappointment seems more threatening to their loving relationship. Announcing a disappointment is often sufficient to bring girls back into line. One of them said: 'I really care about what my mum thinks. I hate disappointing her, that makes me feel terrible'.

If a daughter frequently 'disappoints' her mother, then the latter can always fall back on harder methods drawn from a previous stage of civilization and education: grounding, no pocket-money, more chores, obligatory homework classes, moving to another school.

During the whole teenage period, a mother pays special attention to her daughter's best friend. Is she the mother's ally or her rival in influencing the daughter? As a result, the friend is vetted minutely before mother gives her approval for the friendship. Once the friend is considered suitable, then the daughter is allowed to intensify contact. However, that contact should lead preferably to the friend's integration in the family circle. She is invited to stay to dinner and to stay the night, calls the parents 'aunt' and 'uncle', and is invited to come on family holidays. By including the friend in the family circle, possible problems are avoided. If the friend doesn't manage to meet with the required approval, then there are mothers who are not above impeding and even forbidding contact. Mothers can impede contact by not passing on messages when the friend has phoned, by not allowing her to eat with the family or stay overnight, by insisting the daughter comes home early from the friend's house, and by being unfriendly when the friend is in their home.

DAUGHTERS: MANIPULATION RATHER THAN CONFLICT

As long as the daughter wants exactly what her mother wants her to want, then everyone is happy. Problems occur when girls try to secure more freedom of movement than is allowed. According to most of 'my' girls, creating a scene is not a sensible course of action; as a daughter, this action rarely gets you what you want. It is more effective to use ways of getting your own way which conform to the parents' educational policy.

Teenage girls acquire more freedoms within the home in exchange for less outdoors. The tangible proof of this freedom is the bedroom decorated according to the daughter's personal taste. Mothers see not only their own homes, but also the homes of approved friends as safe, enclosed places where they do not have to worry about their daughters. The first way daughters get around parental limitations is by making use of friends' bedrooms. Geographic limitations are overcome by staying the night at the home of a friend who is allowed to go places she is not. Smoking and drinking alcohol – often forbidden at home – are possible in the room of a friend with more liberal parents. And first sexual encounters often take place in the home of a friend whose parents have gone out.

A second way friends help each other escape parental authority is by developing common strategies to anticipate mothers who check up on their daughters. I call one of these strategies the 'smoke screen'. By telling fantasy stories about things that happened in class or meetings with strangers, the girls create a smoke screen which hides them from the parental eye. Questions which would provide clarity for the mothers receive purposely misleading answers so that the smoke screen remains intact. As Patricia said: 'No, it's not really lying. . . . You have to look out for yourself a bit, you know'.

Another method is telling half-truths. In this way, girls censure the information mother receives from them. Marjan told her mother she had been to Monica's. She had. But she didn't say there were also two boys there.

Finally, a third method is what I call 'translation'. In this case, girls have borrowed the technique from their mothers. They now manipulate their mothers in the same way they themselves were manipulated (Riesman, 1974). Just as mothers explain all kinds of boring rules as designed for 'your own good', the daughters now present their behaviour in terms which force approval from their mothers. The idea of an expensive item of clothing is 'sold' by saying at least the daughter will now look respectable for a family party. Money for a pop concert is extracted under the guise of promoting cultural development. And taking the bus to school instead of the bicycle is defended by saying that it saves the daughter's energy for the serious business of learning.

By using all these methods, and supported where possible by friends, girls create the illusion that they are doing their parents' bidding, whereas they are secretly living their own lives with their contemporaries. One of my informants summarized the situation neatly: 'If you can't do it in front of them, then do it behind their backs'.

TO CONCLUDE: LIKE MOTHER, LIKE DAUGHTER?

For a mother of a daughter, puberty is a phase during which the daughter appears to come much closer in a very short time, and in which she confronts her mother with her own desires and problems. Menstruation, sexuality, ideals – all are very real themes for the mother too. For some of the mothers, certain differences between them and their daughters almost disappear, for example, when the mothers are again involved in courtship and/or have re-entered education. For the daughter, the mother also appears to have come closer. Frequently, she is a mother who, now her children are grown, is either back in education or looking for a job, and who browses through the same clothing racks as her daughter. And mother's experiences are not much different when following a divorce she again tries her luck in love. It is not surprising that many mothers and daughters today feel a more equal relationship between them is more self-evident than a relationship in which the mother is the traditional font of all wisdom.

Yet it is impossible for mother and daughter to be 'exactly the same', as Alice expressed her relationship earlier in this article. Having a teenage daughter today also confronts many mothers with the lack of options in their own lives. The daughter can go on to higher education, a choice which was not always open to mothers. Daughters can aim for 'male' professions, while in the main mothers were destined for 'women's' jobs. Sexual liberation and contraception mean daughters can experiment with love in ways mothers could not have conceived. When the daughter begins a relationship, she and her partner will share tasks both inside and outside the home, so that she is not sentenced to a life of house and children as many mothers were.

While some mothers appear to be blinded by the apparent unlimited freedom enjoyed by their daughters, others are deeply worried. Some of the mothers of today's daughters fought for the rights and options these girls now have, but they also learnt the hard way that practical circumstances which would enable them to make free choices were rarely in place. In their striving to unite the best of two worlds, they ultimately saw themselves saddled with a double burden.

'Modern' mothers present themselves increasingly as friend of their daughters – as an equal who is never angry, only disappointed. Yet, they are still very concerned about what their daughter does or doesn't do. It appears that in practice all kinds of limitations and codes of behaviour apply for girls; codes which are essentially different in a number of ways from those applying to boys. Using almost imperceptible force, modern mothers try to raise their daughters to do 'spontaneously' what the mother wants. It is no easy task for daughters to discern their mother's pedagogic moral, veiled as it is in reasonable arguments, apparent empathy and shared enjoyment. Thus, even though we may perceive their lives as easier than in early periods, it turns out that teenage girls still have difficulty in developing their own identity separate from that of their mothers.

NOTES

1 As a cultural-anthropologist, I carried out doctoral research on the subculture of teenage girls for the University of Utrecht. For four years, I visited schools, club houses, swimming pools, snackbars, discos, and a lot of bedrooms. I had conversations with around fifty girls, thirty of whom I saw regularly over a one-year period. I followed ten girls for three or more years. My research method was not limited to interviews and observation; I also corresponded with them and analysed personal documents (letters, diaries, photographs). My dissertation entitled 'Meisjes: een wereld apart. Een etnografie van meisjes op de middelbare school' ('Girls: a separate world. An ethnography of girls at secondary school') was published by Boom, Amsterdam, in 1989, and I have also written a number of articles on the subject. The article included in this volume is based primarily on the chapter 'At home' in my dissertation, which includes a summary in English.
2 Normative restriction is described by Greer Litton Fox (805–6) as follows: 'This form of social control over the social behaviour of women is embodied in such value constructs as 'good girl', 'lady', or 'nice girl'. As a value construct, the latter term connotes chaste, gentle, gracious, ingenuous, good, clean, kind, virtuous, noncontroversial, and above suspicion and reproach. (...) Here the method of administration of control is largely internal – self-control through the internalization of values and norms – rather than externally imposed'.
3 De Vries' study (1990) also demonstrates the power of gossip as social control for Turkish girls living in the Netherlands.

REFERENCES

Brinkgreve, C. and Regt, A. de (1990) 'The disappearance of family relations that are taken for granted; on the consequences of individualization for children'. *Jeugd en Samenleving*, 324–34.
Fox, G.L. (1977) ' "Nice Girl": social control of women through a value construct'. *Signs*, 2, 805–18.
Riesman, D. (1974) *The lonely crowd. A study of the changing American character*. New Haven: Yale University Press.
Swaan, A. de (1988) *In care of the state. Health care, education and welfare in Europe and the USA in the modern era*. Cambridge: Polity Press.
Swaan, A. de (1989) *De mens is de mens een zorg*. Amsterdam: Meulenhoff.
Vries, M. de (1990) *Roddel nader beschouwd*. Leiden: COMT.
Waal, M. de (1989) *Girls: a separate world. An ethnography of girls at secondary school*. Amsterdam: Boom.

Chapter 6

Whatever happened to gender?
Female subjectivity and change in a generational context

Harriet Bjerrum Nielsen and Monica Rudberg

What is happening to gender in modern society? When this question is debated (both popularly and academically), conflicting impressions emerge. On the one hand, it seems as though nothing has changed, while on the other there appears to be a total disintegration. When our on-going research project, 'Girls and boys in change?', was introduced to the eighteen-year-olds who were to be the subjects of our study, we soon picked up the nickname of 'sex-role ladies'. The girls' reactions were divided along the following lines: some overwhelmed us with stories purporting to tell the TRUTH about the sly and dominating boys in their environment – 'we'll be quite disappointed if you don't record their covert power techniques!' And there were those who listened to us with a polite, but knowing smile. They were clearly wondering how on earth we were to grasp anything as complex as adolescence today, using the extremely old-fashioned concept of gender – 'you see today, we are all individuals first and foremost'. And both groups were right, of course; psychological gender is both recognizable across generations, and yet changing constantly. How are we to understand this process? The primary aim of this article is to raise a few tentative theoretical points on this question.

CLARIFYING THE THEORETICAL POSITION

Before we approach this main issue, however, we wish to clarify our theoretical position on three points that are more or less implicit premises of our line of argument, and essential to the debate between feminist scholars today. (In our view, this debate should not merely be regarded as an academic discourse, but reflects generational shifts in both the feminist movement and in women's studies.)

Our first point is that change in gender is a complex phenomenon that involves both rapidly and slowly changing structures. This is not the same as saying that 'psychology' is more inert than, for example, social power structures or cultural symbols of gender. The point is that within the 'psychological field' there is something that undergoes rapid change, and something else that changes slowly. Our concepts of change are often too massive and non-dialectical – either there is nothing new under the sun, or everything is completely and strangely different (cf. the girls cited above). Stereotypes produced in the heat of generational struggles could be seen as examples of this non-dialectical view of change: for instance, we often depict our mothers' generation as archaic and stifled, while experiencing the generation to which we ourselves belong as new, and also as a result of our efforts. However, our mothers are probably more modern, and we ourselves more old-fashioned, than we would care to admit. But the point is really that the 'old' and the 'new' can exist side by side, because change in all social phenomena is a process which lacks contemporaneity.

Second, we believe it is important to stress that cultural representations and individual psychology cannot be reduced to the same formula. There are many researchers today, both within women's studies and in youth research, who rightly emphasize that the symbolic representation of gender has become more manifold and ambiguous than before. A lawyer can look like Marilyn Monroe, and Rambo can be a nurse. But this doesn't necessarily imply that gender has become a masquerade, or that in a psychological sense identities are more volatile and unstable. In our view, the post-modernist assertion that there is nothing but discourses is both problematic for empirical research and psychotherapeutic endeavour. People are not texts, even though they are full of them, and could be interpreted as such. Individuals have life histories, bodies, feelings and potential for development; texts do not.

Third, in our view it is futile to try to avoid every concept of femininity for fear of being accused of essentialism. Of course, this doesn't amount to the same as saying that there is a universal femininity, or that there is no need to study differences between women in a given cultural and historical context. However, as the American feminist Susan Bordo (1990) put it, the grand post-feminist 'Law of Difference' should not be allowed to block small theories of similarity (and every empirical study must look for such similarities or patterns in one or several dimensions). Post-modernist deconstruction is inspiring in so far as it makes empirical 'truth-telling' less pretentious, but not if it intimidates empirical research on women and femininity. In the latter case it may, according to Bordo, imply that the old positivist 'view of nowhere' is simply replaced by the post-modern 'dream of everywhere'. This could result in a sort of closing of the circle, where post-modernists and positivists unite paradoxically: the one who sees everything simultaneously is in fact standing nowhere.

To summarize, our point of departure involves a view of change that stresses lack of contemporaneity in all social phenomena; a view of individual psychology which cannot be reduced to either social structure or to cultural representations; and a view of female subjectivity as 'essence' in the sense that it represents an individual reality with some sort of continuity across time and context. With these points in mind, how can we grasp change in psychological gender? Let's look at this question from two different perspectives of change: in the first place, from the perspective of individual development, second from the perspective of generational transformations.

CHANGE IN THE PERSPECTIVE OF INDIVIDUAL DEVELOPMENT

Object-relations theory – a theory of change or reproduction?

Our approach to this research area has been influenced mainly by the object-relations theory – as it was applied to, for instance, development of gender identity by Nancy Chodorow (1978) and Luise Eichenbaum and Susie Orbach (1983). Some years ago, we wrote a book trying to tell the story of gendered development from infancy to the age of twenty, mainly using this theory as point of departure. (The title alone would make any post-modernist choke: *The Story of Boys and Girls* (Bjerrum Nielsen and Rudberg, 1989).) The main attraction in this theoretical framework was its attempt to trace the connections between the social and the psychological worlds – taking 'patriarchy' into account, without erasing the specific character of psychological understanding. However, as some critics have pointed out, this search for connections between outer and inner worlds might also represent the main weakness of this theoretical endeavour. Walkerdine and Lucey (1989) have argued that, contrary to the professed goal of this approach, it might result in a sort of environmentalism, with heavy weight put on mother as both cause of and solution to women's problems. According to these authors, this environmentalism could in its turn result in an unintentional reduction of the psychological world to a mere reflection of the outer – for instance, where drives are banished and thereby 'action, passion, violence and conflict are replaced by passivity, receptivity and nurturance'. Thus, one could say that the theory is at risk of reproducing a socially acceptable 'good girl' image of women with 'mother-hood' as the supreme state and in tune with patriarchical ideology. The relationship between mother and child once again becomes the symbol of what is good in human relationships.

In our view, the feminist version of the object-relations theory is not at all blind to ambivalence and conflict, both in female subjectivity and in the relationship between mother and child (criticism on this latter point often tends to stereotype its opponent). However, admittedly there is a weak spot connected with the 'environmentalist' streak in the theory: women are not portrayed as 'good', but our shortcomings are seen as associated with the fact of patriarchy, which perverts female subjectivity and prevents the joy of the mother–child relationship being realized to its full potential. Walkerdine and Lucey (1989) call this tendency a feminist 'fantasy of harmony', where the father is removed rather aggressively from the psychological scene. In developmental psychology, the trend of replacing the male-biased theory of separation with an emphasis on female 'connectedness' is indeed often related to such a reduction of the father's significance, both as power and resource (cf. Apter, 1990). One could say that there is a lot of denial (men don't mean a thing) and splitting (men are evil, women are good) going on in this kind of theorizing – tendencies which can hardly be helpful in the struggle against oppression (cf. Bjerrum Nielsen and Rudberg, 1991a).

So to what extent is the feminist object-relations theory able to grasp change in psychological gender? Although environmentalists are often seen as possessing the means of change because the environment is malleable, more often than not their theories seem to grasp only individual adaptation and social reproduction. The psychoanalytic version of this environmentalism could be even more deterministic because the psychological gender that is historically produced – and therefore fits the social power-structure so neatly – will in itself become a motor in the reproduction of this structure. As we ourselves have put it: women learn not only how to do what they should, but also to want it (Bjerrum Nielsen and Rudberg, 1989). To avoid this deterministic fallacy, Walkerdine and Lucey (borrowing from Jacqueline Rose) argue that psychoanalysis is not to be used as a theory of socialization, but as a theory which tells the story of the failure of socialization. In our view, it could be both; however, if this ambivalence is not built into the theoretical framework, the story of psychological gender can only be altered through an external force producing a change in socialization practices (for instance through 'shared parenting'), which in turn produces a change in the 'wants' or 'identity projects' of girls.

We certainly think that such external forces are important – compare the changing family structures of white, middle-class, Western society – but that they cannot tell the whole story, because there must be a sort of 'internal' readiness for this external influence to have effect. In fact, internal psychological change can precede external changes, at least as a sort of unrest and vague longing. There are not only 'good mothers' and 'good girls' waiting for their release, but all sorts of passions and cravings in conflict with one another (as every mother certainly knows). Of course, psychological gender is not a conflict-free zone, where desires are moulded into mere devices for adjustment, functioning at the beck and call of the patriarchical system. However, there is no denying that adjustment is also a salient feature in individual development. Furthermore, that adjustment is not always resisted, but experienced as fulfilling individual needs and projects. Thus, Chodorow, for instance, is quite right in pointing out that 'mothering' often represents such an intricate weave of personal desire and social demand – just as there is ample evidence to suggest that the wish to become a mother represents one of the more inert structures of female subjectivity, quite unshattered by the fact that so many women today are not at all content with being just a mother. There are both conflicts and lack of contemporaneity in psychological gender.

Gendered subjectivity and gender identity

To grasp the conflicts as well as the lack of contemporaneity, we suggest that it is meaningful to differentiate between gendered subjectivity and gender identity. 'Gendered subjectivity' is loosely defined here as 'gendered being-in-the-world', i.e. those gender-specific and often unconscious ways of relating to the world and one-self, which have been registered in so many empirical studies of boys and girls of different ages. (In this context we will not elaborate on the psychological complexity which such a concept implies, but in line with the above mentioned criticism of the object-relations theory, we most certainly include sexuality, body and aggression in this 'gendered being-in-the-world'; cf. the contributions by Sayers and Flax in this book.) In this context, 'gender identity' refers to the personal construction of 'what gender means to me'. Of course, 'gender identity' could be seen as the most inflexible part of psychological gender, the immutable fact of belonging to one and only one sex. This basic 'fact of life' does not, however, exhaust our identity as gender, which is constructed throughout life on the basis both of our gendered subjectivity and the cultural conceptions of masculinity and femininity that are available to us. On the other hand, this construction of gender identity is not to be understood as just a matter of adjustment to a 'gender role' that could easily be modified as we 'outgrow' it. It is a process with substantial psychological consequences, as it renders to us identity as gender, where the question of our femininity becomes interwoven with the question of who we are.

Maybe one can put it this way: as gendered subjectivity, psychological gender is something you are; as gender identity, psychological gender is something that you have. In Gestalt terms, one could say that gender identity is the figure and gendered subjectivity is the background. For instance: girls who choose to become nurses can do so either in order to confirm their gender identity (it is feminine to help others) or because their gendered subjectivity makes them feel that it is meaningful to help others. This means that girls can go on choosing caring professions, even though doing so is no longer culturally defined as specifically feminine. This lack of contemporaneity is an important fact to bear in mind, not least for those of us who are involved in education, where we often struggle with the 'depressing' fact that girls tend to drift into jobs that seem to reinforce their traditional role and status. However, choices that could be regarded on the social level as conforming, could be both personally motivated on the level of gendered subjectivity and, paradoxically, combined with untraditional conceptions of femininity on the level of gender identity. (This distinction between gendered subjectivity and gender identity bears some comparison to the Marxist concepts of the working class 'an sich' and 'für sich', and could also be seen as related to historical change in somewhat the same way: it is only as 'für sich' that the working classes can be instruments in social upheaval.)

The moratorium as site of change

This lack of contemporaneity could perhaps be understood as related to difference in tempo between gendered subjectivity and gender identity. Our suggestion is that gender identity, defined in this way, is the aspect of psychological gender that undergoes the most rapid changes – both with regard to the content of such identity and with regard to the importance of being confirmed as a woman. Gendered subjectivity, on the other hand, will be a more inert and continuous structure – both historically and individually (Bjerrum Nielsen and Rudberg, 1991b).

This difference in rapidity of change between gender identity and gendered subjectivity is possibly related to their 'timing' in the developmental process. Gendered subjectivity is, of course, constructed throughout life, but in our view the early unconscious formation of self as both connected and separate forms the 'basics' of this construction. Gender identity is involved in this construction from the beginning; in fact, the rudimentary sense of being a boy or girl can really be seen as the 'start' of the whole process of gendered development. Nevertheless, the construction of gender identity is a specifically important project in youth, the million dollar question being: what does it mean to me to be a grown woman or man? What desires can be accommodated – and at what cost? The construction of gender identity in adolescence as a phase of both adaptation and creation has, in our view, been neglected in women's studies in general and in theories of gendered development in particular. This might also be an important reason for the difficulties of grasping change in psychological gender within those theories.

It is our suggestion that this construction of gender identity takes place in the moratorium (Erikson, 1968). Even though youth was not invented along with the steam engine, the psychosocial moratorium as a specific phase before reaching adulthood is connected quite clearly to the historical fact of modernity. This is the time in life when the young person is supposed to be most 'individualized', both psychologically and socially. On the psychological level, the moratorium implies a new kind of 'inner' freedom to administer oneself in both adaptive and creative ways, following the psychological separation from the parent figures. This psychological freedom goes hand in hand with the societally prescribed freedom for youth to engage in exploration of different cultural possibilities. This individualization also makes it possible for young people to relate to gender in a reflexive way.

Of course, as it has been pointed out repeatedly, this psychosocial moratorium is indeed a very class- and gender-specific path towards adulthood. However, we find it important to stress that it will nevertheless become a sort of 'requirement' for the development of individuals in modern society. Thus, the status of women as individuals (as opposed to mere gender) in this society is in fact determined partly by their success in slowly gaining access to this kind of moratorium. Girls have certainly constructed gender identities before this, but by participating in this more or less free-floating phase, the girl is provided with a historically new possibility of reflexively handling this construction. As the cultural analyst and youth researcher Thomas Ziehe (1989) has suggested, 'individualization' and 'reflexivity' are two important cultural tendencies in modernity, and in our view 'psychological differentiation' of the kind discussed here is clearly connected with those cultural modes. Thus, to the modern girl, gender will become not only something that she is, a more or less automatic prolongation of her gendered subjectivity, but something that she herself can take possession of and view from a reflexive distance: Is this me? Is this what I want? And what are the alternatives? Such a reflexive handling of gender identity will, in its turn, be an important precondition for subsequent change in gender relations.

As Walkerdine (1986) has pointed out, the discourses of child and girl are partly incompatible because the 'child' in the modern bourgeois discourse has been an active, exploring boy. Of course, the same point can be made with regard to the discourse of youth – where there is a contradiction between being young and irresponsible, and being an almost grown girl who is supposed to take care (both of others and of herself). Therefore, one way of getting a picture of social change is to study the processes through which these two contradictory discourses actually become mixed (because evidently they do), and what the consequences are for the further youth/girl discourse, as well as for the girls involved. For instance, when middle-class girls in our mothers' generation acquired access to the moratorium (often a short and stifled version of it), something important obviously happened – even though they ended up the 1950s as the most housewifely housewives of them all. And even though young girls of today are more individualized than the generations before, they are not at all individuals in the same way as boys. In the final part of the article we will try to give a hint as to how this 'mixture' could come about.

CHANGE IN A GENERATIONAL PERSPECTIVE

A model for understanding generational change

If we are to summarize the points made so far concerning change in psychological gender, we can say that it involves the relations between three different 'aspects': gendered subjectivity, gender identity and cultural/social possibilities. In our view, it is the lack of contemporaneity between those aspects that makes change come about. But different generations experience different forms of uncontemporaneity. The model can indicate where the main contradictions might be found for the three generations of mainly middle-class women in our study (and what is said here has the status of a tentative suggestion, and not an empirical result):

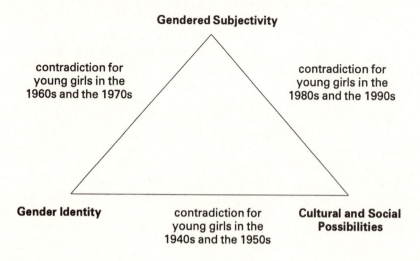

Gendered Subjectivity

contradiction for
young girls in the
1960s and the 1970s

contradiction for
young girls in the
1980s and the 1990s

Gender Identity

contradiction for
young girls in the
1940s and the 1950s

**Cultural and Social
Possibilities**

Grandmother, daughter and granddaughter

Let's take a look at the 'grandmothers' in the study, who were young in the 1930s and 1940s. There is reason to believe that they, as middle-class girls during the 'war-generations', were in fact pioneers. In their stories we can discern the beginnings of youth cultures as we know them; we can identify the loosening up of sexual morality; and we encounter – maybe for the first time in history – girls telling us that they want to 'live' before they marry (which didn't prevent them from marrying extremely young). In all this there is the seed of a new individualization, which makes it possible for them to relate to what kind of women they want to be. This individualization in the moratorium is still very much in contradiction with the 'gendered destiny' that awaits those girls. There are no cultural or social possibilities to break out of it: no jobs or arrangements for child care, and very limited cultural options for expressing grown-up femininity (mother, girl, tart – or a man?). And in many ways their gendered subjectivity will be in agreement with their social task as mother, even though they certainly also desired other things for themselves. Thus, for the grandmothers one important contradiction might be between a sort of modernized gender identity (increased individualization) and the cultural and social options available to them.

So what happens to our own generation – the daughters born in the 1940s and 1950s? On the one hand, we will experience the unrest in our mother's identity projects, and on the other, we will have quite different social/cultural possibilities to make a life for ourselves outside the home. One can say that the experience of the 'new' and the 'old' is there as an ambiguous streak through our whole socialization: unconsciously, mother transferred her gendered subjectivity to us, while she told us about a more modernized version of gender identity. We must not forget that it was often mother who encouraged us to choose a different way of life from her own, for instance, by insisting on education – quite contrary to what we constructed later as our maternal burden (cf. Åström, 1986; Apter, 1985).

Thus, one can say that we, the daughters, 'inherit' both our mothers' 'updated' gender identity and her 'old-fashioned' gendered subjectivity. But the contradiction between those two aspects of psychological gender is much more noticeable in this generation, as the outer restrictions slacken. For instance: the daughters (supported by mother) are quite set on getting an education – but what on earth do they want for themselves? Thus, the educational stories of our generation (even those of us who made an academic career, see e.g. Rosenbeck, 1987) often reflect what has been called a 'syndrome of non-planning' (Bech-Jørgensen, 1985), where important choices are determined more often than not haphazardly by the preferences of a good friend or the pamphlets that happened to be in the mailbox the day before application. An important contradiction for this generation could be formulated as one between a modern gender identity on the one hand, and an old-fashioned gendered subjectivity on the other (which for instance is seen in their relations to men and motherhood). The psychological importance of the feminist movement could perhaps be understood as the collective elaboration of this contradiction, when the daughters reach their late moratorium and adulthood. An elaboration which most certainly also had important effects, as it sustained us in our extra-familial projects (even though not without ambivalence) at the same time as we chose to become mothers.

This will also result in changed conditions of socialization for the granddaughters, young girls of today – which might also have an effect on the more inert structure of gendered subjectivity. Some studies seem to suggest that the heterosexual relationship is no longer associated with psychological autonomy for girls in the way it used to be, and that same-sex friends are evaluated in quite a new manner, even though girls could ridicule such concepts as 'sister solidarity' (Vik Kleven, 1991). Gender identity is also more culturally manifold – and the construction of it is more than ever a personal project for the girl. This will have both positive and negative consequences for her: she will be able to play with gender in ways that her mother couldn't even dream about, but at the same time, when it comes to quality of performance and self-control, the demands on her could be quite insurmountable. What is even more important, however, is that this construction of gender identity now seems to be part of a more comprehensive project, namely, to be confirmed as an individual. In fact gender might be used to get such confirmation without the constant fear of being 'tarty' (grandmother's fear?) or 'objectified' (mother's fear?) – to have a gender could be part of human rights for a girl in the 1990s!

The 'granddaughters' will not experience the same conflicts between new gender identity and outer possibilities as their grandmothers did: gender can be expressed in many ways. Neither will they experience their mothers' conflict between old gendered subjectivity and new gender identity: the modern girl can be both individual and gender. Maybe one of their most important conflicts will lie in the third axis of the triangle – between the new gendered subjectivity on the one hand and the cultural and social possibilities on the other. The modern girl will not necessarily experience her gender as a limitation – she wants everything and she thinks she can do anything. But is it possible? Or is it just another female fantasy of harmony?

It is difficult to tell a story of change without wavering between nostalgia and heroic optimism. In our view, there most certainly are both gains and losses in the process of change, and paradisaical visions of either sort are really quite lifeless. The generations to come will at least have one thing in common with their mothers and grandmothers: they too will live within the dialectics of uncontemporaneity. But exactly where those contradictions will make themselves most felt is, of course, impossible to predict.

REFERENCES

Apter, T. (1985) *Why women don't have wives*. New York: Schocken.
Apter, T. (1990) *Altered loves. Mothers and daughters during adolescence*. New York: St Martin's Press Inc.

Åström, L. (1986) *I kvinnoled* (Of female descent). Stockholm: Liber.

Bech-Jørgensen, B. (1985) *Noget med mennesker eller noget på et kontor* (Something with people or something at an office). København: Samfundsfagnyt.

Bjerrum Nielsen, H. and Rudberg, M. (1989) *Historien om jenter og gutter: Kjønnssosialisering i et utviklingspsykologisk perspektiv* (The story of boys and girls: gender socialization in the perspective of developmental psychology). Oslo: Universitetsforlaget. (Paper available in English.)

Bjerrum Nielsen, H. and Rudberg, M. (1991a) 'Kön, modernitet och postmodernitet' (Gender, modernity and postmodernity). *Kvinnovetenskapligt Tidskrift, 1*. (Paper available in English.)

Bjerrum Nielsen, H. and Rudberg, M. (1991b) *Halløj tykke! – Jenter på vei* (Hi there, chubby! Girls in change). Unpublished manuscript, University of Oslo.

Bordo, S. (1990) 'Feminism, postmodernism, and gender scepticism'. In L.J. Nicholson (ed.), *Feminism/Postmodernism*. New York/London: Routledge.

Chodorow, N. (1978) *The reproduction of mothering. Psychoanalysis and the sociology of gender*. Berkeley: University of California Press.

Eichenbaum, L. and Orbach, S. (1983) *What do women want?* Glasgow: William Collins.

Erikson, E.H. (1968) *Identity: youth and crisis*. New York: Norton.

Rosenbeck, B. (1987) 'Kvindekøn'. In *Den moderne kvindeligheds historie fra 1880–1980* (The history of modern femininity. 1880–1980). København: Gyldendal.

Vik Kleven, K. (1991) *Vi er ålreite jenter, ikke sant?* (We are OK girls, aren't we?). Oslo: Universitetsforlaget.

Walkerdine, V. (1986) 'Post-structuralist theory and everyday social practices: the family and the school'. In S. Wilkinson (ed.), *Feminist social psychology. Developing theory and practice*. Milton Keynes: Open University Press.

Walkerdine, V. and Lucey, H. (1989) *Democracy in the kitchen*. London: Virago Press.

Ziehe, T. (1989) *Kulturanalyser* (Cultural analysis). Stockholm: Symposion.

Part II

Mothering in context

Chapter 7

Mothering in context
Female subjectivities and intervening practices

Liesbeth Woertman

Social and economic divisions between the sexes have led to different worlds for men and women. Women perform unpaid labour in the private sphere of the home, while men have paid work in the public sphere. The woman was mother and wife; the man breadwinner. These specific divisions of labour appear to be gradually breaking down as increasingly more women and mothers enter the labour market. The traditional women's occupations were always permeated by implicit and/or explicit 'motherly' skills. Take for example nursing. However, in the 1990s, women may still be overrepresented in the traditional women's professions, but they are also gradually gaining ground in higher positions and in 'men's' occupations. This has resulted in the emergence of the working mother and symbolic motherhood. The expectation of 'motherly' skills of women in work outside the home is known as symbolic motherhood. The term 'working mother' refers to biological mothers.

In this section of the book, the emphasis lies on fantasies, symbolic meanings and myths about mothers. The presupposition is that every contact between women is influenced by mother symbolism and by experiences in the primary mother–daughter relationship. This common ground – analysis from a symbolic maternal perspective and of the primary mother–daughter relationship within a non-biological context – is new. But before I go on to outline the articles in this section, I would like to introduce them using a short historical sketch of thinking on mothers and motherhood from the perspective of the women's movement.

FROM NATURAL MOTHERHOOD TO CONTEXTUAL MATERNITY

We do not become mothers simply by bearing a child. We are made into mothers. Obviously, I'm paraphrasing Simone de Beauvoir here, who broke the traditional, automatic link between womanhood and motherhood in her classic analysis in *The second sex*, resulting in the notion that anatomy did not necessarily determine destiny.

It was more than 20 years before de Beauvoir's voice was heard and recognized by large numbers of women. A major factor was undoubtedly the introduction of the Pill, and the fact that women were gradually enjoying higher levels of education. For the first time in history, Western women from all classes had the opportunity to decide for themselves whether they wanted to become mothers, and if so, how many children they wanted. Motherhood thus became an option rather than a fate.

At the same time, during the 1960s and 1970s women were still raised and socialized almost exclusively to acquire the skills, qualities and personal characteristics traditionally linked to the female subject (i.e. mothers and wives), such as nurturing, self-sacrifice, self-denial, empathy and emotionality.

Since the 1970s, motherhood has been an issue in the women's movement. For the first time in history, books on the limitations, frustrations, disappointments and loneliness of motherhood appeared in the US and the UK. One of these was authored by Adrienne Rich. The following fragment is taken from her diary in November 1960.

> My children cause me the most exquisite suffering of which I have any experience. It is the suffering of ambivalence: the murderous alternation between bitter resentment and raw-edged nerves, and blissful gratification and tenderness. Sometimes I seem to myself, in my feelings towards these tiny guiltless little beings, a monster of selfishness and intolerance. Their voices wear away at my nerves, their constant needs, above all their needs for simplicity and patience, fill me with despair at my own failures, despair too at my fate, which is to serve a function for which I was not fitted. And I am weak sometimes from held in rage. There are times when I feel only death will free us from one another, when I envy the barren woman who has the luxury of her regrets but lives a life of privacy and freedom.
>
> (Rich, 1976: 1)

I think this quotation is a prime example of the ambivalence between the reality of motherhood as experienced by women and the ideal – which she can never match. The word 'fate' demonstrates that woman and mother were inextricably linked at that time and that there was little question of choices or options. The books written by Rich and other mothers (Friedan, 1964; Dinnerstein, 1976) led to an awareness in large groups of women that they were not alone in feeling as they did. And they created a growing insight into maternity. Rich wrote:

> But for most of what we know as the 'mainstream' of recorded history, motherhood as institution has ghettoized and degraded female potentialities.
>
> The power of the mother has two aspects: the biological potential or capacity to bear and nourish human life, and the magical power invested in women by men, whether in the form of Goddess-worship or the fear of being controlled and overwhelmed by women. We do not actually know much about what power may have meant in the hands of strong, prepatriarchal women.
>
> (Rich, 1976: xv)

In 1981, the French writer Elisabeth Badinter added her analysis of motherhood to that of the American Adrienne Rich (1976). A comparison of the two books is interesting because they appeared at around the same time, were – and are – both influential, and both offer a different perspective. In this sense, they can be considered as representations of two important approaches within women's studies. Rich emphasized differences between women and men (the alpha bias), whereas Badinter focused more on the presupposed similarities of men and women (the beta bias). In essence, Badinter is elaborating on de Beauvoir's blue-stocking tradition. Badinter and Rich write from their own experiences as mothers of three children, and both central premises are almost the same. They both criticize the social myths of maternal instinct and the idea that motherhood is woman's only satisfaction. However, their arguments, supporting evidence and conclusions are very different. Badinter concentrates on a limited historic period; Rich uses her personal experience more fully and draws from more varied historic sources. But perhaps the greatest difference between the two books is the role of the man and the father. Rich's book reflects the Anglo-Saxon utopian vision of the lonely, intimate bond between mother and child. In contrast, Badinter's ideal family is based on absolutely equal responsibility of men and women in raising the children.

At around the same time, the experiences of mothers were being charted through studies on chronic over-burdening and lack of space for individual activities. Feminist women and some Marxist-oriented men were also analysing the institution of motherhood. This analysis was primarily socio-economic, and aimed at exploring the reproduction of existing labour relations. The results showed a complex of self-maintaining circles – boys were raised to become bread-winners, who would later perform alienating labour; girls would be educated to perform the role of wife and housewife who would be responsible for animating the tired man in preparation for the next day's labour. But women also had an additional function – bearing and caring for children. The first feminist socialization analyses were rather global, and did not examine different contexts and situations in which women were expected to perform this maternal task. Nor were differences between women explored. This would have to wait for the 1980s.

The different ways of mothering have hardly been explored by psychology. Motherhood is usually isolated from other experiences in life (Birns and Hay, 1988).

To recap here, we can describe the 1970s and 1980s as a period in which individual experiences of women with regard to maternity were revealed in all their ambivalences by feminist women. The 1980s were also a time when motherhood as an institution was criticized, but the insight that mothers are made within a social context had to wait for the 1990s.

MOTHERING IN CONTEXT

By using this title as heading for this section, we hope to indicate that the following articles attempt to take distance from the notion that there is such a thing as 'universal motherhood'. This is achieved using two methods. First, mothering as (biological and social) practice is situated in time and place, i.e. in an historic and cultural (or ethnic and geographic) context. Second, mothering as practice is divorced from a biological or social necessity. It becomes a package of independent skills, activities and attitudes that are expected from women, or which women expect from themselves if they are placed in a power and/or confidential position. This can mean work situations, but also love relationships or friendships.

The object-relations theory again occupies a prominent position here, but not essentially to describe psychosocial development. It is used as an explanatory model for interactions that can be considered repetitions or continuations of the primary woman–woman relationship between daughters and mothers. One of the work situations focused on here is the therapeutic setting. This is a situation *par excellence* where the ideal mother is evoked. But it also appears to be an area where 'ideal mothers' (read: therapists) have found their niche in life.

Orbach and Eichenbaum especially have had the courage to examine their own role as therapists. They approach this examination by analysing their projection onto their clients, whereby they 'signify' this projection in a mother–daughter context. Halldis Leira uses the myths of Demeter and Clytemnestra as examples of ideal mothers who live in the unconscious of women. Sayers explores what the first women psychoanalysts have to tell us about maternal and phallic power. Deutsch, Horney and Klein are examined before Sayers passes on to provide a number of examples of maternal power drawn from her clinical experience.

Krips has developed a programme for child-therapists so that they can explore the mother images from which they work and project onto clients. Groen asks if a multicultural future is possible for practical and symbolic motherhood. She shows how the Western preoccupation with 'I', in both society and science, excludes the 'Other' (including other mothers). One of the examples she provides concerns single motherhood. She shows how a network of aunts and other relatives surrounds Surinam or Antillian children and could provide a possible alternative form of organization, and concludes by asking: how can we develop multiform identities?

A common problem in all the essays is the link between the notions woman, mother and object, and the strong emphasis in Western society on the values of a person as autonomous subject. All authors attempt to represent mothers as autonomous subject, and also to allow the autonomous subject to be perceived as a relational subject. In other words, to reveal the ingrained notions which brought 'the mother' into being. A further common aspect is that all the writers have made visible differences between women. Which difference is accentuated depends on the (sub)discipline of the author, but the prevalent dichotomies are questioned by all: I and the Other, society and the individual, Western and other cultures.

The strong emphasis in this second section on images, myths, fantasy, the (collective) unconscious on women as mothers provides an insight into the complexity women have to deal with, and brings to prominence the tight interweave of the concepts woman and mother. Even in terms of language, it appears incredibly difficult to transcend dualistic thinking.

The articles illustrate how difficult it is to relinquish an objectivizing approach to mothers. The object-relations theory actually invites this kind of objectivization of the mother (as object of her child). Mother is represented as a fixed entity and not, as in the case of other people, as someone who is busy developing/constructing her identity in an interplay with others. Orbach and Eichenbaum pick up on this pitfall and subsequently elaborate its consequences for the therapeutic process.

The leading question is and remains 'who identifies with the mother?' The following articles show that this also implies the question 'who relinquishes paradise lost?' As long as the mother is considered essentialistic and is objectified, all unfulfilled desires can be projected onto her. However, if it is accepted that mothers are also subjects-in-development, we will have to say a definite farewell to 'the mother' as centre of existence, as anchor, as point of reference from which we name ourselves.

In the chapters that now follow, a start has been made on this long goodbye to the mother as surrogate for godly care.

REFERENCES

Badinter, E. (1981) *The myth of motherhood.* London: Souvenir Press (E & A) Ltd.
Birns, B. and Hay, D. (eds) (1988) *The different faces of motherhood.* New York: Plenum.
Dinnerstein, D. (1976) *The mermaid and the minotaur: sexual arrangements and human malaise.* New York: Harper & Row.
Friedan, B. (1964) *The feminine mystique.* New York: Dell.
Rich, A. (1976) *Of woman born.* New York: Bantam.
Ussher, J. (1990) 'Negative images of female sexuality and reproduction: reflecting misogyny or misinformation?'. *Psychology of Women Newsletter,* 17–29.

Chapter 8

Maternal and phallic power
Fantasy and symbol

Janet Sayers

Recent feminist psychoanalysis, at least that informed by the work of Nancy Chodorow (e.g. 1978) and Luce Irigaray (e.g. 1985), has tended to focus on, and celebrate women's mothering. In this it is at one with many men psychoanalysts who now variously idealize mothering in terms of empathy (e.g. Kohut, 1977), holding (Winnicott, 1960), containment (e.g. Bion, 1977), and transformation (e.g. Bollas, 1987).

But this is to neglect the power, negative as well as positive, vested in fantasy in the mother as effect of the child's sexual impulses as described by psycho-analysis's leading women pioneers. It also overlooks the power vested in men as symbol, *qua* phallus, by virtue of the economic and political dominance enjoyed by ruling-class men in male-dominated society. I will illustrate this point below. First, however, what of early women psychoanalysts' account of the power vested in the mother?

WOMEN ANALYSE MATERNAL POWER

To begin at the beginning. Helene Deutsch was arguably the most important of the first-generation women psychoanalysts in Vienna. Certainly she was the first psychoanalyst to devote a book to women's psychology. In it she very much drew on the power battles she experienced with her mother that in turn sensitized her to those of her women patients. She described her mother as beating her 'not to punish me, but as an outlet for her own pent-up aggressions', so embittered was she that Helene was not the son she wanted and desired (Sayers, 1991: 25). Deutsch likewise records a woman patient telling her of her mother punishing her childhood masturbation with binding while her father simply looked on, just as Helene felt her own father passively gave way to her mother's torment of her as a child. Drawing on such experience, Deutsch emphasized the fraught identification of mothers and daughters so overlooked by Freud – an identification that is now often assumed by feminist psychoanalysis to be unproblematically reproduced by their shared sex (e.g. Chodorow, 1978).

By contrast with Helene Deutsch, Karen Horney, the only woman founding member of the Berlin Psychoanalytic Institute and the first to mount a woman-centred critique of Freud's penis-envy theory of female sexuality, felt much more warmly toward her mother. Like Deutsch however she also experienced her mother, not her father, as the most powerful figure in her childhood home. This in turn alerted her to her women patients' similar histories. It culminated in her account of a patient she called Clare – actually a composite of her own and her women patients' mother–daughter experiences. Clare, Horney wrote, had a self-righteous mother who demanded her daughter's admiration and exclusive devotion. The father was no help. He was absent – physically and emotionally. His only affection was for Clare's mother whom he worshipped with blind admiration. Yet she despised him. Judging 'it was much safer to be on the powerful side' (quoted in Sayers, 1991: 131), Clare repressed the hostility her mother's narcissism evoked in her under a facade of submission first to her mother and then to a succession of male lovers. In sum: through this and other clinical tales of mother–daughter interaction Horney thereby prefigured today's account by Alice Miller (e.g. 1979) of power and its abuse – sadism and masochism – in parent–child relations.

Like both Deutsch and Horney, Melanie Klein, arguably the single most influential figure after Freud on British psychoanalysis, also characterized her mother as the most powerful force in her childhood home – the one who did most to make ends meet unlike her impotent-seeming father. But whereas Deutsch and Horney attended to the seeming realities of the mother's power, Klein drew attention to the way images of maternal power are refracted through fantasy fuelled by the child's bodily preoccupations and impulses – oral, anal and genital. In this she drew on her pioneering work applying Freud's theory of unconscious fantasy and infantile sexuality (now deplored by Alice Miller and many feminists) to the treatment of children, first in Berlin and then in London where Klein settled in 1926.

Examples included two-year-old Rita who transferred onto Klein the terror she felt each night lest something come through the window and bite her genitals just as she had earlier wanted to attack her mother when she was pregnant with her baby brother. Indeed so frightened was she of this imagined retaliating, orally attacking maternal figure, Rita initially could not bear to be alone with Klein – not, that is, until Klein took her outdoors and put her fear and its maternal origin into words.

Another patient, three-year-old Trude, construed her mother's power in anal terms. In therapy she repeatedly pretended it was night-time and that she and Klein were asleep. She would then come over to Klein and threaten her, saying she wanted to hit her in the stomach, take out her poohs and make her poor. No sooner said than she hid terrified behind the sofa, covered herself up, sucked her fingers and wet herself. In this, says Klein, Trude re-enacted every detail of the way, when she was not quite two, she used to run into her parents' bedroom at night as though wanting to rob her pregnant mother of her babies and kill her – just as she now attacked Klein and wanted to rob her of her poohs. This then generated fear lest her mother likewise attack her. Hence her nocturnal fears – like those of Rita.

By contrast four-year-old Ruth's fantasies were more genital in content. One day she played at feeding her dolls jugfuls of milk only to cry out at Klein when she put a wet sponge by one of them, 'No, she mustn't have the big sponge, that's not for children, that's for grown ups!' as if she could not bear what her grown-up mother enjoyed, the sponge seemingly representing her father's big penis (quoted in Sayers, 1991: 220).

Generalizing from such cases, Klein concluded that the child's deprivation by her mother's relationship with the father, and the very real power she exercises in weaning and potty-training, give rise to wishes in the daughter to attack this power both orally and anally. This in turn elicits fantasies about the mother's power – of her oral and anal retaliation against the daughter's actual and imagined attacks on her sexuality.

Furthermore, argued Klein, since her genitals are internal the girl, unlike the boy, cannot so easily reassure herself that her mother's imagined attacks on her sexuality have not taken place. Hence, she claimed, women are never so confident of their femininity and childbearing capacity as are men of their phallic masculinity, albeit through their work and creativity, and through sex and having babies, girls and women may assuage fear of having been destroyed by the mother's power while also repairing damage done her by their attacks. It is these attacks – and the oral, anal and genital fantasies they involve – that Klein maintained constitute the mother as first castrator in the child's mind, not the father as Freud assumed on the basis of his patients' transference to him as patriarch. In both sexes, she stressed, 'it is the mother who in the deepest strata of the unconscious is specially dreaded as castrator' (Klein, 1926: 129).

PRESENT-DAY CLINICAL EXAMPLES OF MATERNAL POWER

Women continue to dwell on the power of the mother – or at least they often do as patients in therapy as I shall illustrate from my work as a clinical psychologist.

First forty-year-old Daphne. She came for treatment because of lack of confidence, particularly when reporting to her female, seemingly matriarchal superiors at work. The childhood story she recounts is one dominated by maternal tyranny involving repeated beating and chastisement by her adoptive mother for Daphne's supposed crimes at home and school. Her criticism never seemed to cease. Internally it still continues, as it does in our relationship. Daphne feels that, like her mother, I hold the whip hand over her. And in a sense, of course, I do. For it was my decision to take her on for therapy, and the timing of sessions, holiday breaks and the ending of therapy are all under my control. But Daphne also imagines I despise her, that just as her mother witheringly compared her unfavourably with her older brother, I likewise disparage her as completely boring compared to my other patients. So saying she lapses into silence – curbing and cutting off whatever she might say as too stupid, thereby destroying all spontaneity and liveliness just as she felt her mother so powerfully did in the ruthless regime she instituted in Daphne's childhood home.

Fifty-year-old Pat, by contrast, illusorily appropriates the seeming power of the mother to herself. She then seeks to bolster her powerfulness by making her mother and myself the powerless and envious spectators of her sexual prowess. She emphasises her ageing mother's disability and, on this basis, tries to command her life by doing all her housework, shopping and entertaining. So much so her mother recently sent her packing – a response with which I can sympathize having myself also been subject to Pat's somewhat cloying, suffocating and paradoxically disempowering hospitality. Whereas Klein's child patients felt enviously excluded by the mother's powerful seeming possession of the father, Pat has her mother and I envy her. Her mother, she suggests, coveted her husband. Indeed I can well believe it. The glowing terms in which Pat depicts him to me are enough to awaken anyone's envy of the power she seemingly enjoyed in possessing his single-minded devotion.

Unlike Pat, Anne, now in her late twenties, confers this power on me. She idealises me, as Klein describes the toddler's idealization of the mother, as omnipotent – lacking nothing – as replete with milk, faeces and father's penis too. Anne tells me I have everything 'sussed out', unlike her mother whose weakness she deplores: specifically her failure to stand up to Anne's violent father; and her blindness to her brother-in-law's sexual abuse of Anne. Not that Anne does not also recognize her mother's actual power. After all it was her mother who first took her to school and abandoned her there, as it seemed. Anne still remembers asking herself, as if it were yesterday, 'How could she do it to me?'. Now she similarly bemoans my power in leaving her for my summer holidays. Indeed she would complain more vehemently were it not that she deals with my absence by imagining me as an omnipotent, omnipresent figure, forever there for her in the Clinic, unlike her mother whose unavailability at the time of her younger daughter's birth still remains a painfully vivid image in Anne's mind. No wonder she abhors women's power in childbearing.

Horney and Klein rightly drew attention to this power and the envy it evokes. So too have a few recent feminist writers and therapists (e.g. Rich, 1976; Chernin, 1985; Maguire, 1987). But this has often involved overlooking the quite different power symbolized by men *qua* phallus.

PHALLIC POWER – CLINICAL EXAMPLES

While women control children's day-to-day lives and thereby seem to exert the most powerful formative influence on their psychology, economic and political power is concentrated in the hands of ruling-class men. More visible than class, men and masculinity thereby come to signify power, albeit most men's power is negligible. Nevertheless, as feminists influenced by the work of the French psychoanalyst Jacques Lacan put it (e.g. Mitchell and Rose, 1982), man – or the phallus – is a central symbol of the law in patriarchal society. But as a symbol nobody can have or be the phallus. Nevertheless the illusion of having or being a man – and the power equated with manhood – exercises a tenacious hold. It has very real effects, not least on mother–daughter relations as I shall illustrate by returning to the above-mentioned patients.

First Daphne. Her father and husband are in no way powerful. Quite the reverse. Daphne derides them both as 'wimps'. Her father, she tells me, was completely under his mother's thumb. He did not even dare offend her by marrying. He only married after her death. And then, it seems, he merely traded one maternal tyrant for another – or at least that is how Daphne puts it in telling me his honeymoon with her mother put him in mind of death. It drove him to write his last will and testament. But what Daphne most holds against him was his failure, when she was a child, to intervene and protect her from her mother's abuse.

Given the weakness Daphne ascribes to the men in her life, it is perhaps surprising that, like other daughters, she looked to, and continues to look to, men as the only figures sufficiently potent to save her from herself and her mother. Or it would be surprising were men not endowed with such power, whatever their actual characteristics, by virtue of the material power enjoyed by a few men in our society. In this respect it is perhaps not so surprising that Daphne looked first to her father and then to her husband to rescue her from her mother, just as she now takes refuge both from her and me in actual and imagined affairs with men. She even contemplates self-abusive breast implant surgery to win men's affection, so readily do her heterosexual affairs become imbued with the destructive and self-destructive perversion of power she suffered, and still suffers in fantasy, in relation to her mother.

Next Pat. Her late husband, John, seems an unlikely candidate to embody phallic power. In life he was a bureaucratic underling, forced by ill-health to take early retirement whereupon he sank into self-defeating gloom. But in her mind Pat reverses this impotent image. She recalls John as a 'pillar of strength'. Imbuing him with all the traits she feels her mother lacks, she characterizes him as a paragon of virtue, as looking after all their friends, relations and neighbours – 'Nothing was ever too much for him'. No wonder she cannot bear to give him up, to acknowledge his loss. Three years after his death a name plaque by the front door still informs visitors, 'John and Pat live here'. His toothbrush remains in the bathroom rack, his dressing gown on the bedroom peg, as if he was just about to return. Otherwise Pat feels she would be as impotent and frail as her also recently bereaved mother seems to be. She cannot bear to be without him – to suffer the absence of a man. Hence her rejection of the emasculation seemingly signified by being called a 'widow' – like her mother. Yet, fettered to the illusion that seemingly buoys up her potency of having an ideal man represented by her now dead husband, she is imprisoned in the past, and thereby rendered powerless to move forward, as she herself admits.

Last Anne. Like Pat, Anne characterizes the men in her life as big and strong. But she depicts this strength in more negative terms. She tells me how, as a child, she would stay awake at night dreading yet excited by the thought of her father's imminent return when he might well beat up his wife, Anne's mother. Anne also recalls her maternal uncle – large and fat – getting into bed with her when she was just 9 years old, or driving her into the country where he would inveigle her into masturbating him. Similarly she evokes an image of her present boyfriend as immense and aggressive. Unlike Daphne, who repeatedly seeks out a powerful man to intervene between her mother and herself and her self-destructive identification with her, Anne finds herself, both in her dreams and in sex, distancing herself from her weak-seeming mother by wanting to be one with the brutish men of her life. Pregnant, she identified the child inside with her boyfriend. Then, terrified of the damage she associates with men's power, she had the baby aborted. Now she finds herself again imagining herself to be a bestial man. Physically she confronts me – large, solid, sullen – while experiencing herself with her boyfriend as the physically powerful, violent figure she takes men to be. Dreading the harm she might thereby do him and herself she turns her back on him and sex. Yet she wants both it and motherhood. Indeed this is the reason she first sought therapy – in effect, to overcome the obstacle posed by illusory identification with the power symbolized by men that prevents her having sex or babies like her mother.

ANALYSING PHALLIC POWER

This brings me back to the early women psychoanalysts. One of the effects of today's feminist and psychoanalytic idealization of mothering has been to lose sight not only of power but also of sex, including phallic sexuality. Yet, as indicated above, this is also often central to mother–daughter relations.

This was recognized long ago by the Dutch psychoanalyst, Jeanne Lampl-de Groot. As a result of the mother–daughter transference her sex invited in her women patients she came to appreciate, unlike her male colleagues, the primacy of the daughter's desire sexually to possess the mother in the only way she knows how in male-dominated society, namely through having a penis.

Lampl-de Groot recounted, for instance, the case of a woman referred to her because of unresolved transference issues with a male analyst. At first she was hostile to Lampl-de Groot. Then she became enamoured of her, and actively wooed her. She dreamt that Lampl-de Groot's analyst was castrated so she could take his place and possess her for herself. In this context she recalled childhood hatred of her father, particularly when, after many nights of getting her parents out of bed to attend to her, he came in and boxed her ears. Then she remembered a dream, from when she was 4 years old, of lying in bed feeling a sense of supreme bliss with her mother beside her, saying 'That is right, that is how it ought to be'. At that she awoke, having wet the bed, feeling extremely disappointed and unhappy – a response Lampl-de Groot attributed to her recent discovery of sexual difference, which she construed as signifying that without a penis she could never sexually possess her mother.

Lampl-de Groot's (1927) account of women's transference on to her of their early sexual desire for the mother led Freud (1931) radically to revise his claim, based on his women patients' patriarchal transference to him as male analyst, that the first object of the daughter's desire is the father. Thanks to Lampl-de Groot he now recognized that women's first desire is for the mother.

But he took Lampl-de Groot to task for overlooking the daughter's hostility to the mother. Not that he paid much attention to this, or to the fantasies of maternal power involved. Nor did he or Lampl-de Groot attend to the power symbolized by the phallus in male-dominated society that arguably makes it such an object of desire. In this they differed from Klein (1926), and more recent psychologists (e.g. Dinnerstein, 1976), and psychoanalysts (e.g. Chasseguet-Smirgel, 1964), who argue that the daughter looks to the phallus to escape the mother rather than to possess her sexually. But all alike ignore the political and economic dominance of men that makes the phallus such a powerful symbol in this respect – whether of flight or possession. They overlook the material factors evoking women's persistent illusion, illustrated above, that if only they or their menfolk could embody the power symbolized by the phallus all their troubles, including those involved in mother–daughter relations, could be solved.

CONCLUSION

From its inception psychoanalysis has sought to help patients put into words and thereby undo the fantasies and symbols expressed in dreams and neurotic symptoms. For only through their deconstruction – and of the omnipotent illusions therein involved – can we begin to know and struggle to meet our wants and desires, actually and in fact. But in the case of the illusions bred by phallic symbols of male power more is at stake than individual therapy. What also has to be exposed, challenged and undone is men's command of economic and political resources that so much evokes and reinforces these illusions. And this, as feminism recognises, calls for collective political action. All too often, however, this becomes stymied by primitive fantasies of maternal power, some of which I have described in this chapter. These too therefore have to be confronted and dispelled if our struggles to change the social reality reinforcing the symbolic equation of men with power, and the illusions to which it is heir, are to be effective – a project that cannot be achieved simply through idealizing mothering as is the case in much of today's psychoanalysis.

REFERENCES

Bion, W.R. (1977) *Seven servants*. New York: Jason Aronson.
Bollas, C. (1987) *The shadow of the object*. London: Free Association Books.
Chasseguet-Smirgel, J. (1964) *Female sexuality*. London: Virago.
Chernin, K. (1985) *The hungry self*. London: Virago.
Chodorow, N. (1978) *The reproduction of mothering. Psychoanalysis and the sociology of gender*. Berkeley: University of California Press.
Dinnerstein, D. (1976) *The rocking of the cradle*. London: Souvenir Press.
Freud, S. (1931) 'Female sexuality'. In *Standard edition of the collected works of Sigmund Freud. 21*. London: Hogarth.
Irigaray, L. (1985) *That sex which is not one*. Ithaca: Cornell University Press.
Klein, M. (1926) 'The psychological principles of early analysis'. In *Love, guilt and reparation*. London: Hogarth.
Kohut, H. (1977) *The restoration of the self*. New York: International Universities Press.

Lampl-de Groot, J. (1927) 'The evolution of the Oedipus complex in women'. In J. Lampl-de Groot, *Man and mind*. New York: International Universities Press, 1985.

Maguire, M. (1987) 'Casting the evil eye'. In S. Ernst and M. Maguire (eds), *Living with the Sphinx*. London: Women's Press.

Miller, A. (1979) *The drama of the gifted child*. New York: Basic Books.

Mitchell, J. and Rose, J. (1982.) *Feminine sexuality*. London: Macmillan.

Rich, A. (1976) *Of woman born*. New York: Bantam.

Sayers, J. (1991) *Mothering psychoanalysis: Helene Deutsch, Karen Horney, Anna Freud, Melanie Klein*. Harmondsworth: Penguin Books, 1992.

Winnicott, D.W. (1960) 'The theory of the parent-infant relationship'. In *Maturational processes and the facilitating environment*. London: Hogarth.

Chapter 9

Feminine subjectivity, countertransference and the mother–daughter relationship

Susie Orbach and Luise Eichenbaum

Over the last 30 to 40 years a significant literature around countertransference has built up and countertransference is now widely understood to include all the responses that are aroused within the therapist when working with a particular patient. In other words, the psychotherapist's disposition to feel certain kinds of ways; to incline towards particular behaviours; to experience certain kinds of wishes in relation to a particular patient are now seen as being as much the nitty gritty of the analysis as the content the patient brings.

> My thesis is that the analyst's emotional response to his (sic) patient within the analytic situation represents one of the most important tools for his work. The analyst's counter-transference is an instrument of research into the patients's unconscious.
>
> (Heimann, 1950: 81)

Transference interpretations once given on the basis of the manifest and latent content of the analysand's material are now given extra credence because they reflect the analyst's examination of the countertransference as well. That is to say, the analyst confirms their hypothesis about the patient by reference to their scrutiny of their own feelings about the patient; what is aroused in them; what they feel *vis-à-vis* the patient; what relational melée they feel drawn into by the patient and so on.

Psychoanalysis, once a practice of historical discovery, is now more commonly understood as an endeavour in which the relational aspects, the intersubjective field between the analyst and the analysand are at the centre of 'talking cure'. What occurs within the therapy, between the therapist and patient, the feelings the patient has for the therapist, the feelings they in turn arouse in the analyst and the working through of those have now taken centre stage. Clinical practice sees the therapy relationship as a re-enactment (Mitchell, 1988) of previous significant relationships; as a defence against the experience of early object relations; as containing in nuance the emotional shape of former relationships.

Many contemporary analysts and therapists, ourselves included, look to the therapeutic relationship rather than the interpretation, as the site of psychic structural change. What can occur in the interpersonal field between analyst and analysand during the course of therapy is seen as curative. The countertransference is used as a diagnostic tool by practitioners. It tells us about the internal world of the patient, provides clues to the level of her object relations and it alerts the clinician to the defence structure of the patient. For us (Orbach and Eichenbaum, 1987) the use of the countertransference provides us with a way to relate to those aspects of the person that are hidden behind their defence structure. To give a simple example: the patient is extremely negative both about what she is talking about and towards the therapist. She feels hopeless as though nothing can get better. She communicates this to the therapist in a way that arouses in the therapist very negative and hopeless feelings. The therapist recognises this communication from the patient, feels herself embroiled in the negativity, feels even turned off by it and feels an impulse to withdraw attention away from the patient and abandon her with her own distress. By recognizing the countertransferential nature of the feelings, the therapist is able to intervene in her own responses. She uses them to understand how the patient might be feeling. She doesn't reject her, rather she wonders about why the patient feels the urge to set up an intersubjective field in which she encourages rejection from the other. As she reflects upon this she begins to talk with the patient about the despair she imagines may be behind the negativity. She attempts to encounter the patient behind her defence structure and to provide a mode of relating that allows the patient to meet that unconscious despair – a despair that has remained buried and split off for many years – in a relational context that will allow that despair to be felt and to be integrated.

The analyst's wish to withdraw is understood as what the patient is able to create: a situation in which she pushes people away. But beyond this defensive structure, the analyst is also able to conjecture and theory-build about the patient and the operations of her internal world. She begins to draw a picture for herself about the shape of this person's psyche, how she experiences the environment, how she came to be this way, what her original relationships felt like to the patient and so on.

As we monitor our countertransference reactions we are continuously challenged by the fact that each therapy relationship is unique, just as each individual within any given therapy relationship is unique. Each therapeutic encounter creates its own particular pattern, a pattern marked by a variety of emotional exchanges within the interpersonal field. No two patients reproduce the same relationship with an analyst, nor do any two patients engender identical feelings and responses in the analyst. Each therapy relationship is always being created between the two participants. And within the analytic relationship there is a tension between a re-enactment of the familiar patterns of relating – that is the way the person knows how to be in relationship – and a transcendence of that way of being in the new relationship.

And at the same time, when one works within a social and gender-conscious framework, one is well aware of the fact that there is a commonality of emotional responses and internal object manifestations shared by patients which derive simply from their living in a common culture. There is, in many ways, more uniformity to the cultural influences which contribute to the shape of a person's psychology than interactions with the varied and numerous permutations of individual family constellations. So within the therapy setting one is not only engaging with the array of family interpersonal connections, but with the internalizations of the culture as well. Cultural prescriptions for gender, along with race and class, powerfully insert themselves into the very essence of who we feel ourselves to be.

We need to insert the fact of gender into the heart of relational theory and clinical practice. Just as there is no such thing as a non-relational subject, there is no such thing as a de-gendered subject. Subjectivity, a sense of selfhood, occurs in developmental time coincident with the recognition of personal gender and the gender of other(s). Personal pronouns may be neuter in the English language, but 'I' always refers to a masculine or feminine subject. 'You' always refers to a masculine or feminine object (Stoller, 1978).

Recognizing the notion of the gendered subject, clinicians and feminist theorists need to understand the particular issues achieving differentiated selfhood involves and means for women – both for women patients/clients and women psycho-therapists. Psychoanalysis has only recently turned its attention to the implications of the notion of the gendered subject and yet this is a crucial area for both clinical practice and feminist research (Chodorow, 1978; Dinnerstein, 1976; Eichenbaum and Orbach, 1982).[1] Many women will say that they don't know who they are when they are in a relationship, that they lose themselves. That the person they are, the person who is revealed when they are in an intimate relationship is a different 'self' from the self they know outside the relationship. They have an unstable and, perhaps we might add, a defensive concept of self. It is as though they feel themselves to be taken over in a relationship.

This phenomena, an instability in the sense of selfhood occurs within the transference–countertransference aspects of the therapy relationship. The psychotherapist's reaction within the countertransference alerts us to the particular problems that the intersubjective field holds for women. Subjectivity, inter-subjectivity, the achievement of what we have called an autonomous self or a separated attachment is shaped in a particular way.

Women patients/clients, we have observed (both in our clinical practices, in our colleagues' practices and in the work of those psychotherapists whose work we supervise) crave a certain kind of relating that is at the same time quite hard for them to tolerate. The closeness and intimacy they desire is hedged in with defensive rejection, with shame, with conflict about the desire for relating. They project onto the psychotherapist prohibition, disapprobation and censure for that wanting. And then when they allow that wanting to materialize there is a worry that they will merge with the other/the psychotherapist never to emerge as their own person again (Eichenbaum and Orbach, 1987; Orbach, 1987; 1990).

As we have argued elsewhere, a crucial aspect of the development of a feminine psychic structure has depended upon the denial of a girl's, later a woman's needs, desires and wants. She has had to shape her needs, in line with those needs that will find approval or recognition in those around her. This creates a situation in which the most personal aspects of self demand denial or recasting leaving the individual with a wary relationship to desire that arises from her. This denial of needs can take all sorts of forms. The person can present themselves as need free, as confused about personal needs, as lacking in the words to know those needs, or by worry that she is overwhelmed or will overwhelm others with her needs.

This latter response can produce a particular interaction if the therapist only cursorily reviews what is going on in the countertransference. For example if the woman presents in such a way that is extremely needy, it may produce a frisson or rather more, an impulse to reject. The therapist may feel, even if she doesn't want to, a wish that the patient contain herself better and manage her neediness in a less voluminous way. She, who has also been raised as a woman, may be aware of the way she herself contains her own neediness and she may find the expression of it in the client disagreeable and even threatening. The client's neediness hides the real need by saying in effect 'I'm too much, I can't be helped, I'm hopeless, my needs are ugly, see you can't stand them/me either'.

Because this defence of super neediness is effective at an emotional level it can work. The therapist can collude with the patient by refusing to recognize that what is being presented is actually a defence, a defence of excessive neediness against the woman's internal conflict over her need. In other words by producing this form of defence she elicits discomfort in the therapist and the exasperated therapist can feel 'Yes, you are too needy', rather than doing what is required, which is to talk with the woman about how this defence is designed to reiterate this state of affairs, rather than allow them both to work on the woman's projected-out internal conflict.

So within the countertransference, the inclination of the psychotherapist may well be to take up the countertransferentially-induced demand to collude with a prohibition, disapprobation or censure at that wanting. But these inclinations are what lie at the heart of the problem of the woman's subjectivity in the first place. To do so, to act on the countertransference rather than receive it, process it and respond to those aspects of self hidden behind the projective identification would be to reinforce the very problems that the woman who has come to therapy sought relief from. In other words, the problem with achieving a feminine subjectivity – a self who is related to other distinct but interrelated selves; a self that has boundaries that are flexible rather than transgressable – arises because aspects of self have not been received and accepted by others. Those unwelcomed aspects of self have had to be split off and repressed. This is Winnicott's 'true self', Fairbairn's 'schizoid split', Eichenbaum and Orbach's 'little girl'. In order to achieve feminine subjectivity those split off parts of self need to be received within the therapeutic relationship, in the intersubjective field between analyst and analysand and through this process re-integrated into the person of the analysand.[2]

We have written extensively elsewhere (Eichenbaum and Orbach, 1982; 1983; 1988) about the social requirements of femininity and their impact for the psychological development of girls. We have examined the ways in which a gendered psychology is reproduced from generation to generation with a particular emphasis on the mother–daughter relationship as the pivotal transmitter of the culture. In our work we have proposed that women, as the people responsible for the emotional and physical welfare of others, come to feel troubled about their own needs for nurturing, dependence, initiative, agency and subjectivity. Although we did not describe it as such in our first writings it was first within the transference–countertransference configuration that we became aware of the predicament posed for our women clients around the issue of emotional dependency.

Our clinical finding that our patients' refusal of our offering of a relationship in which their needs for care, love and attention could be accepted and welcomed led us to think about what this meant and why this was so. Repeatedly we witnessed our women patients' minimizing their needs after the initial crisis which brought them into therapy had passed. Repeatedly we experienced their surprise that we actually found their needs reasonable and understandable. Repeatedly we witnessed their disbelief that we found them to be worthy people. And repeatedly we came up against a defence which essentially kept us at a distance. We began to understand a defence structure in which the woman kept aspects of herself hidden and off limits to the relationship for fear of being rejected by or overwhelming to the therapist. And we understood that our task was to gain access to what we called (taking it from our clients' language) the little-girl inside by repeatedly making interpretations which spoke to the conflicts about recognition and acceptance of that fuller self. We understood our goal, in some sense, to be the integration of that split-off part of the ego thereby enabling the woman to be more fully and authentically her own person.

In those early years we were well aware of our part in the provision of a new experience for our women patients. Influenced by Winnicott, Fairbairn and Guntrip's work on the developmental struggle from infantile dependency to the development of an individuated self, we surmised that the early dependency needs of female infants had been thwarted contributing to a feeling of illegitimacy in relation to needs that arose from within her thus producing enormous difficulties with experiencing a subjectivity.

We laid great stress on the provision of a relationship that could accept and work through an early problematic merger, a merger that we read off from the transference–countertransference matrix 'marked, not only by the daughter's need of mother, but with the mother's need for psychological merger with her daughter' (Eichenbaum and Orbach, 1988: 51). The therapy relationship could be used not only to explore the conflict around dependency for women but also to provide a relationship where a woman was not constantly shoring up her false boundaries by fleeing into pseudo-separation (Eichenbaum and Orbach, 1987). Within this context we acted as the container (Bion) of our patients' anguish, desire, omnipotence, rage and so on. We often had to work hard to get these emotions into the intersubjective field, but once there, we knew we could tolerate and survive them. We knew, too, that we were being made use of through our interpretations which spoke to the conflicts about needs and desire, which spoke to the feelings of hopelessness at ever being met or understood emotionally and by offering the possibility of a relationship with another woman which, we thought, could challenge the inevitability of complicated and restrictive mother–daughter transference dynamics.

In recent years a more detailed reading of the countertransference has confirmed many aspects of our early theory building. It has also allowed us, however, to question more closely our participation in the transference–countertransference configuration. From this current vantage point we see that in order to transcend the interactional pattern of the patriarchally shaped mother–daughter relationship, a relationship in which each woman's subjectivity is restrained and denied, more is required of us than merely the ability to contain and survive.

What do we mean by this? In order to answer that we must first address the most critical of problems feminist theorists have been grappling with: that of the subjectivity of women. For we cannot speak of woman, mother, daughter, analyst or patient as subject without first addressing the reality of woman as object – non-subject – both within patriarchal culture and within psychoanalytic theory.

In those early years, unbeknown to us, in offering ourselves as the container, the one who could tolerate and survive, we were perpetuating the ideal of woman (mother) as object. Rather than be an object who disappointed, failed or could not tolerate the daughter's needs for dependency or initiative, we could now be the object who could be there to provide and bear witness to the difficulty that providing caused, to the defences it threw up, to the anguish it provoked.

It wasn't so much that we saw ourselves as the replacement mothers or perfect objects that we perceived our patients required in order for their own subjectivity to emerge. That's to say we didn't see that we were being the perfect mothers they wanted/needed (which was incidentally a criticism flowing from a misreading of our work), it was more that for many of our patients their very fragile sense of existing meant that to impose ourselves as separate subjects within the therapy was technically unfeasible. In other words, their developmental level meant that we were only experienced as their objects we couldn't be experienced as separate subjects without a concomitant experience of their obliteration.

Clearly this was not the only way *we* experienced ourselves within the therapy, because even if we were being used by the patient as their object we nevertheless still had agency and our own subjectivity and our engagement in the therapeutic endeavour were active. We were not simply the sum of our patients' projections, we were an important part of the therapy relationship. They could only make use of us as an object if we could simultaneously retain our sense of ourselves as subjects too – subjects who could experience a version of the feeling states our patients were in and give it back to them in digestible form.

But a further technical problem ensued directly, we believe, related to our gender. For us to absorb the countertransference without becoming ourselves submerged within it required a subjectivity of our own in which our boundaries were flexible without being violated. That assumed a far greater sense of internal solidity than we might often have felt. In essence in trying to find a way to be both the patient's object and a subject we were grappling with the issue of the therapist's subjectivity.

We suggest that recognition and presentation of oneself as a full subject within the therapy relationship and within the mother–daughter transference–countertransference configuration may be problematic for the woman analyst. In our own work as well as in the work of many women we have supervised, we are well aware of the struggle these issues represent. Women therapists talk about feeling too pushy or too self-important if they articulate their presence within the inter-subjective field. They feel far more comfortable being the object who is there to listen, to nurture, to contain, to accommodate, tolerate and survive.

A woman therapist can feel enormously pleased with herself for being exquisitely aware of her patient's needs and desires and yet uneasy with the expression of a different viewpoint or the assertion of an interpretation that includes self-reference. To differentiate in this way and to insert oneself into the therapy is to assert one's subjectivity. Mindful of the power of the analyst's position and perhaps reticent about her own legitimacy and subjectivity, this can feel extremely complicated for the woman therapist.

So then we must ask how does the transference–countertransference configuration change when the woman analyst/mother emerges as a whole subject? We suggest that this powerfully effects the experience that both female and male patients have in the treatment and shakes up, at a very deep level, the internalized object representation of woman/caregiver.

Therapist and patient both exist within internal and external worlds structured by a feminine gender identity. The creation of the relational matrix in which the analysand lives and the involvement, both conscious and unconscious, of the therapist within that relational matrix is saturated with the meaning of gender. A woman analyst will have a somewhat predictable range of responses to her women patients stemming from her own gendered subjectivity (Orbach, 1990). In some sense we might say they have lived in a shared experience, an experience of being a girl and a woman in a patriarchal culture. The consequences of that experience are something they each, in their own way, have adapted to. Each will inevitably have points of vulnerability around a set of culturally prescribed social and psychological edicts for women.

For example, both client and therapist will experience her own internal negotiations with the expressions of desire, entitlement, agency, emotional needs, recognition, envy, differentiation, attachment, intimacy, boundaries, anger. Obviously their personal relationship to each of these states will vary, but the common denominator they inevitably share is that each of these emotional states poses some sort of psychological dilemma for a woman and achieving a position of safe, authentic, and entitled subjectivity is a veritable feat for women. For subjectivity is more than a developmental or interpersonal achievement for women. It is a cultural and political taboo. This is no less true for the woman analyst than for her patient and so what this means is that both the transference and the countertransference will contain the dilemmas, conflicts, prohibitions and struggles of achieving or maintaining a secure subjectivity. The analyst's subjectivity (as opposed to her use value as the patient's object) now presents itself as a critical component of a successful analytic experience. For what is required in the analytic relationship is not only the holding by an object (mother) of the patient's developing subjectivity; what is required is an encounter with another subject.

Subjectivity itself is only achieved in the context of relationship. Stolorow and Atwood argue that subjectivity is always an aspect of intersubjectivity. That is to say, we are who we are because of relationship:

> The concept of an isolated, individual mind is a theoretical fiction or myth that reifies the subjective experience of psychological distinctness ... the experience of distinctness requires a nexus of intersubjective relatedness that encourages and supports the process of self-delineation throughout the life cycle ... the experience of differentiated selfhood is always embedded in a sustaining intersubjective context.
>
> (Stolorow and Atwood, 1991: 193)

Stolorow and Atwood's work, based on both clinical practice and the important observational work of Stern, coincides with concerns of feminist psychoanalysis.[3] What we have frequently witnessed in our clinical practices is the difficulty that distinctness, a differentiated selfhood, a knowing of oneself in relation to self and others poses for women. For us, as gender-conscious psychotherapists, a number of questions present themselves: in what ways are we re-enacting earlier mother–daughter dynamics by denying (consciously or unconsciously) our own subjectivity within the analytic relationship? In what way does introducing analyst/mother as subject into the relationship affect the woman patient's struggle with her own subjectivity? How does a gendered perspective alter our theory and technique in relation to what we so commonly refer to as a mother transference? How does this analysis help us to both analyse and use our countertransference differently?

We would like to turn to some clinical material and an examination of the countertransference which exemplifies two different fairly common categories of countertransference response in woman-to-woman psychotherapy relationships. First as an example of the struggle of a daughter for recognition of her subjectivity and in the second and third brief case descriptions examples of a mother's lack of subjectivity. In each of the examples it was an understanding within the countertransference that allowed us to know what was going on.

Mary is a forty-one-year-old woman who is very successful in her career. She is the curator of a well-known gallery in New York City at the centre of the modern art scene. In many ways she has quite a lot of power and is thought of as a leader in her field. Mary, in fact, is herself a painter, but increasingly over the past 5 years since she got this high-powered and demanding job, she has painted less and less. Mary came to therapy after an eight-year relationship came to an end. Although she was the one who terminated the relationship, she was in a great deal of pain and felt she had to struggle on a minute-to-minute basis to keep herself from re-entering this highly unsatisfactory, exploitative relationship.

In the therapy we have worked together to understand the ways in which Mary is the midwife to the productions of others while she always berates herself for not producing her own work. She clearly gives to others what she herself yearns for: support, encouragement, a belief in their abilities and an appreciation of those abilities.

Whenever I have commented on anything remotely complimentary to Mary that is specifically about her (as opposed to how good she is in her abilities to help others) – whether that be about her ability to create beautiful visual images in her descriptions of things, the sadness I felt in hearing about her mother's view of her as an unattractive little girl or the moments where it is obvious by my tone and my words that I value and appreciate who she is – she stares directly into my eyes in a very confrontational manner and becomes furious. With hostile eyes she criticizes me, questions my authenticity, even questions my rationality, says I can't possibly know these things to be true and so on. At these times I experience quite a powerful countertransference reaction.

I feel as if I am in the hot seat, attacked and thrown off balance by a sense that I have just done something terribly hurtful or that I have unintentionally humiliated her. I feel I can either try to justify myself or just shut up and get back into my place as observer or person to be entertained. I become aware of having stepped outside of a relational matrix I was not aware of being in in the first place.

In other words Mary's rages at those moments helped me to discover myself within the countertransference. Through the process of understanding more clearly the drama I was a part of, I understood that I was supposed to stay relatively detached and from that position of judge and observer I was to experience Mary as charming, witty, intelligent and even gifted, but ultimately unsuccessful and a failure at realizing her true potential. This is the way she felt seen and was ultimately who she felt herself to be. The wit and charm were never felt by Mary to be deriving from her true self, to use a Winnicottian concept, but rather as defensive adaptations necessary for survival in a family where external appearances and impressions are what mattered.

Although on the one hand Mary is able to brush off her ease with words, her knowledge of literature and art, her worldly and sophisticated qualities as if they were all unimportant, we both know them to be the only attributes that mattered within her family. Mary felt she was always a disappointment, particularly to her mother, and could never be enough of what her parents expected and needed her to be. She experiences her mother as consistently commenting on ways she feels Mary is lacking or difficult and her father as unable to see her at all although he continuously pontificates about how everything she does is wonderful and blessed. The feeling one has about Mary's parents are that they are very distant, remote and formal. False self presentation is very strong, seemingly successful and lived out to its fullest. Each has a very clearly delineated image of who they want Mary to be and the success of her false self presentation is what is given any recognition. When Mary confronts any of these dynamics (which she does quite intuitively), they see her as difficult, always needing to upset people and cause trouble. Mary as subject in her own right, with her own vision, interests and soul, is not allowed to exist.

Within the transference–countertransference configuration unbeknown to me I was a person who, in a sense, was also blind to Mary. I could feel entertained by her, impressed by her job and the circles of people she knew, but I must not forget that she no longer painted or produced. When all was said and done I must continue to see her as a failure. Like her father I would be blind to and competitive with Mary's true self and like her mother I would always see her as not fulfilling her potential. But if I resist transformation (Levenson) and actually see Mary as creative, loveable, acceptable – experience her more fully and appreciate her – then, as I described earlier, I get attacked.

Thankfully, I was able to stay outside of the relational re-enactment just enough to actually feel very strongly appreciative of Mary. My responses to her at those times genuinely reflected what I felt about her. In other words I did not make those comments as reparative provisions that I saw as lacking and therefore needed, but rather as authentic spontaneous responses within our relationship. My recognition and appreciation of Mary's subjectivity was transformative because it was outside of the familiar pattern of her interpersonal dynamics. Edgar Levenson puts this very succinctly: 'Therapy proceeds not so much by virtue of the therapist's capacity to provide the patient with a de novo experience, as by his capacity to resist being converted into an old and familiar experience' (Levenson, 1991: 64). Mary attacked me at those times because it was threatening her only familiar schema. As I understood these moments between us, so we were able to discuss them. I shared my (countertransference) feeling and put it between us for analysis and understanding. Mary as subject was now in the room with us. We had words and actions to attribute to her. Gradually we were able to speak more directly to her desires, her need for recognition, and we continued the process of moving from Mary as object to Mary as subject.

If one were working within a more classical model which looked for the mother transference within the relationship, one would have been less willing to accept the inevitability of my falling into the transference–countertransference drama. Instead one would be looking for Mary's perception of me as someone expecting a particular kind of success from her or alternatively Mary's perception of me as critical of her. These aspects would be zeroed in on and interpreted as Mary's distortions of me in the transference. By clearing up Mary's distortions and having her experience me as having different intentions than her mother, our treatment would be well on its way towards its goal.

The contribution that a gender-conscious perspective brings to the interpersonal, object relations and classical interpretations is the understanding that it is not just a coincidence of individual destiny that Mary suffered from issues of self-denial and humiliation in relation to her need for recognition, acceptance and subjectivity, but that these feelings reflect the patriarchal paradigm for women's internal object relations. My ability to enter into a re-enactment in which Mary's subjectivity was denied not only came about because of Mary's unconscious forces within our relationship, but because of my own particular stance and susceptibility if you like to go along with it all. And, perhaps it would not be all that different for a male practitioner who might have to struggle inside of himself with his own deeply held images of woman as subject or non-subject. Clearly the gender of the therapist is significant and alters and shapes the transference–countertransference constellation and the outcome of the interpersonal experience.

I will briefly speak of two other patients both of whom engendered similar responses in me. In these relationships the transference–countertransference configuration allows for a re-reading of the mother–daughter transference dynamics in the light of the mother/analysts as a non-subject or subject.

Kerry is a thirty-eight-year-old commercial artist, married with one child. Joan is a forty-year-old journalist who has lived with her woman lover for twelve years. Both women talk repeatedly about the dissatisfaction they feel in their relationships – they get little in the way of emotional or sexual satisfaction and feel extremely unrelated. Their partners are like distant roommates, each very involved in their work and often working well into the evening hours. Each of my clients also feels extremely dissatisfied with her work. In other words things are going badly both in the love and work departments. They experience very little satisfaction and feel stuck in a rut. Any attempt I have made to examine the fears of moving out of these deficient daily life experiences is met with utter defeat. Nothing I say or do seems to make a difference and although both women agree with me in many of my interpretations, no movement seems to come out of it. They present themselves as victims of circumstances they cannot possibly begin to change.

In the countertransference I feel a range of emotions including extreme frustration, fury, boredom, hopelessness, defeat. Sometimes I feel they have convinced me – it is hopeless, nothing will change. I feel as stuck as they feel. But more than that I feel as if I am losing my self in an atmosphere of merged depression. I feel victimized. My reading of the countertransference tells me that each of these patients has successfully communicated the feelings she has felt in relation to a mother who was very unhappy, trapped in relationships, and lacking a sense of subjectivity, of visibility, of agency (in Kerry's mother's case it was within her marriage and with Jill's mother it was with her own mother). Through the transference–countertransference I have been included in a dyad of women who feel furious at how lost and overwhelmed they feel, how powerless, how oppressed they feel by their circumstances and relationships in which change seems impossible.

Each of my patients describes their relationships with their mothers as very close and loyal. Kerry remembers herself at her mother's side at all times and has conscious memories of trying to make her mother happy so she would not leave the family. Jill, at the age of thirty-seven was still going home to visit her mother every weekend. Each time I experienced this merged depression and defeat in the countertransference I would try, sometimes successfully, to remind myself that what I was experiencing was an externalization of the patient's inner world and that all was not lost. It became apparent that my task was to remain sufficiently outside of the merged stuckness to maintain my own sense of subjectivity and my own differentiation from the non-subject mother enough to be a presence (a subject) within the relationship. When I moved outside of the stuckness I felt as though I was abandoning my patients to the black hole. It was a case of sink or swim and I had to save myself to stay psychically alive. I knew that this was their dilemma in relation to their internal mothers. Any attempt at differentiation, agency and establishing a subjectivity, that is coming psychically alive, felt like an unthinkable abandonment. In understanding my countertransferential dive into the black hole and my struggle to stay outside of it, I could then discuss with these patients how strong a pull I knew they felt. The articulation of that understanding was experienced by both of us as an act of breaking the familiar pattern and as such moved the therapy forward. Although we had spoken prior to that point about how difficult it was to have a life different from mother, to be an agent in one's life, to be a sexual woman, we could now talk about these same issues with a very different feel in the room.

Where Kerry and Jill emotionally knew attachments that were based on misery and helplessness we had the task of redefining attachment. That had to be done before psychological separation could take place. Technically it meant that we had to live through their felt abandonment by means of me. I had to refuse an attachment based on commiseration and fusion in the black hole and offer instead one based on my separateness.

The countertransference experience and its articulation enabled us to experience a change from words and intellectual understanding to an aliveness (sometimes fear and anxiety) between us.

In each of these relationships I was challenged to do two things. First to become the non-subject mother, the woman lost inside of a relationship, powerless, dissatisfied and feeling hopeless. And second to maintain enough of myself – to resist transformation sufficiently – to maintain myself as a subject within the relationship. If we compare this stance to the one we spoke of earlier – of container, of good object – then we can see why more is required of us than we thought ten years ago. For although unquestionably one part of the treatment with each of these women has been to hear the despair, the anger and the hopelessness, and to survive the feelings of victimization and powerlessness, perhaps more important is my own struggle to maintain myself as a subject within the analytic relationship. I need to be able to do that for them (for if I am merged I am useless) and I need to be able to do that for me.

Again, a gendered reading of these transference–countertransference configurations reminds us of the commonality of women's experience in patriarchy. We are not surprised by these psychological internalizations and adaptations because they are part of a paradigm – a paradigm which denies women's subjectivity. One part of our job must be to be aware of the ways we are inevitably living within that paradigm with our women patients so that we can struggle to learn to be outside of it. As we struggle to create and find ourselves outside of the paradigm we benefit as much as our patients do.

NOTES

1 Also see the work of the French school who take up these issues from a slightly different perspective.
2 'When a child's affective experiences are consistently not responded to or actively rejected, the child perceives that aspects of his own experience are unwelcome or damaging to the caregiver. Whole sectors of the child's experiential world must then be sacrificed (repressed) in order to safeguard the needed tie. This defensive walling off . . . is the origin of the dynamic unconscious' (Stolorow and Atwood, 1991: 185).
3 We refer to the work of The Stone Center, The Women's Therapy Centre, etc.

REFERENCES

Chodorow, N. (1978) *The Reproduction of mothering. Psychoanalysis and the sociology of gender*. Berkeley: University of California Press.
Dinnerstein, D. (1976) *The mermaid and the minotaur: sexual arrangements and human malaise*. New York: Harper & Row.
Eichenbaum, L. and Orbach, S. (1982) *Understanding women: a feminist psychoanalytic approach*. London: Penguin.
Eichenbaum, L. and Orbach, S. (1983) *What do women want? Exploring the myth of dependency*. London: Michael Joseph.
Eichenbaum, L. and Orbach, S. (1987) *Bittersweet: facing up to feelings of love, envy & competition in women's friendships*. London: Century Hutchinson.
Heimann, P. (1950) 'On counter-transference'. *International Journal of Psychoanalysis, 31*.
Levenson, E. (1991) *The purloined self*. New York: Contemporary Psychoanalysis Books.
Mitchell, S. (1988) *Relational concepts in psychoanalysis*. London and Cambridge, Mass.: Harvard University Press.
Orbach, S. (1987) 'A note on Vivien Bar's comments on Outside Inside Out'. In S. Ernst and M. Maguire (eds), *Living with the Sphinx*. London: The Woman's Press.
Orbach, S. (1990) 'Gender & dependency'. *Journal of Social Work Practice, 4*.
Orbach, S. and Eichenbaum, L. (1987) 'Separation and intimacy: crucial practice issues in working with women in therapy'. In S. Ernst and M. Maguire (eds), *Living with the Sphinx*. London: The Woman's Press.
Stoller, R. (1978) *Sex & gender: on the development of masculinity & femininity*. New York: Science House.
Stolorow, R.D. and Atwood, G.E. (1991) 'The mind & the body'. *Psychoanalytic Dialogues, 1*.

Chapter 10

Revealing cultural myths on motherhood

Halldis Leira and Madelien Krips

Revealing cultural myths is a way of understanding psychological problems and possibilities. Of necessity, it is a work of detection because the myths are tabooed, as effective myths usually are.

This chapter breaks down these taboos in several respects. Halldis Leira[1] analyses the mythological, cross-cultural and modern models of motherhood, their scientific legitimitization and the double-bind in which they hold women.[2] Her contribution is followed by an unravelling and consciousness-raising programme for child therapists described by Madelien Krips.

Culture as background for self-understanding

Halldis Leira

Mythology and historical psycho-cultural patterns have always influenced and dominated our lives, even though we are not always aware of the fact. Themes from ancient mythology still command our attention, and these same themes are retold in modern literature and the arts. They are compelling because they mirror our own lives and the dramas which are enacted in our minds and experiences. As a result, people have been moved by the same themes for thousands of years, even though they do not always know why. Jung (1984) has referred to this aspect of human life and thought as the 'Collective Unconscious'.[3]

In the search for self-respect and dignity, we are bound by our culture. The question then arises as to what are the conditions in a particular culture which give rise to feelings of dignity versus shame (Ødegård, 1992). This is a psychological process involving cognitive–emotional work within the context of our own cultures. We must make a psychological choice, and in fact we are continually making a choice, as to what to internalize and what to reject of the various values, norms and ideals which are embedded in our culture. The outcome of this life-long, and often unconscious process (and other variables), be it either self-respect or self-contempt, is determined by a number of external historical and cultural forces. These may include, for example, different politico-economic systems (peace versus war, fascism versus democracy, employment versus unemployment, patriarchy versus matriarchy, etc.), varying mythologies (Greek, Roman, Norse, etc.), but also what cultural position the individual occupies.

These external relations give rise to varying backgrounds for the inner dialogue of the woman with children. The interaction between the mother's dialogue with this outer world and the dialogue with her inner voice will give birth to questions such as: 'Who am I?', 'Where am I going?', 'What is the meaning of my life?' and: 'What are the opportunities available to me?', and: 'Out of the possibilities I can see, what is the choice I want to make?' These questions may continually bring new possibilities for new answers to her questions on her self-understanding. A continuous dialogue thus arises between the mother's questions and the opportunities open to her.

Mothers' position in culture

In most cultures, women who have children, i.e. who are mothers, have a different cultural position than women who do not have children. In addition, the meanings associated with motherhood and how it is valued culturally, will vary both in respect to social status of mothers and their practical functioning.

It is as if the woman, the mother and culture are bound in a dialogue, with her acting as figure against the culture's backdrop. Different backgrounds will produce different figures, and vice versa. What possibilities are then available for dignity versus shame in our culture which are expressed through the different psycho-cultural 'models of motherhood'? And what are the cultural conditions which mean mothers have to qualify themselves to deserve dignity rather than shame? The aim of this essay is to reveal some of the varying cultural conditions for mothers' self-understanding and actions.

Modern psychology and motherhood

How does psychology deal with different models of motherhood in meetings between therapist and mother–client? Is psychology capable of understanding the mother 'in her individuality', which Freud defined as the job of all therapists in their relations with their clients (Freud, 1912)? Or is psychology, itself a product of our culture, blind to the individuality of the mother? Freud also claimed that psychology is able to expose the oppressive myths held by a culture, without legitimizing these myths and giving them a quasi-scientific status.

There are a myriad of old and new myths on the theme of motherhood. Is psychology today capable of exposing those which are oppressive, or are these myths still given quasi-scientific legitimacy? I cannot see that it is possible to escape this dilemma. Is psychology itself a product of our culture equipped to perform this task? And if psychology fails, then psychology itself must be viewed as no more than another oppressive force in therapeutic work with mothers. But the task of revealing myths in this very emotional area is problematic. One main problem for psychology in this field is that Western rationality denies our own magical thinking. This denial makes us blind. It is difficult to reveal mythological thinking if its existence is not acknowledged.

It is a fallacy to believe that mythical and magical thinking ends with childhood. Magical thinking is also a part of adult and educated people's lives. This fact is illustrated by the example of a writer who, when criticizing a film on the burning of witches, argued that the film did not reveal whether the main female character *really* was a witch. This writer is not exceptional. The point is that we easily forget that mythological themes and figures are human constructions. This also happens partly because we are so fascinated by the gods and goddesses in Roman, Greek, Norse and other mythologies that we too readily lose analytical distance, and believe these figures to be real and not the constructions of human fantasy. Mythological figures always 'mirror' human problems, passions, wishes, hopes, conflicts and needs. They offer different solutions to these aspects of human life. Mythology is a scene in which the expression of human power is drawn into conflict with human needs. In mythology, oppression is legitimized, but also the possibilities of rebellion are shown (Fo, 1989).

By rejecting human mythological thinking, however, Western rationality weakens Freud's claim that therapists are able to reveal myths. In order to be able to do this, it is necessary to first acknowledge that mythological thinking and fantasy figures are human creations. We carry them as part of our own mental psycho-cultural baggage, and moreover, they represent a driving force in our mental life.

Mythology on motherhood

The task of revealing mythological thinking is especially difficult in relation to themes of high emotional content. As a result, revealing mythological thinking on motherhood and understanding it in relation to mother–clients is particularly difficult. The emotive tenor of our magical thinking, as it relates to the motherhood-theme, is particularly high.

Women with children – mothers – have a myriad of models, which they may copy or reject, to choose from. This is the case even if this part of life is seldom discussed because it belongs to the realm of our Collective Unconscious. It is time to develop some collective consciousness in this field. Four mythological models of motherhood are described below, followed by a presentation of some historical and cross-cultural patterns of motherhood. Women's choices of how they function as mothers do not emerge in isolation from their cultural, historical and mythological context.

MYTHOLOGICAL MODELS OF MOTHERHOOD

Four of the different mythological models of motherhood are presented here: the myths of the goddesses Demeter and Clytemnestra, the myth of The Ideal Mother, and the myth of the Yiddish Mama.[4] The stories of Clytemnestra and Demeter differ from the Ideal Mother model and the Yiddish Mama model in terms of expressions of power. The latter two are models of omnipotence, whereas the former figures represent different versions of the theme of subordination to patriarchal power, exemplified in Clytemnestra's relationship with her husband, King Agamemnon, and Demeter's relationship with Zeus. Clytemnestra and Demeter have in common their lack of omnipotence. But the myths of Clytemnestra and Demeter reveal different models with respect to the strategy a mother who loves her child adopts towards patriarchal power, when this power represents a threat to her child.

The myths of Demeter and Clytemnestra

Once upon a time in Greek mythology, there were two goddesses and their names were Clytemnestra and Demeter. Both were mothers and moreover each had a daughter whom they loved dearly. No mother could have felt a deeper or greater love than these mothers did for their daughters. Clytemnestra's daughter was called Iphigenia and Demeter's daughter was called Core (also called Persephone). In spite of their mothers' love Iphigenia and Core were to meet different fates, for Greek mythology is not populated by mothers and daughters alone.

What would Iphigenia's fate have been if her father, King Agamemnon, had acted differently? Agamemnon, a bold king, was obliged to sail to Troy to take revenge on the beautiful Helen because she had been unfaithful to her husband, his brother. Initially, the wind was unfavourable. Agamemnon killed his daughter as sacrifice to gain favourable winds so the fleet could sail to Troy. What part does Iphigenia's mother, Clytemnestra, play in the story? Agamemnon knew that Clytemnestra would never permit the slaying of her daughter, so he deceived his wife. He told her that Achilles wanted to marry Iphigenia, and that Clytemnestra should bring her daughter to the fleet. When Clytemnestra finally discovered the plot, she attacked him verbally and physically, but her actions were in vain. She was unable to prevent the murder. Subsequently, Clytemnestra took revenge on Agamemnon and killed him before ultimately committing suicide.

Demeter's daughter's fate is quite different. Core was also taken away from her mother. She was abducted by Hades and taken to dwell with him in the realm of death. Unlike Clytemnestra, Demeter won her daughter back. Demeter was the goddess of life and she reacted to her daughter's abduction by going on strike and telling Zeus that her strike would not end until her daughter was returned. As a result, all growth on earth ceased. Neither flowers nor grass grew and the rivers died. Only the desert flourished. The people and animals of the earth appealed to Zeus because they were dying. Demeter, however, was adamant and refused to end her strike until she was reunited with Core. Zeus was therefore forced to relent, and Demeter's beloved daughter was returned to her mother. The famine on earth ended and, as a result, Demeter won the love of its inhabitants for helping them.

Clytemnestra does not love her daughter any less than Demeter does. The differences between them are on other levels. Demeter and Clytemnestra differ with respect to strategy and their use of power, but not in the quality of their love. If Clytemnestra had strengthened her alliance with Achilles, she may have gained more power, but that would have meant rebellion in the army, making the outcome of the battle uncertain. Clytemnestra fights Agamemnon with both words and fists, but she loses. Demeter, however, goes on strike, and because her inaction threatens all life on earth, Zeus is forced to relent and Demeter is reunited with her daughter. Demeter and Clytemnestra are equal in their maternal love. They differ in their chosen strategies and use of power, and consequently their struggles have opposite outcomes.

The point illustrated by these two stories is the following: it is impossible for observers – therapists, social workers, or others – to draw conclusions about a mother's love for her child based solely on her actions. It is necessary for observers to understand both what kind of power oppression her actions are related to, and what possibilities she has to realize her motherly love. As models, Clytemnestra and Demeter suggest different ways in which a mother can handle her motherhood. It is possible, therefore, for mothers to act differently despite equal values of love for their children.

The myth of the Ideal Mother

The definition of, or the meaning of, the Ideal Mother is that of the mythical figure who sees, understands and fulfils her children's every need. The essential distinction between Demeter and Clytemnestra, as mythological models, and the Ideal Mother figure, is that the Ideal Mother is omnipotent (Haavind, 1974; 1987).

The Ideal Mother myth is benevolent; she answers the human need for support. Paradoxically enough, the need for the care and comfort of an Ideal Mother is felt most strongly by rational atheists living in today's tough world. Moreover, Lutheran protestantism offers little in the way of care and comfort from an Ideal Mother, since it has no feminine goddess. The myth of the omnipotent Good/Ideal Mother answers a need for comfort, and in this way we are able to heal ourselves in fantasy, as children do in fantasy play. This is one of the most valuable aspects of our magical thinking. It is also optimistic: it is never too late to acquire a good mother, she can be created in one's own fantasy.

Problems arise, however, when we misunderstand 'Her' to be a real participant in life, and when we forget that 'She' is a part of our fantasy baggage, i.e. when we lose analytical distance. When we forget that 'She' is a magical fantasy figure and we incorrectly misunderstand Her to be a part of real life, 'She' is not a good instrument for analysing reality; nor is 'She' a good model for real-life mothers to copy. If, for example, a child's every whim is met, including those which are egoistic and aggressive, they may develop into egoists, and do not develop the ability to care for others. Moreover, children who are not limited in their aggression may also develop a partly evil self-understanding. The Ideal Mother never withstands her child's aggression and egoism. In addition, in real life it is clear that this model will not allow the mother room of her own. In this sense 'She' will be an incompetent mother model because 'She' will be a model of self-denial (Dahl, 1984).

The need for the mythological Ideal Mother is a legitimate one, for everyone, not least for social workers. The conscious recognition of this legitimate mythical need may weaken the tendency among social workers to be moralistic in their dealings with mother–clients. The conscious recognition of this need may prevent it being projected onto the client.

The myth of the Yiddish Mama

The Yiddish Mama is also a mythical figure who represents omnipotence.[5] She is different from the Ideal Mother, however, in that she is an invasive figure. She is omnipotent, for better (Chagall, 1967) or for worse! If she disapproves of her children's life-projects, she will always make them change. Her omnipotence has no limits. It is near and far, and it pervades life and death. Woody Allen has demonstrated this point humorously in his film 'New York Stories'. The Yiddish Mama who engulfs the entire skyline of the screen tells her son from her very heavenly position what to do, and what not to do – and of course he does what she wants, whether he wants to or not. The cinema audience smile in recognition! The Yiddish Mama is the cause of her children's choices.

The myth of the Yiddish Mama is the mythical model of the cause of everything. Used as a tool to analyse reality, this type of mythical thinking results in reductionism. One is blind to other determinants such as patriarchal power, socio-economic and political factors and the will and creativity of the next generation, etc. This myth, though, remains influential. Just as the critic of the witch film, we often unconsciously adopt this mythical way of thinking even when we believe we are objectively analysing reality. At an exhibition of paintings, all expressing pessimism and anxiety, the viewers concluded that the artist 'must have had a bad mother'. This is another example of 'analysing' by magical thinking. Other experiences had possibly inspired the artist to paint such gloom, for example the Holocaust or the Gulf War. The film critic and the exhibition visitors mistook their magical thinking for an objective analysis of reality. Not so with Woody Allen. He reveals his insight into his own magical world by exposing the Yiddish Mama's dominance by placing her in a position occupying the entire skyline of the cinema screen.

Was Woody Allen's insight – the recognition of the difference between the mythical Yiddish Mama model and the real world – clear to the Jewish pioneers of psychology? The myth of the Yiddish Mama was necessarily vivid and powerful among the pioneers of modern psychology. Many, including Freud himself, were Central European Jews living in Vienna until Nazi anti-semitism made it difficult to stay.

Freud's claim was that psychology should aim to reveal myths and not give them a quasi-scientific legitimacy. However, it is questionable as to whether this aim has been successful in revealing the myth of the Yiddish Mama in psychological theory and practice. Perhaps in the mythical thinking of the Yiddish Mama we can discover one important origin of the 'motherhood model' in academic psychology. This unrevealed mythical thinking gives legitimacy to the mother-blaming tradition found in academic and clinical psychology.

The myths of Clytemnestra, Demeter, the Ideal Mother and the Yiddish Mama are all our own fantasy creations, and at the same time they serve as models for modern mothers to copy or to reject. A central question will therefore be: just what validates oppression in these myths, and moreover, what can these myths offer modern mothers in the way of help and support?

CROSS-CULTURAL MODELS OF MOTHERHOOD

Models of motherhood do not exist in mythology alone. Women with children have lots of foremothers – and forefathers – to learn from, and cross-culturally and historically there exist myriads of models of child care. Collective female child-care patterns and paternal child-care responsibility have existed side by side with cultural designs such as the professional maid, the housekeeper and the nanny.

Collective forms

It is not always clear from reading psychology textbooks that outside of Europe and the US many different collective forms of motherhood exist. Collective forms of motherhood suggest that 'the mother–child dyad' is neither a natural nor a bio-social law. In fact, the mother–child dyad is only one of many cultural patterns of organizing child care. A tendency exists, however, among Western intellectuals to believe that the mother–child dyad is the only universal pattern. This universalization of a cultural pattern is a theoretical construct, and moreover, whether we like it or not, this concept depends on Eurocentric provincialism.

Paternal responsibility

It is neither inherently natural nor a bio-social law that the responsibility for child care falls on the mother. This is also a cultural pattern, and because child care is so interwoven with female value and identity, this is not always apparent. The socio-biologists like to look to the animal world to 'prove' their thesis. Let's take a look at the animal world then, and use the hypo-deductive method in which deviation is enough to prove that a thesis is false. Is the mother in charge of child care in the animal world in every case? Not so with lions. The male lion cares for his offspring while the lioness hunts. Penguins use the same system. Among the birds, the Norwegian wagtails adopt the same pattern in caring for their young. Finally, in the world of humans, in Africa there still exists a tribe which organizes its child care in a similar paternal manner.

It is a question of whether paternal child care has played a more important cross-cultural role in history than we have been able to determine so far. In any case, it has played enough of a role to lead us to conclude that the thesis of the mother–child dyad as the one and only pattern nature and culture have produced is a false thesis.

WESTERN MODELS OF MOTHERHOOD

In Europe and the US there are several concepts of motherhood models other than the mother–child dyad stereotype. The Inuit child, the child growing up in Catalonia, in rural France or east-end Oslo – all provide different and alternative models of motherhood from those in central or northern Norway, or in families where five generations have had educated mothers with paid jobs. The influential and determinant factors are many and complex. For instance, why did Norwegian women get the right to vote in 1913, while French women had to wait until 1949, 36 years later, to exercise this kind of power? What kind of influence on infant care organizing may come from political conditions? Nevertheless, one pattern is hegemonious when it comes to status in Europe and the US: this is the stereotyped mother–child dyad. This is possibly originally a patriarchal way of organizing caretaking in society. And this strong mother–child dyad is possibly one source of the tendency to strong separation anxiety in the Western personality.

Double-bind

Patriarchal culture gives the woman as mother a double-bind message she cannot escape. If she unconsciously internalizes this message, she will always be wrong. In this cultural context it is impossible to be a good woman and a good mother at the same time.

The first message in this double-bind is the point that a married woman's value lies in motherhood. This is a cultural taboo but also a culturally powerful aspect in our Collective Unconscious. A married woman who does not want children represents a threat to the patriarch, whereas in the eyes of the patriarch a married woman who is unable to bear children is to be pitied and/or held in contempt (Leira, 1985). For couples, not having children is taboo; one never dares to ask why they are childless. If the barren woman internalizes this cultural contempt, she will experience shame, depression, inferiority and, in some extreme cases, develop a psychosis (Emecheta, 1982). So, unconsciously, the married woman in our culture knows that in order to gain self-respect and gratitude from her context, she had better bear children, and thus attain dignity and the respect of her culture.

The second, contradictory message relates to the same culture's gender code. This gender code says that masculinity is dominant and that femininity is subordinate. This gender code is expressed most fully in our visions of romantic heterosexual love, and marriage is a primary scene for systemizing it (Haavind, 1985). According to Foucault, it is precisely this lack of unegalitarian code which makes lesbian and homosexual love such a threat to our culture. An important institution which maintains this code is marriage. Moreover, the source of the legitimacy of the subordination of the woman in marriage can possibly be found in motherhood. In the patriarchal picture, the woman achieves her personality simply by bearing and caring for children – i.e. in her motherhood (Leira, 1985). Motherhood, therefore, gives the married woman cultural dignity and respect, while simultaneously providing the validation of her subordination.

Thus, culture tells the woman that a) to have value as a woman in marriage, she must be a mother; b) a valuable feminine woman is subordinate to her husband; c) this subordination is validated by her motherhood. It is a classic example of Catch 22. In this system, it is impossible to be both a competent mother and a feminine wife at the same time. A subordinated woman is a mother without authority. A feminine wife is an incompetent mother, and a competent mother will be not a feminine wife. Catch 22. A good mother is a bad wife, and vice versa.

Unable to avoid this double-bind message, the mother may try to find the solution in one particular way: she may try to be omnipotent in subordinance strategies. The cleverest women with especially high levels of social skills will be very good at responding to the cultural double-bind message by becoming expert and omnipotent in subordinance strategies. This will be hard work, demanding both a lot of activity, authority, creativity in developing strategies and hiding activity, authority and strategy, so that she does not break the subordinance code.

These high-level social skills and hard work may be misunderstood by observers. They may perceive her as passive, or without authority, or as negligent, or they may even perceive her to be masochistic, because they are not aware of the double-bind message she is handling with so much wisdom and courage. Observers may be blind to the content of her actions because they do not understand what is behind her performance. The reason why these observers are blind is the same as why mothers become trapped in the double-bind message. This reason is the cultural taboo – a cultural taboo based on the patriarchal value of the married woman. There are others. It is a cultural taboo that we still need the 'Ideal Mother'. And finally, it is a cultural taboo that the 'Ideal Mother' will be a mother without authority.

Psychological problems, as well as psychological possibilities, are determined by which problems culture allows to be seen and worked through, and which problems culture makes taboo, i.e. 'non-existent'. As long as the patriarchal myth of the married woman is taboo, the woman and her culture are not free to break the double-bind.

The married woman with children cannot be a good wife and a good mother at the same time. However much she tries to be both, the task is impossible. And when she attempts to understand herself, her inner dialogue will also always relate to this cultural double-bind. How can she be both valued and subordinated through this value? If she uses authority or does not bear children, she is breaking the cultural code. Value and subordination are then opposing aspects of the same message. The life projections of married women today, which are related both to motherhood and to participation in society (the latter is relatively new compared to the former), represent a conflict with the old patriarchal pattern. In modern culture today no consensus exists on the meaning of the married woman with children. We are witness to and participants in a struggle on this topic. What is obvious, though, is that the meaning and value of a married woman in our culture is a patriarchal concept. No woman could create a concept of this kind because it confronts the married woman with children with a cultural 'double-bind' message. The 'classical' double-bind concept, as Gregory Bateson (1972) elaborated it, is a highway to schizophrenia. The person in question receives two contradictory messages communicated at the same time, and is not able to choose the right response. If the person responds to one communicated message, she/he is blamed for not answering the other. Escape is impossible. So, given her cultural background, how can the mother orient herself in order to develop her self-confidence? In the patriarchal context, she is cornered – damned if she subordinates, and damned if she uses authority. How then can dignity be attained and shame avoided? And how can therapists be prepared to support children and women in this struggle if – or when – the therapists themselves are participating in the same struggle?

Revealing cultural myths is a way of understanding psychological problems and possibilities. Of necessity, it is always a form of detection because to be effective these myths have had to be tabooed. They belong to what Jung called our Collective Unconscious. Questioning cultural taboos can be dangerous, as Freud pointed out, and learnt personally (Masson, 1984). Many have defined the danger, but let me give Bernal's formulation here: 'In the whole written and oral history of mankind it has been dangerous to look too closely at how one's own society functions' (1969: 1022). On the other hand, revealing tabooed cultural myths creates new opportunities for development. When it comes to the taboos of the motherhood myths I cannot see how we can avoid the dilemma Freud pointed out: either revealing them, or giving them a quasi-scientific legitimacy. To be effective the myths have to be tabooed. Thus, breaking the taboo of the motherhood myths will be of great help, both to the mothers, and to the therapists.

Educating child therapists in helping mothers

Madelien Krips

The interests of the child tend to be the primary (emotional) focus for therapists involved in youth care, and in family therapy. However, therapists are often irritated by the mothers of their young clients: the – frequently single – mothers 'moan and complain', and every piece of advice seems only to make mothers feel more inadequate, resulting in more problems for the children, and more irritation in the therapists.

The introduction of women's interests in their work means a real shift of emphasis from the child to the mother. Five themes turned out to be very helpful in exploring the mothering side: the position of mother and daughter in the therapists' own families; the 'ideal' mother and the 'ideal' therapist; the mother in allochthonous (migrant) families; the mother in a family where incest occurs; and especially the mother 'without authority'. The following provides an impression of how a group of seven women therapists involved in youth care dealt successfully with these themes at five meetings, and outlines the meetings.

Mother and daughter in the therapist's life

At the first meeting, the whole group was asked to make drawings of their parental family (not a family tree, but a representational drawing). In the ensuing discussion, the drawings showed few words were needed to see how the mother's position determined the mother-image ingrained in the daughter-therapist, and in her experience of motherhood.

Two different types of mother positions emerged from this group: a dominant (we should note here that this dominance is limited to the family) or subordinate position. The main aspect reported by daughters of 'dominant' mothers was rivalry for the father's affection, or rivalry among siblings for the mother's love. The daughters of 'subordinate' mothers talked about a lack of mother love and 'parentization' as a way of making up the lack. The father is sketched larger than life, but at a distance. Brothers and sisters appear to play no significant role.

The ideal mother

In the assessment sessions on the 'ideal' mother and the 'ideal' therapist, incompatible desires were tabled amidst great hilarity, such as 'she should have her own life, but always be there when I want her'. All the therapists became aware that each and everyone of us is still under the spell of a desire for an 'ideal' mother, and how this collective desire is validated and reinforced by social attitudes (see also Flax in this volume). The perception of a link between one's own unfulfilled desires and the way personal content is given to the job of therapist was a logical subsequent step.

All of the therapists described their great emotional efforts on behalf of their young clients, and concern for their well-being. They also discerned a kind of concerned 'bossiness' with regard to the mothers of these children. The 'rival' daughters gave more open expression to their impatience, and offered advice more frequently, while the 'parentized' daughters transformed their bossiness into excess concern.

Beyond identification with the victims

During the next two meetings – on mothers in migrant and incest families – more identification with the position of mothers emerged by trying to imagine how the therapists themselves would feel if, for example they had to relocate to a different country and didn't speak the language: what would they miss most of all and what would they do to feel more at home? A possible pitfall in this work-method is that identification arises with the victim element only. An atmosphere of mutual impotence would be the result, and ultimately threaten the progress of the helping process.

For example, during role playing 'the therapist' began to give advice, hoping to find solutions quickly. However, this solution ultimately reinforced a sense of impotence in 'the mother' and devalued her in the eyes of 'her child'. 'Therapist' and 'mother' appeared to choose – unconsciously – the most primitive solution to a conflict between 'therapist', 'mother' and 'client': divisions into 'good' mothers (the therapists) and 'bad' mothers (the 'real' mothers). This 'solution' thus confirms the status quo.

This consciousness-raising paved the way for attention to the often hidden survival strategies and power strategies used until then by the mothers of the client children. An extensive arsenal of indirect power strategies could be listed, such as complaining, nagging, sulking, development of somatic complaints, transferral of aggression ('Wait until your father comes home!'), and, in addition, concern can also have an imperative and even suffocating nature.

Mothers without authority

Many of the mothers who seek help have no clear self-image. Motherhood is often a first step towards an identity and position of their own. 'Caring for' is their source of strength and knowledge. Therefore, direct exertion of power or direct expression of aggression does not tally with their perceived binding function of good wife and good mother. They perceive motherhood in terms of a specific myth, a collective magical solution that functions as a survival strategy. This myth is characterized by an emotional dichotomy with, on the one side, the image of the ideal or good mother being synonymous with love without authority, and, on the other side, the image of the bad mother, or the non-mother/witch, symbolizing authority without love.

But in the meanwhile, the reality of motherhood demands that they provide both love (read: care) and authority (read: establishment of boundaries). The development of a child during various age phases requires direct authority to test her or his own strength, and assist in her or his search for autonomy. However, therapists' advice such as 'stand up for yourself' or 'you have a right to a life of your own' or 'get really angry with him/her' meet with little response from a large group of clients, or even results in a boomerang 'guilt' effect. So the gateway to changing this one-sided type of motherhood must be found in the 'caring for' frame of reference.

The development game

Table 10.1 Motherhood diagram

Age phases: BABY Tasks:	TODDLER	PRE-PUBESCENT	PUBESCENT	ADOLESCENT
BOUNDLESS	BOUNDARY	RECOGNITION	LETTING GO	. . . . . .
nurturing	caring	confirming	restriction	agreements
caring	restricting	protecting	trust	conflict-
protecting	stimulating	challenging	care	management
	space	explaining	experimentation	

A simple development graph has been worked out which uses the different age phases to show that 'caring for' has various aspects: both an aspect of love and an aspect of authority. The alternatives of these aspects can be emphasized by working together and by using colours for the completion of the diagram; e.g. red for tasks that are linked to love and blue for tasks that are linked to authority.

This motherhood diagram demonstrates that the maternal characteristics of the first age phases – nurture and care – are valued the most within our Western socio-cultural attitudes.

Those characteristics which are related more to having and exercising authority, such as setting boundaries for oneself or for others and letting go, can count on much less support and even censure.

The advantages of this motherhood graph are multiple. The therapists identify personally and professionally with the graph as regards care and knowledge of the children. Moreover, it also does more justice to the position of the mother.

Results

After the programme, the therapists report that working with the mothers is much easier. For example, they feel there is more real pleasantness in their negoti- ations with a 'stubborn', impotent mother who continually asks for advice. In addition, a number of therapists indicate they are now discussing the graph regularly with mothers, a practice that means less words are needed to reach understanding. Many mothers recognize themselves in the graph, suggest corrections or additions. The point of departure – that caring is not only bonded loving but also setting boundaries and letting go – struck a chord. The mothers feel as if their authority as mother gained more recognition. They are tackling their own confining myths.

NOTES

1 Her research was financed by the Norwegian Research Council. It was written in very inspiring surroundings; at the Centre for Women's Research at the University of Oslo.

2 'Model' in this text refers to the conception of the *psycho-social example*. It has a
   different connotation from the 'model' connotation in science. The model concept here
   is inspired by, but also differs from, the sociological model concept used in A. Leira:
   'Models of motherhood' (1990).
3 The term 'Collective Unconsciousness' was coined by C.G. Jung. In this text, it refers
   to psycho-cultural processes and is not based on the assumption of biological
   archetypes.
4 The themes in mythology are told in various ways. For instance, Euripides and
   Aeschylus tell the story of Clytemnestra and Agamemnon in opposite ways.
5 The myth of the Yiddish Mama refers partly to a myth, but is also a social tradition
   among Jews. 'She' is the one of these four examples which comes closest to real life.

REFERENCES

Bateson, G. (1972) *Steps to an ecology of mind*. New York: Ballantine Books.
Bernal, J.D. (1969) *Silence in history*. Harmondsworth: Penguin Books.
Chagall, B. (1967) *Brœndende Lys*, trans. (1989) *Burning light*. New York: Schocken
   Books.
Dahl, S. (1984) *De andre – meg selv* (The others – myself). In I. Anstorp, E. Axelsen, and
   R. Ingebretsen, (eds), *Kvinne(p)syke*. Oslo: Universitetsforlaget.
Emecheta, B. (1982) 'En kvinnes strste glede', Oslo: Cappelen. trans. Emecheta, B. (1988)
   Joys of motherhood. New York-Huntington: Fontana Books.
Fo, D. (1989) *Manuale minimo dellàttore*. Odense: Drama.
Foucault, M. (1980) *The history of sexuality. Volume 1: An introduction*. New York:
   Vintage.
Freud, S. (1912) 'The dynamics of transference'. In *Standard edition of the collected works
   of Sigmund Freud. 12*. London: Hogarth.
Freud, S. (1913) 'Totem and taboo'. In *Standard edition of the collected works of Sigmund
   Freud. 13*. London: Hogarth.
Haavind, H. (1974) *Myten om den Gode Mor*. Oslo: Universitetsforlaget.
Haavind, H. (1982) *Makt og kjærlighet i ekteskapet* (The myth of the love in marriage). In
   R. Haukaa, M. Hoel and H. Haavind (eds), *Kvinneforskning: Bidrag til Samfunnsteori*.
   Womensresearch. Oslo: Universitetsforlaget, 138–71.
Haavind, H. (1985) 'Changes in the relationship between women and men'. *Materialisten*,
   4, 33–48.
Haavind, H. (1987) *Liten og stor. Mødres omsorg og barns utviklingsmuligheter* (Little and
   big. Mothers' care and children's developmental possibilities). Oslo:
   Universitetsforlaget.
Jung, C.G. (1984) *Mitt Liv*. Stockholm: Wahlstrøm & Widstrand.
Leira, H. (1985) 'Ufrivillig barnløshet, en usynlig psykososial krise (Unwilling
   childlessness – an invisible psychosocial crisis). *Nytt om Kvinneforskning*, 4: 4–13.
Leira, A. (1989) *Models of motherhood*. Oslo: Institutt for Samfunnsforskning.
Leira, H. (1990) 'Fra tabuisert traume til Anerkjennelse og Erkjennelse, del 1 (From
   tabooized trauma to recognition and conception). In *Tidsskrift for Norsk
   Psykologforening, 27*, 16–22.
Masson, J.M. (1984) *The assault of truth*. New York: Fremad, Farrar, Strauss & Giroux.
Ødegård, T. (1992) 'Den elsk-verdige kvinnen: Monster og Mangfold' (The love-worthy
   woman: patterns and variety). In R. Haukaa (ed.), *Nye Kvinner – Nye Menn*. Oslo: Ad
   Notam.

Chapter 11

Mother–daughter, the 'black continent'
Is a multi-cultural future possible?

Martine Groen

More than a decade ago, in 1979, Audre Lorde stated that any discussion of feminist theory would be a particular academic arrogance if this discussion failed to examine 'our many differences and [was] without a significant input from poor women, black and Third-World women and lesbians. Those of us who stand outside the circle of this society's definition of acceptable women, as we, those of us who have been forged in the crucible of difference; those who are poor, who are lesbians, who are black, who are older, know that survival is not an academic skill'.

Opportunities for the development of a multi-cultural future appear to be decreasing all the time. One only has to switch on the news to hear of more measures to restrict the introduction or decrease the roles of ethnic minorities into our Western societies. The lines of demarcation are becoming broader rather than narrower as the possibilities for communities to become multi-cultural come under ever greater pressure, and the chances of success are being increasingly questioned by all concerned. Is the process of integration actually possible in a society such as ours – a society that already comprises so many diversities? Are these differences really so great and so divisive, or are we in fact looking at an economic problem?

In the light of these questions, we see the tension between the individualization process and belonging to a community with different cultural notions as one of the bottlenecks in the whole acculturation process. How do we find models for this problem? What do other cultures have to offer? Is it in fact possible to maintain a different culture, which is more collective and differently organized in our over-individualized society? And what is women's role in this culture process? Women are, after all, essential in the socialization process of future generations. In many cultures mothering is organized and valued differently than in our (Western) culture. Can we adopt such traditions, and would that be desirable?

The central question is: whether other forms of motherhood should be recognized as a first step towards accepting other socialization processes. Exclusion mechanisms can exist in subtle ways, in all kinds of guises. Subsequently, I want to show that Western women have gained a great deal from the different ways of thinking about sexual differences in the context of the mother–daughter dynamic. Women from non-Western cultures have different relationships with their daughters, and they most probably need different theoretical notions to enlarge the sphere of their existence. Stuart Hall, the Jamaican sociologist, offers an opening for a different approach in dealing with differences. I will also give some examples to serve as an impulse towards more research in order to gain a clearer insight into the dynamics of mother–daughter relationships.

EXCLUSION MECHANISMS

At conferences, women from cultures other than white, Western cultures are usually conspicuous by their absence. Are the same exclusion mechanisms at work here that have always affected women in an academic world dominated by men? Is there now a danger that thinking on these aspects is becoming dominated by white women?

Exclusion mechanisms operate at numerous levels. Sometimes they are patently clear and recognizable. And sometimes they are the result of a very subtle process.

Prejudices which incarcerate women in roles such as 'the mother', 'the witch' and 'the madonna', not forgetting 'the whore' have dominated thinking for centuries. Fears and desires were projected onto the unknown and the strange, and were defended by Reason. The rationale on which our society is structured cannot tolerate minorities as defined by the philosopher Deleuze. These are minorities in the sense that they are chronically excluded from power, and that they have found different forms in which to move, in other words different from the dominant form.

Is it the case that we now talk about black or ethnic groups in the same way women have been discussed for centuries? Do the dominant images obscure to such an extent that women other than white are excluded, or are we talking about a different kind of power here? In her correspondence with Mary Daly (writer of *Beyond God the Father*), Audre Lorde expresses her dismay at the lack of religious examples, however abstract, in which she feels at home. In the same way, I think it is very difficult for women from a matrifocal structure to recognize themselves in a patriarchal mother. We also find subtle exclusion mechanisms in blanket theories when they apply to differences between women.

A great example of exclusion is a study carried out on single motherhood. In our Western society, this form of family organization has all manner of negative connotations. It is perceived as bad for both mother and child. It denies the child access to the symbolic order, etc. The fact that for us 'single' parenthood is problematized is linked to a totally different view of motherhood. The network of aunts and relatives which encircles, for example, a Surinamese or Antillian child is never described as an essential and possible alternative form of organization. The strengths of this matrifocal family structure are rarely, if ever, mentioned. Forms of mothering other than the Western form are generally problematized in research. Moreover, all kinds of deviant behaviour are pointed out, for which mothers are held responsible. The research, both anthropological and psychological, is 'coloured' primarily by the 'cultural paradigm'. Emphasis is placed on the otherness of incomers and this is seen as the root of the problems (Hull, Bell Scott and Smith, 1982; Rath, 1991).

I think the following example demonstrates in a nutshell the differences in culture and the dilemmas arising from a multi-cultural society.

A Surinamese woman went to a Dutch social work department. She was having disagreements with her mother about raising her child. Her mother had come over from Surinam to look after the child so her daughter could work. The social worker's analysis was that this problem was caused by a disruption in the individuation–separation process. The daughter was seen as excessively concerned about her mother and should think more about herself. She was subsequently encouraged to generate conflict situations with her mother and to establish her boundaries. Later, a Surinamese social worker talked to mother and daughter and defined the situation as a loyalty problem in which both mother and daughter's mutual concern and interests had to be balanced (Babel, 1991). She approached the problem from a matrifocal perspective, while her Dutch colleague saw it as an individuation problem.

This example demonstrates the tension between an individualized society with its impersonal rules and the warm nest woven from a close-knit network of relatives in the broadest sense of the word. It's a gap which is difficult to bridge. Women who emancipate themselves seem best able to express isolation. (Women who come from fundamentalist, patriarchal communities have, of course, to confront very different cultural problems than women from a matrifocal tradition.)

Up until now, differences have been obscured by guilt. For example, guilt about racist thoughts and actions can have a paralysing effect and be transferred into concern. Guilt feelings could be the mainspring behind the problematization of everything which is different. Another way of dealing with things that are different is to glorify them. Few manage to see 'the other' as a source of inspiration.

DIFFERENT 'DIFFERENCES'

Differentiation can be discussed in a variety of ways. French philosophers particularly, have seriously criticized traditional duality thinking: duality thinking excludes, and it creates the illusion that only one type of thinking exists. Women and other minorities do not enter the picture at all; they are excluded, they do not count. In her book *Patterns of Dissonance*, Rosi Braidotti (1991) provides an excellent summary of the positions taken up by women in the current Lacanian/philosophical debate. Some see sexual differentiation as the future image; others see more advantages in analysing social power relations and dominant ideas.

There are female thinkers who borrow from the Lacanian school and choose to place the recognition of difference in the strength of the pre-Oedipal. They glorify the oceanic as a creative source from which women can draw strength. Julia Kristeva, for example, sees the pre-Oedipal mother bond as a replacement for the symbolic order. The power and value of reproduction remains of necessity obscure. The mother-body is rejected, the physical is defined as mysterious and magical. Others see the strength of the pre-Oedipal as a means of breaching the symbolic order. And yet another school of thought, with thinkers like Luce Irigaray in its ranks, rejects the link between reason and the masculine. They advocate a different symbolic system based on the feminine. Every woman comprises a symbolic multiformity and therefore offers resistance to a unilinear phallic representation. Like Deleuze, Irigaray describes the body as a libidinal surface that makes possible the construction of subjectivity through the complex interaction of identifications. Differences can continue infinitely and offer openings to all manner of possible theoretic options and strategies without lapsing into synthesis or analysis.

A number of Anglo-Saxon philosophers, discussed in Braidotti's book, more or less dismiss thinking in terms of sexual differences. The question is whether or not a new term should be coined for the physical, the physical space. It could lead to a new body politics which is and was central to the struggle for, say, abortion on demand, etc., but which could also be a place for new conceptions and identities. Adrienne Rich (1977), for example, stresses the theoretic and political importance of the notion of corporeality because it offers the opportunity to criticize the exclusion mechanisms of dualism. The bodies of ideas expounded by Rich and Irigaray offer a number of openings to absorb other elements from different cultures. Thinking in open, flexible subjects creates space.

Besides this discourse, there is yet another line of thought on the nature of differentiation. The French philosopher Finkelkraut (1987) treats differences within a cultural perspective. He does not see sexual difference as a preferred leitmotif, but stresses differences in culture and their consequences in our Western society. He argues that people who advocate the multi-cultural are often trapped in guilt. Advocates of the multi-cultural cry: 'those who want to help immigrants should in the first place respect them for what they are, for what they want to be within their national identity, their culture and their religion'. However, in pursuing his line of thought, he raises questions such as should we allow all kinds of cultural usages which are violent, such as abuse of women and children? Can we tolerate the treatment of women as property? In this sense, he argues against throwing away with the bath water what we have achieved in individualization, and he rejects cultural relativism at any price. In a way, Finkelkraut defends Western culture and points out the dangers of both nationalism and the glorification of other cultures. Respect for differences has boundaries; intolerance of violence is one of them. In Finkelkraut's approach we are still closed subjects and he thinks in polarities, thus excluding other options.

Stuart Hall (1991) takes the concept 'difference' still further, and in my view makes the discussion more interesting. He adds a further dimension, opening up ways to overcome exclusion mechanisms and move towards a multi-cultural way of thinking. The guilt-ridden colonization philosophy which suppresses ethnocentrism hides behind guilt and replaces it with a 'Not I'. In other words, the

whites are bad and the blacks are good. Hall attempts to combine political thinking
and the power of the philosophical concept of 'difference'. One way of achieving
this is by introducing a different terminology. He advocates reclaiming the concept
ethnicity from its colonialized usage. 'Ethnicity recognizes the place of history,
language and culture in the construction of subjectivity and identity; moreover, it
also recognizes the fact that every discourse is placed and positioned, and that all
knowledge is contextual. New forms of representation politics will develop
alongside a new ideology focused around the term ethnicity.' Hall wants to
re-theoreticize the concept 'difference'. To him, it is a slippery concept. It can be
used to indicate a radically unbridgeable division, to refer to sexual difference, but
also to mean a difference in position, condition and circumstance. The latter
approach offers more openings to give shape to the concept ethnicity. Hall argues
that we are all ethnically localized and that our ethnic identities are crucial for our
sense of self. He calls the black experience a diaspora-experience with all the
consequences that entails for processes of extrication, reunification and
hybridization. According to Hall, nothing creative can occur if experiences from
the past are not re-experienced once again and reassigned meaning through
categories of today. Hall sketches flexible subjects, ethnicities, which can
comprise compositions of different elements from other ethnicities. What does
such an ethnicity concept mean in the light of other socialization models and do
other forms of mothering have a chance of surviving in the West?

MOTHERING DIFFERENTLY

Over recent decades, women in the West have tried to secure space by demanding
equality. There is also another strategy for creating space; the emphasis of
differences between the masculine and the feminine. (And perhaps it is the case
that differences can only be designated when a certain level of equality exists.) The
redefinition and creation of an own area is very prominent in thinking about the
mother–daughter relationship. The eternal mystifications surrounding mothers
were demythologized. A process began, and in both feminist-psychological
language and philosophy women were allotted an important place as mothers and
thus as guardians of a cultural heritage. These two theoretic traditions have in
common a search for new formulations. Reformulations are sought to give women
a place and a space, and to validate these with regard to the 'major theories'. In
psychology use is made of psychoanalytical 'process classifications', such as
pre-Oedipal and individuation–separation, but we also find concepts like
autonomy and alliance in the psychology literature. Philosophy talks about
subjects, and the feminine and the masculine, deconstructed or not, and sees them
more as abstractions rather than as coupled to men or women. At the root of the
conflict between these two traditions is, among others, the relationship between the
unconscious and sexuality. The psychoanalytical concepts individuation and
separation are now receiving more emphasis in feminist psychoanalytical theory
formation than before. Using these concepts women could theoretically emerge

from the shadows and become subjects. This individualization process has borne many fruits for us white women, but isn't it time to look further afield?

Every culture ascribes another meaning to motherhood. There is no such thing as a 'European' mother, whereas we all know a more or less patriarchal mother in the sense that power is generally exerted by men with support and recognition from women. An Italian mother has a different place and space in Italian society than a Dutch mother. A Belgian mother differs from the northern-Dutch model, and so on. The meaning, the place, the space and the value of motherhood is closely linked to women's sense of own worth. Italian, French and Belgian mothers are not perceived as minorities, nor are they treated as such. They still belong to our imaginary European community. This does not apply to 'foreign' newcomers. If they do not behave according to the prevailing norm, they are confronted with a socially constructed dividing line. They are ascribed a different meaning, and are thus different and problematic (Rath, 1991). This socio-cultural exclusion is such a powerful mechanism that it forms a real obstacle to further thought and to seeing where opportunities lie which would disband the imaginary community and make room for other ways of living.

The reality is that when we are confronted with these communities in our midst, we reject them. I'd like to give you two extreme examples of mothering differently – the first, the Creole experience, is right on our doorstep; the second is rather more distant.

As a result of the Creole people's history of slavery, the absence of men was one reason to organize society matrifocally, however reluctantly. Close-knit networks were means of survival in the colonial age during which poverty and violence had to be averted. One of the strengths of this survival strategy is the close ties between women. There are rituals and codes which socially endorse this respect. For example, a study on menopausal complaints showed that older Surinam women had far fewer than their Western counterparts. This was considered due to the high social standing these women enjoy as they grow older. Motherhood also enjoys a very high social standing. Sexuality is not mentioned in the pronounced manner used in the West. It is ambiguous and is not named, but it is ever-present. Relationships come and go; family networks go on for ever. A good illustration of this point is the position of the 'mati'. Although there is a social fear that daughters will become matis, the fact that women love each other is tolerated. Love between women is celebrated in ritual and is surrounded by initiation dances. A further important difference between customs is a different way of approaching the physical. Besides the high level of physical contact common in every-day life, there is also a different relationship to the body, a relationship we do not know here. Repressed circumstances forced them to become financially independent, but it is now seen as a major advantage. A great number of disadvantages also adhere to close-knit networks. You have to follow the rules and arrangements and if you fail to do so, ostracism can follow. These close-knit networks in Surinam are less stifling, there is more space. Apart from the disadvantages, we can say that a relationship between mother and daughter occupies greater space and has a positive meaning.

Before going into the question of whether this example is transferable or could be implemented as a process in which ethnicities could be mutually inspiring, let me give you just one more example.

The Malinese Dogon culture is described as kind and friendly, also because it is a less complex society. The psychoanalyst Paul Parin studied this community and discovered that a number of phenomena common to our cultures do not occur among the Dogons. It appears that observation and physical innervation in this people goes hand in hand with a much greater integrative quality because children are carried by their mothers until they are three years old. This continual skin contact provides a richer variety and differentiation of observation which develops in dialogue with the mother. The 'I' has time to develop an emphatic sensibility. A possessive affinity with valued objects, resentments or affective reserve is considered pathological by Dogons. A clan conscience exists, which only operates in the community. The guiding principle of behaviour is controlled by fear, shame, identification or various forms of dependence, and to a much lesser extent by punishment or guilt feelings.

The Dogons appear to have developed an extremely strong identity which is immune to the acculturation process of an advancing Islamization and economic change. As an individual, the Dogon's chances of survival are bad. This conclusion ties in with the sombre thought that qualities which come into their own in a 'we' community have only a bare chance of surviving in the individualized West.

The close mother–child bond which emerges from these two examples flourishes in a 'we' culture. There exists, as it were, a group conscience. When people from 'we' cultures are placed in an individualized society, the two cultures clash, creating tension. But this very tension is seen in the West as the greater good; 'the individualized society and the welfare state' as opposed to a community based on a group culture. However, a number of cultures exert a great attraction because they are diametric opposites of our impersonal culture. They offer the possibility of projecting our desire for a warm community. A matrifocally organized community, with its orientation towards life, nurture and the earth, appeals to the imagination. Life is in women's hands.

As I have already noted, Hall (1991), Irigaray (1977) and Rich (1977) offer openings for further thought. Irigaray sees the mother–daughter relationship as an explosive core of woman's becoming a subject and of her subjugation. Because she falls outside the symbolic, she does not yet have a right to exist. According to Irigaray, this creates a basis for the passionate bond between women which is often broken by fierce jealousies. But passion and recognition are also part of the feminine identity. Irigaray sees a new mother–daughter relationship as a potentially revolutionary bond. Women, daughters, can become active subjects if they identify positively with a mother, an identification which could give rise to new forms of communication. In her future scenario, she sees the recognition of otherness in people of the same sex as a condition which makes the woman–woman relationship subversive. Rich suggests a re-evaluation of the bodily roots of all subjectivity, a new body politics, which, in addition to campaigns against sexual violence, could also create a physical space to determine new identities, such as lesbian mothering. Irigaray offers as option a new mother–daughter bond which has a positive tint and Rich emphasises physical space. Both notions have their roots in individualized thinking but they may, perhaps, link up to life-styles in other cultures; similarities can be found with the qualities carried in the Creole mother–daughter bond.

HOW CAN DIFFERENCES AND ETHNICITIES BE RETHOUGHT?

Socio-cultural exclusion is such a powerful mechanism that it forms a real obstacle to further thought and to seeing where opportunities lie which would disband the imaginary community and make room for other ways of living. In a welfare state such as the Netherlands, government has a far-reaching involvement in everyday life. Although it would be untrue to say government determines all social processes, it does structure and regulate many of them. But even so the influence of government policy is limited. The origins of exclusion lie very deep. It would seem to be of great importance to study the discrepancies and similarities between Western and non-Western socialization models. It is important for future generations to understand what this cultural gap's role is in the socialization process, and how they can deal with it. Perhaps constructive use could be made of the tension between different ethnic cultures. The slogan integration with respect for ethnic identity has been replaced by the idea of integration whereby, supposedly, each ethnic identity dissolves into one big melting pot. At the same time, nationalistic attitudes are gaining unheard of support under the pressures of European integration. Clearly, there has been insufficient reflection concerning ethnic identity divergencies. The point is not how to maintain an ethnic identity, but how to develop plural identities. As far as I know, there has been no research on the precise nature of the conflict in the mother–daughter dynamic. What qualities can be found in the type of motherhood introduced into the Netherlands by the Surinamese community? Why is it that my black colleagues and black women friends don't complain about their relationships with their mothers? My Dutch women friends moan about the mother–daughter relationship frequently. Why is it that self-respect has a different connotation for my black friends than for my Dutch (white) friends? Is it that shame, guilt and loyalty are experienced differently? Or does it have more to do with the psychological structure of the Dogon culture? Research relating to these questions could help demystify the misperceptions we in the Western world have of other cultures. More information and the creation of other images could be a tool for acculturation. This comes very close to Hall's idea of finding other forms of representation, such as cinema, which offer more possibilities for different ethnicities. Traces of all kinds of cultures can be found in the music business, in advertising and in sport. The African beat is one example of how commercialization, advertising techniques and the life-style of the homeland have become merged. Our police force is a good example of an organization effectively working towards a multi-cultural composition.

And now motherhood. It is time to work at all the alternative ways of mothering in the hope that a broader perspective can contribute to the process of acculturation. Until now, our worlds have been segregated. An opening towards a different type of society will have to include actions and not just words. If no steps are taken to change the socio-economic situation of (ethnic) minorities, if they are not in a position to share power equally with us, then the prospect of integration is indeed very sombre. And surely, if these pre-conditions are not met, a change in attitude will be unattainable.

REFERENCES

Babel, M. (1991) *Is vrouwenhulpverlening ook toegankelijk voor zwarte vrouwen?* Amsterdam: Stichting De Maan.

Braidotti, R. (1991) *Patterns of dissonance*. Cambridge: Polity Press.

Deleuze, G. and Parnet, C. (1977) *Dialogues*. Paris: Flammarion.Hall, S. (1991) *Het minimale zelf en andere opstellen*. Amsterdam.

Finkelkraut, A. (1987) *La défaite de la pensée*. Paris: Editions Gallimard.

Hall, S. (1991) *Het minimale zelf en andere opstellen*. Amsterdam.

Huijbrechts, V. (1990) *Hulpverlening aan allochtone vrouwen. Verslag van een literatuurstudie*. Utrecht: NCB.

Hull, T., Bell Scott, P. and Smith, B. (1982) *But some of us are brave*. New York: The Feminist Press.

Irigaray, L. (1977) *Ce sexe qui n'est pas un*. Paris: Minuit.

Janssens, M-J. and Wetering, W. van (1985) 'Mati en lesbiennes'. *Sociologische Gids, 32* (5–6), 394–415.

Kuiperbak, M. (1986) 'Een demon in de stortkoker'. *Sociologische Gids, 33* (4), 233–52.

Lorde, A. (1979) 'The master's tools will never dismantle the master's house'. In C. Moraga and G. Anzaldua (eds), *This bridge called my back*. Latham, NY: Kitchen Table.

Rath, J. (1991) *Minorisering: de sociale constructie van 'ethnische minderheden'*. Amsterdam: SUA.

Rich, A. (1977) 'Motherhood as experience and institution'. In *Of women born*. London: Virago.

Wetering, W. van (1986) 'Een sociaal vangnet'. *Sociologische Gids, 33* (4).

Part III

Daughtering and mothering

Chapter 12

Daughtering and mothering
Female subjectivity rethought and reevalued

Janneke van Mens-Verhulst

After reading through Parts I and II, it can be concluded that scientific thinking on daughters and mothers has been blinded in several ways. Following these critiques, many new components were identified for the construction of more differentiated images of daughters and mothers. However, the prevailing frame of analysis – the object relations theory, with its orientation on separation – remained almost unchallenged. Neither the connections between concepts, nor their evaluations were disputed, and no alternative frameworks were exposed.

The strategy of reframing has been reserved for the third part of this volume. Two 'fresh' frameworks for daughtering and mothering are presented: the relational paradigm and the multiple subjectivity paradigm. The frameworks are new in several respects. First, they share a dynamic way of modelling: 'time' is incorporated as an essential variable that undermines the idea of a complete rehearsal in human development or its reversibility. Second, both frames abandon the idea of fixed boundaries of the self, understood as the core of personality. In this respect they both question the existence of a separate, autonomous subject, though they don't agree on an alternative conceptualization of boundaries in space and time. Third, both frameworks offer alternative norms and strategies for a healthy development of women. Together they reveal fascinating new realms and processes for enquiry.

THE RELATIONAL PARADIGM

The relational paradigm stresses connection and mutuality between people – especially mothers and daughters – as starting point of the human self and as essence of human life. This framework originates from a psychology based on 'the voices and experiences of women', and implies an upgrading of connection. It is applied and explained in the contributions of Surrey, and Gilligan and Rogers.

Jordan's contribution demonstrates the complexity in rethinking female subjectivity. It clarifies how theories on the development of female subjectivity are 'disciplined' by the assumptions of a Western science honouring separateness, autonomy and objectivity. As a consequence, the relational and empathic nature of women's sense of themselves has been almost neglected. Then, it depicts how men's and women's experiences of their ego boundaries reflect the same gender split between separateness and connection; this is attributed to the differences in identification of boys and girls with their fathers and mothers. Finally, it alerts us to psychological epistemology and language as obstacles for a relational understanding of subjectivity development, male as well as female.

Together, these contributions represent the following shifts in points of departure (see Table 12.1): from static to dynamic modelling; from a focus on steady states to a focus on processes; from a concentration on identity to development; from theorizing about a separate and contained self to theorizing about an intersubjective self; from a mental health norm centring around autonomy to a morality of clarity-in-connection; from an objectifying therapeutic strategy to a mutual cognitive–affective empathy approach; from using one perspective to holding more perspectives, and alternating and integrating these.

The relational paradigm, as represented by the second terms in this set of basic assumptions, offers consciousness-raising potential for clearing up the first terms which represent the more traditional assumptions of psychology. In contrast, the first part of the basic assumptions almost impedes the view of new possibilities implied in the second part.

However, this positive evaluation of the relational paradigm must not dazzle us and veil inherent pitfalls and dangers. First, the relational paradigm could easily lead to the exclusion of thinking about disconnection and conflict. Hate and envy could be defined away as 'not genuine' forms of relatedness, as Flax points out (p. 151). Second, the relational paradigm has no built-in protection against essentialist applications which tell women that by nature, and in contrast to men, they are nurturing, caring and relating beings (Davis, 1992). Third, the relational paradigm is rather naive in linking its characterizing dichotomies directly to the distinction between healthy and non-healthy personal development. In addition, no doubts are raised on the strict separation constructed between movement and non-movement, or on the values attributed one-sidedly to movement, dialogical learning, open boundaries and clarity-in-connection. It appears that this way of reasoning produces another collection of 'shoulds' for healthy women that may turn an initial release into the opposite. The outcome could be the creation of a new dogma on superior subjectivity, albeit female-oriented.

THE PARADIGM OF MULTIPLE SUBJECTIVITY

The paradigm of multiple subjectivity belongs to the post-modernist tradition (Nicholson, 1990) and rejects the idea of only one mode of subjectivity. Within this paradigm, it is too straightforward to consider daughterhood and motherhood as no more than mirror images, or to depict maternity as the inevitable destiny of daughterhood. As a consequence, daughterhood and motherhood are dismissed as supreme ways of understanding female subjectivity. Instead, the multiple subjectivity paradigm asks why mothers have been construed as central agents in the constitution of subjectivity.

Following this paradigm, healthy subjectivity is judged by persons' abilities 'to tolerate ambiguity and ambivalence and their desire to seek out, develop and preserve multiple forms of difference that are truly multiple and not merely variants of one same superordinate ideal'. From a feminist point of view, an additional criterion is identified: women, and men, must be able to recognize the perverting influences of unequal relationships, and be capable of resisting these – actively and effectively (Flax, 1991). Anyhow, mutual ambivalencies between daughters and mothers are not regarded as pathological.

COMPARING THE PARADIGMS

Comparing the two paradigms' theoretical capacities, the multiple subjectivity paradigm seems to be superior. Analysis of the scheme of frameworks (Table 12.1) reveals that the third column can encompass, 'understand' and explain the other two paradigms – the separational alongside the relational. The multiple subjectivity paradigm is also more powerful in another respect: it can explain correspondences as well as differences between women, and between men and women.

Comparison of the frames of reference could be complicated, however, by the choice between alpha and beta bias, as Hare-Mustin and Marecek (1986, 1990) call it. In origin, the relational paradigm happens to be linked to the (alpha) assumption that women are more in need of, and have a talent for, connection than men, whereas the multiple subjectivity paradigm appears to go hand in hand with the (beta) assumption that women and men have the same needs and talents. In clinical practice, these combinations of paradigms and 'biases' persist. Nevertheless, it would be a mistake to conclude that each paradigm is linked restrictively to one particular set of suppositions about similarities and differences between men and women. The relational paradigm does not exclude the theoretical possibility that

Table 12.1 Comparative overview of frameworks

Perspective	Traditional	Relational	Postmodern
Modelling style	static	dynamic	dynamic
Focus on	steady state	process	process
Concentration on	identity	development	development
Nature of self	separate unitary contained	intersubjective	multiple
Mental health norm	autonomy self-determination	clarity in connection	ability to tolerate ambivalence and ambiguity
Therapeutic approach	objectifying	mutual empathy	supporting on-going self-construction
Point of view	one perspective	alternating and integrating multiple perspectives	alternating and integrating multiple perspectives, but politically localized

women and men are alike in their competence for connection, and the multiple subjectivity paradigm does not prevent the hypothesis that women will construct their subjectivity essentially along other paths than men.

From a therapeutic point of view, the multiple subjectivity paradigm may be a good theoretical programme to support when thinking about all sorts of clients, female as well as male. However, the accompanying ideal of mental health – as the ability to tolerate ambivalence and ambiguity – may often prove too sophisticated. In daily practice, reduced models may be sufficient for many types of clients, and could make a better and quicker match. Therefore, the opposite question has to be posed: which paradigmatic 'narrative' is best suited to which category of (wo)men – clients and therapists?

The relational narrative implies an underlying attitude of optimism about human beings and the world they live in. It seems to be in accord with several mainstream religions promising a better future, especially because it justifies the fostering of mutual empathy. The narrative offers insights into the unhappiness, anxiety and anger of female clients who seem to have individuated and separated successfully. It explains the forced relinquishment of connection, and love between women, while exposing the 'patriarchal perversion' in societal arrangements and standards. Presumably, it suits the cognitive schemata of (women) therapists from a background which values harmony and development, and with beliefs in the progressive evolution of humanity and society.

The multiple subjectivity narrative offers a valid scenario for women who had both the chance and the capacities to define or select their own environments. Of course, it also fits those who do not come from privileged backgrounds, but managed to escape their origins through their intellectual, emotional and physical competencies. The narrative may serve female clients experiencing problems in defining and realizing their subjectivity and identity. It emphasizes the necessity of deconstructing the gendering influences of both social environments and mental constructs. 'Living the narrative' requires a lot of fighting spirit in women, therapists and clients (as does the object-relational narrative on individuation and separation). The narrative will probably confirm the cognitive schemata of therapists who share the humanist and liberal values of the upper middle or upper classes, and who live in matching circumstances. It supplies no tools for analysing power relationships between individuals or social categories (see van Mens-Verhulst, 1991).

Evidently, the answers to the question on the match between narratives and categories of therapists and clients resemble Hare-Mustin and Marecek's (1986) conclusions after they analysed the therapeutic goals of autonomous or related subjects. It turned out that each therapeutic narrative inevitably confirms the values held by the group(s) the therapist belongs to. Therapists are not super(wo)men; they cannot be expected to escape from their social position and personal prejudices. The best way they can perform is by basing their actions on self-reflexive responsibility in order to avoid unjustified projections and transferences.

REFERENCES

Davis, K. (1992) 'Towards a feminist rhetoric: the Gilligan debate revisited'. *Women's Studies International Forum*, *15* (2), 219–31.

Flax, J. (1991) 'Multiples: on the contemporary politics of subjectivity'. Paper presented at the annual meeting of the American Political Science Association, 21 August 1991.

Hare-Mustin, R.T. and Marecek, J. (1986) 'Autonomy and gender: some questions for therapists'. *Psychotherapy, 23*, 205–12.

Hare-Mustin, R.T. and Marecek, J. (1990) *Making a difference. Psychology and the construction of gender.* New Haven and London: Yale University Press.

Mens-Verhulst, J. van (1991) 'Perspective of power in therapeutic relationships'. *American Journal of Psychotherapy, 45*, 198–210.

Nicholson, L.J. (1990) *Feminism/Postmodernism.* New York and London: Routledge.

Chapter 13

The mother–daughter relationship
Themes in psychotherapy

Janet Surrey

TRADITIONAL PERSPECTIVES: THE PROBLEM OF MOTHER BLAMING

The mother–daughter relationship has consistently been considered of major significance in understanding women's development and especially in formulating women's psychological problems. This focus on pathology is, unfortunately, still with us, and there has been little attention paid to the strengths or potential strengths emerging from this relationship. Even Freud, early on, acknowledged his lack of understanding of the pre-Oedipal dynamics of this relationship, which he described as part of the 'dark continent' of female psychology. He did postulate that the girl's pre-Oedipal stage of development persisted longer than the boy's, and suggested that girls never really achieved a total shift away from the mother, due to problematic Oedipal resolution. Thus, the girl's attachment to her mother was seen as regressive and infantile, and leading to psychological 'immaturity'; masochism, passivity, narcissism and weak moral development. Such norms still underlie our clinical theory – valuing the separation of mothers and daughters. Freud essentially saw female Oedipal development as mirroring that of the boy, with this exception: the girl's problematic task was to make an identification with her mother, who was anatomically deficient. Conflicts between mothers and daughters were viewed as rivalrous and Oedipally based, and healthy resolution was based on this problematic identification. Stiver (1986) has critiqued powerfully such a formulation of female development as reflecting a basic and profound misunderstanding of the mother–daughter connection.

Especially in America during the past fifty years, clinical formulations have shifted to the study of the early pre-Oedipal relationship as a basis for understanding development and developmental difficulties. The assumption of an early symbiotic, undifferentiated phase of pre-Oedipal development, followed by the separation–individuation phase, supported by separation from mother and identification with father (who 'carries' the values of the larger culture) has been widely accepted in American psychiatry. Such formulations are, I believe, derived from theoretical models of male development where separation, disidentification and disconnection from the mother are seen as hallmarks of achieving male gender identity. In the light of such androcentric thinking, women's psychological development has frequently been seen to be held back by the vicissitudes and failures of separation from their mothers. Very often, pathologies of the 'self', i.e. identity confusion, failures of autonomous development and boundary problems are conceptualized as the core developmental deficits in explaining women's problems with what are called 'dependency', 'passivity', 'caretaking fixations' and most recently 'co-dependency'.

There has been a pervasive tendency for clinicians to view psychological problems as arising within the early mother–child relationship, and especially within the mother herself, with no contextual analysis. It is important that we begin to integrate biological and genetic as well as contextual explanations, e.g. family systems theories, and the impact of race, class, sexual preference and ethnic group experiences in all our case formulations. Multi-cultural perspectives may be of special importance in understanding the development of the mother–daughter relationship; and for helping us learn to appreciate the ways in which cultural and systemic power structures impact relational development.

It is alarming how frequently mothers are still 'blamed' for psychological problems by both patients and treaters, and it is not clear to what extent this represents a white male privilege bias in our professions. Caplan and McCorquodale (1985) studied 125 articles in major clinical journals for the years 1970, 1976 and 1982 where etiology and treatment of seventy-two different forms of psychopathology were discussed. When any dynamic etiology was formulated, it was seen almost universally as residing in mothers. Mothers were also blamed for children's problems ranging from sleepwalking, ulcerative colitis, hyperactivity, peer avoidance, delusions, poor language development and inability to deal with colour blindness.

In reviewing my own outpatient case reports over the past 15 years, causal factors for problematic separation from mothers is frequently cast in very blaming language. Mothers are described as 'engulfing', 'controlling', 'intrusive', 'enmeshed', 'seductive' and 'unempathic', 'distant' or 'depleted'. Often, the mother is described in a very oversimplified, negative way, e.g. mother was 'abusive' or 'crazy'. According to Smith: 'The indictment of mothers in the psychological literature has historically been so nasty, so massive, so undifferentiated, and so oblivious of the actual limits of a mother's power or her context that it precludes a just assessment of real responsibility' (Smith, 1990: 17). Part of our work as therapists must involve helping our clients to see and to name strengths as well as difficulties. Paula Caplan (1989) has made a major contribution toward this in her recent book, *Don't blame mother*. Fathers are also mentioned with increasing frequency today, especially in relation to incest, sexual and physical abuse. However, father-blaming is not the antidote to mother-blaming! We need new models of relational development which more accurately describe both the impasses and the possibilities for the optimal development of the mother–daughter relationship.

RELATIONAL DISCONNECTIONS: 'KNOTS' IN MOTHER–DAUGHTER RELATIONSHIPS

I'd like to describe a number of frequently encountered relational 'knots' that can either be an impetus for positive development within the relationship, or, under other conditions, can lead to serious derailments, wounds, sickness, or non-vitality in mother–daughter relationships.

'Be like me – don't be like me'

The mother's double message to her daughter reflects an internalizing of conflicting cultural values around women's ways of being, and especially of mothering. This leads both mothers and daughters to feel anxiety that the connection between them will be threatened by any change. Differences become feared as a source of potential disconnection, and so do similarities, as daughters become afraid of 'being like mother'. This can keep the relationship from moving forward and encompassing both differences and similarities.

Conflicts between protectiveness and authenticity

Many mothers and daughters of all ages express the wish to respect each other's privacy, and to protect each other from criticism, anger or pain. However, the desire for authenticity and the sensitivity to each other's feelings make it difficult, sometimes impossible, to 'hide out' or remain silent. Mothers may try to protect daughters from their pain, or the intensity of their own needs (especially if they feel trapped in a painful or unfulfilling marriage). At the same time, even very young girls are 'tuned in' and feel their mother's feelings. Unspoken, unrepresented or denied feelings can be very destructive.

Daughters also feel a wish or need to hide their experiences, and often their own pain, from mothers, to protect both their mothers and themselves, and are frequently outraged when their mothers sense the feelings and involve themselves. This tension between 'truth-telling' and protection of oneself, the other and the relationship can be a major source of relational growth. However, it is particularly problematic between mothers and daughters and can lead to major disconnections: 'brutal' or burdening honesty, criticism and anger or, on the other side, aloofness, superficiality and lack of authenticity in relationship.

'Compulsive care-taking' or 'co-dependency' patterns

The tendency for girls to remain more open, sensitive and responsive to their mother's feelings (and vice versa) can make for psychological difficulties. Learning to tolerate and bear painful or 'unacceptable' feelings in ourselves and those we love is one of the most difficult trials of life and relationships. It is one thing to desire another's happiness, it is another to deny their pain. Often, mothers try to defend against or deny their daughter's pain or anger because they have not had a relational context which allows them to know and to act on their own painful feelings. As women, they have learned to survive in a culture which frequently makes women's experiences invisible, distorted or pathologized.

A further difficulty here is the very common misrepresentation of empathy as a care-taking orientation. Often in our culture, mothers have been made to feel responsible for children's feelings, responsible for creating bad feelings in the first place, and then responsible for making the child 'feel better'. This over-responsible pattern of mothering has been encouraged by the standards of the culture as well as by psychological theories which promote mother-blaming. When daughters feel psychological pain (as they inevitably will), mothers may move into taking responsibility or blaming themselves, and acting to change the feelings ('to make her feel better') rather than helping the daughter experience the feelings and become empowered to act herself. Such 'compulsive care-taking' is not synonymous with empathy. Empathy involves understanding, joining, or moving with the person in their experience which facilitates empowerment. Mothers may become depressed or angry as a result of their inability to 'fix' the daughter, which may also lead to overt or covert 'daughter-blaming'.

Through identification with this relational stance, many women develop a conflictual and overdeveloped sense of responsibility for their mothers. They feel deeply responsible, burdened and resentful of either 'causing' the problem, or for not being able to sufficiently help or empower mother. As clinicians, we often see adult daughters who at present are depressed, angry and highly critical of their mothers. This overlays a terrible lack of self-worth, sense of personal disempowerment and despair about the possibility of ever creating healthy connections. The resentment and criticism do not get to the real source of the pain, which is the pain of the disconnection and the daughter's feeling stuck in the feeling of responsibility for mother's pain.

This overdeveloped sense of responsibility can also lead both mothers and daughters to try to avoid or deny each other's pain as it feels so unmovable and overwhelming. This can lead to 'cheery denial' (Ruddick, 1986), or extreme superficiality and distance in the relationship. In this case, neither mother nor daughter feels capable of moving the relationship towards authenticity.

Fear of connection

A final problem we frequently encounter in clinical practice suggests a fear of the intense feelings evoked in connection. Both mothers and daughters may try to stay away from the depth and intensity of their feelings which are evoked in connection, and this may lead to defensive anger or distant, superficial relationships. This superficiality feels terrible because neither can get to what's real and important. Similarly, we often see a shared avoidance of the terrible hurt and grief associated with the pain of disconnection, and again this can look like chronic irritation, conflict, avoidance of contact or superficiality. There may be chronic anger, complaining and criticizing, yet this is not about the real source of the pain, which is the pain of disconnection.

The following is an example of a brief interchange in psychotherapy which reflects this. Cynthia is a twenty-three-year-old single college graduate in her first year of therapy.

Cynthia: My mother is so difficult, so opinionated. My brothers and father know how to 'manage' her, but I just can't let anything go.

Therapist: Maybe you're the one in the family who takes her most seriously.

Cynthia: (Startled) Well, that's true. But why do I keep picking on her, trying to change her? Why can't I just accept her, it's crazy!

Therapist: We need to think about what you want her, even feel you need her to be like. I think if you knew what was so urgent and important to you, it wouldn't feel so crazy.

Cynthia: I guess I want her to be different so she could accept and understand me better or maybe so I could love her more and respect her – then I'd feel better.

Therapist: Maybe it feels too painful to feel so disconnected and you keep trying so hard to make the relationship feel better, as if something will change if you keep working hard enough, trying to change it.

Sometimes the relational wounds and disconnections in the mother–daughter relationship are major and cannot move. Still, the capacity to grieve the pain, and recognize the depth and meaning of the loss, will help the daughter move out of despair or bitterness.

THE STONE CENTER RELATIONAL PERSPECTIVE

Women's experiences more often evolve through the growth of new connections and relationships which may or may not transform older ones. Our theoretical work at the Stone Center has centred on developing a new language and model to describe development from this relational perspective. A psychology of relationship and relational development stresses the importance of connection, not self, as the primary core element and energy of psychological development (Jordan *et al.*, 1991). By 'growing into connection', we mean the growing sense that can represent oneself freely in relationships and that can contribute to the creation of relationships which hold, sustain, and foster the psychological development of all participants. We are postulating that healthy relational development begins early in life and reveals continuity, increasing complexity and elaboration of connection. The pathway of relational development has not yet been fully described, but clearly, growth in connection applies to the development of particular relationships, to an expanding network of relationships, and to the ways in which individual relationships exist within a total relational context. The capacities for integrating a dyadic relationship within a context of multiple and overlapping relationships is a significant aspect of growth-fostering mother–daughter relationships.

Self–other differentiation or 'separation' is not seen as the core or crucial moment in development. It is not the centrepiece of development, although it certainly has its relevance. Instead, emphasis is on the capacity to grow and to maintain connection, suggesting a more complex, mutual model. Correspondingly, Stern (1985) would talk about the importance of 'self-and-other' or 'self-with-other' experiences.

Mutuality is a key aspect of all healthy connection. This is not the equivalent of equality, reciprocity or intimacy, but rather describes a way of 'being-in-relationship' where both or all participants can be authentically present; able to freely represent their feelings, thoughts and perceptions in the relationship with movement towards greater spaciousness, clarity and clearer manifestation of individual differences. Connections maintained by domination, suppression, distortion, selective inattention or denial are not growth promoting or authentic. What is most important is the 'moveability' or openness in a relationship, not perfect empathy or understanding. This involves a willingness to continually adapt to change, and to accept the frustration of not yet understanding or being understood. There is perhaps no greater change to be negotiated in relationship than in the mother–daughter relationship over the life-cycle, and adolescence may be the period of the greatest change.

Conflicts between mothers and daughters may be reframed as part of the struggle or yearning for connection, or as a frustration or consequence of a disconnection that does not move the relationship in a positive direction towards mutual understanding. The often urgent and frequently lifelong desire and frustration around connection and mutuality in the mother–daughter relationship helps us to understand the terrible anxiety, anger, despair and disempowerment which are frequently part of this relationship, as well as the joy, release and growth in the moments when connection becomes possible.

Mothers and daughters often remain exquisitely open and sensitive to each other's feeling states. When a relational process of clarification through open interchange can occur, it can lead to psychological growth for mother, daughter and the relationship. This relationship can be seen as a beginning process of growing and learning in connection. I will describe three dynamic interactive processes which begin to describe optimal relational development. These processes are mutual engagement, mutual empathy/authenticity and mutual empowerment (Surrey, 1984).

Mutual engagement

This describes the shared interest, attentiveness, joining and focusing together and engaging in a shared process through interaction around feelings. This can be a two-hour intense discussion around the dinner table or a passionate screaming encounter. This helps to understand an adolescent daughter's attempt to get her mother engaged in a real, vital, honest way, sometimes by provoking conflict as a way out of depression, apathy or relational disconnection. She can be seen as trying to 'make' authentic contact or to 'change' the relationship, rather than trying to separate. Mothers sometimes describe their own experience of backing away from this intense level of honesty and sharing.

Mutual empathy/authenticity

The mutual desire to understand – to know the other and to feel understood and known by the other – to see and be seen in the moment and over time. This creates the motivation to stretch our own experience to encompass another's. The motive to join together stretches us to articulate and communicate our experience, thereby increasing and building authenticity. Authenticity and empathy are inextricably interconnected and both are necessary for relational development.

Frequently, mothers have had more difficulty with authenticity than empathy, since mothers in this culture have been made to feel anxious about bringing themselves directly into their relationships with their children. It is the absence of mutual authenticity – where either the daughter's voice or the mother's voice is dominant or silenced – that creates relational disconnection. True dialogue involves two voices listening and responding and able to hold and move with the different subjective realities simultaneously.

Mutual empowerment

This process represents a mutual sense of activation and capacity for responding effectively in the relationship. Both participants feel an ability to impact or move the relationship toward authentic connection, and both are able to be moved and receptive. This can be described as relational empowerment, and describes a 'power-with', power-together or power through interaction model of relationship.

We are only beginning to envision a model that describes the optimal development of connection and mutuality in the mother–daughter relationship. Few relationships fit this exactly. Most relationships are characterized by connections and disconnections. In healthy relationships, conflicts or disconnections can provide a stimulus for relational growth toward connection. The absence of these conflicts may well represent an over-idealized or unauthentic, superficial relationship. Clearly, there can be major disconnections which do not generate such change or movement and become a source of psychological difficulties.

THEMES IN PSYCHOTHERAPY: FOSTERING MUTUAL EMPATHY

I am suggesting that focus on building connection through mutual empathy in relationships can enhance our clinical work. Here I am referring to the movement and opening toward empathic or connected knowing. As Jordan has written

(Jordan and Surrey, 1986), empathy is a complex psychological capacity requiring a blending of cognitive and emotional knowing, a capacity to stretch one's own experience to receive and join with the other. Empathy is not synonymous with liking or being nice to or taking care of or even emotional closeness (although it may relate to some of these). The capacity to respond with empathy does not involve loss of boundaries or boundary confusion. Mutual empathy is based on the mutual capacity to receive, accept and understand the other as they are in the moment, allowing the other's perspective or reality to be part of the movement of the relationship.

Many women clients need to grow in authenticity and empowerment in all their relationships, and often particularly with their mothers. This is the predominant focus of much therapeutic work. We must also emphasize the need to help develop empathy for others, i.e., for developing the relational capacities that foster trust, understanding, acceptance, flexibility, forgiveness and openness to change, without sacrificing or eclipsing real feelings of hurt, disappointment, anger or frustration. This is a complex task, and cultural and clinical models of 'separation' and mother-blaming do not support this.

The mother–daughter relationship is incredibly powerful in its basic connections to the deepest aspects of life: birth, growth, separation, loss and death. The depth and enormity of these issues, the intense feelings and changes to be negotiated over life clearly relate to the tremendous possibilities and challenges to the growth of this relationship. Each life stage for both mother and daughter represents new challenges and opportunities for new relational integrations.

Clearly, both mothers and daughters often have difficulty getting 'current' in their relationship. Mother's memories hold the images of their children as infants, and throughout life they continue to 'see' (and therefore evoke) the child in their adolescent or adult children. A major area of relational development between mothers and daughters is the delicate dance around who is mother and who is child, especially in later life.

The development of empathy for mother appears to reflect an important developmental process. Most empathic development is slow, often imperceptively growing in small increments. At times, however, a daughter's experience of empathy for mother happens in a flash. One client noted with amazement the first time she saw her mother as 'daughter to my grandmother', and this moment initiated a whole new stage of awareness and a sense that knowing her mother in this way reflected her own personal growth and enlarged capacity for connection. Mothers are often seen by children primarily as 'mothers', and growth in perception occurs when they begin to see their mother in larger relational perspectives, e.g., as teacher, doctor, wife and daughter to grandmother. A young woman I saw in therapy, Elizabeth, had worked in prior therapy to relate her own fluctuations in self-worth and confidence to her mother's severe fluctuations in mood. She was finally able to see the contribution of her father's alcoholism to her mother's depression. Frequently, the daughter's sensitivity to her mother's feelings make her mother 'the figure', perhaps – the 'lightning rod', – through which the daughter experiences all the family pain and tension. This is never to deny or suppress her feelings about her mother as she moves toward an enlarged picture, but rather to help her make the larger connections and to learn to see her mother in the larger context.

Many times patients need to learn to accept the limits of their relationships with their mothers, past and present, without sacrificing the validity of their needs. They need to experience the grief in letting go of old expectations and old wounds as they establish an enlarged relational context for themselves. Relational theory stresses the importance of building and focusing on healthy connections, often with the therapist, as a medium of change, rather than working on unmoving or stuck positions. Usually, such a focus in therapy can be accomplished without total separation from mother. Taking responsibility for oneself does not mean giving up on holding others accountable for their behaviour or continuing to voice one's needs or perceptions in a relationship.

Both adolescent daughters and mothers in this culture may internalize the cultural mandate to separate, as this has social sanction. Mothers are often very self-critical and blaming when they recognize their own desires for maintaining connection with their daughters, and often try to suppress or deny their own wishes. We need new models which allow us to validate relational yearnings and strengths as well as difficulties in connections. One woman client, Ruth, a fifty-six-year-old divorced psychiatric social worker, is the mother of two young adult professional daughters, thirty and thirty-three, who are both single and living in the Boston area. Ruth and her two daughters were quite close and involved in each other's lives, and Ruth worried that her involvement with them might be interfering with their getting married. It has been very helpful to validate her and her daughters' desire for and valuing of their connections. She is currently working on building her relationships with her daughters, in addition to other friends, and has begun working towards openness, authenticity and mutuality. As she has accepted her own desire for connection, she is becoming much more effective in expressing her own feelings and needs, and much more open to seeing and appreciating her daughters as adults.

Therapeutic work with mothers and daughters may also involve helping each to understand the other from the other's frame of reference in relation to her generation's standards and challenges. This is particularly difficult at a time when women's lives and roles are changing so dramatically. This is not an easy process for either generation, certainly blaming or labelling mother (or daughter) as unempathic or narcissistic (or even holding this image as we work clinically) will not facilitate this process of change. Often, to help mothers and daughters move out of their personalized sense of misunderstanding and injustice in their relationship, it is useful to suggest intergenerational group experiences for both.

CONCLUDING REMARKS

When I speak about facilitating empathy for mothers, often there is concern expressed about my failure to accept that there are bad mothers, or that there are linear processes or stages of de-idealization. Clearly, the goal of therapy is to help the client develop a realistic perception of her mother, but too frequently the negative or oversimplified perception is what gets emphasized in psychotherapy. Working from a 'separate' self paradigm, we worry about the loss of clarity and authenticity if we try to see from the other's perspective, or see the other 'in context'. This represents a misconception of empathy as either/or proposition. Either I see it through my eyes or I see it your way. A relational paradigm offers the possibility of holding more than one perspective, opening to another's subjective reality without sacrificing or losing one's own. I think this misconception of empathy is based on a model of self/other differentiation, where the emphasis is on finding and holding your own position rather than on being flexible enough to change and grow through interaction. To the extent that mother's voice is seen as potentially threatening to the development of the child's (especially the boy's) identity, mothers will continue to be fearful and guilty about directly voicing their own feelings and perceptions in the relationship. As we have seen, this is especially dangerous for daughters who often begin at adolescence to silence their own voice in relationships, especially with men. If they have not seen their mothers empowered in relationship, they will be more likely to be disempowered themselves.

A common extension of this either/or, self versus other thinking is the worry that empathy will lead us to be further 'bound' to mother, thus limiting our freedom and self-development. Actually, real empathy allows for greater freedom and effectiveness in relationships. Unfortunately, common clinical strategies for fostering separation have often involved emotional suppression through the blunting of emotional sensitivities, or the use of anger, contempt and blame to create distance. When women are encouraged to use any of these strategies to 'separate' from mother, it can alienate them from their own range of affective experiences which can be the source of pleasure, strength and growth in a relationship. Encouraging anger as a means of separation, rather than helping daughters learn to bring uncomfortable feelings into constructive interaction in the relationship can have a negative impact in the long run.

Disidentification with mother is a very frequent presentation of women clients. Daughters often try hard to disidentify, to magnify differences, to fear and exaggerate any sign of similarity, often viewing the mother (and themselves) through the judgements and values of the larger culture (often as mother has internalized herself). The cultural message 'don't be like mother' leaves the girl locked into a cross-generational solution to her mother's problems: 'If I'm not like her, everything will be different for me'. This keeps mothers and daughters from learning from each other's experience and seeing their larger, shared connection as women.

As clinicians, we must begin to examine the ways we implicitly foster mother-blaming, and to appreciate the disservice we do our women clients if we do not respect the potential meaning and power of healing in this relationship. It is essential to help women come to a more balanced, valid understanding of themselves and their mothers as women living within a patriarchal culture.

As we move beyond traditional paradigms of 'self' development, we can more effectively learn to support relational development. Conflict and misunderstanding are perhaps inevitable. What seems to allow relationships to grow can be described as movement towards greater authenticity, empathy and mutuality, through the development of increasing relational competencies, learning to deal with conflict, and the valuing of relational qualities.

Clinically, it is most important that we facilitate these positive changes and do not support premature closure or separation in the name of 'resolution' or oversimplification in the form of mother-blaming. We need to learn more about facilitating connection and mutuality. Finally, we need to inform our clinical work with our awareness of how our culture supports entitlement and unrealistic expectations of women (especially mothers) and devalues and misunderstands women's desire for growth in connection.

REFERENCES

Caplan, P. (1989) *Don't blame mother: mending the mother–daughter relationship*. New York: Harper & Row.

Caplan, P. and Hall-McCorquodale, I. (1985) 'Mother-blaming in major clinical journals. *American Journal of Orthopsychiatry*, *55*, 345–53.

Jordan, J. and Surrey, J. (1986). The self-in-relation: empathy and the mother–daughter relationship'. In T. Bernay and D. Cantor (eds), *The psychology of today's women: new psychoanalytic visions*. Hilldale, NJ: Psychoanalytic Press.

Jordan, J., Kaplan, A., Miller, J.B., Stiver, I. and Surrey, J. (1991) *Women's growth in connection: writings from the Stone Center*. New York: Guilford Press.

Ruddick, S. (1986) *Maternal thinking*. Boston, MA: Beacon Press.

Smith, J. (1990) 'Mothers: tired of taking the rap'. *New York Times Magazine*, 142, 17.

Stern, D. (1985) *The interpersonal world of the infant*. New York: Basic Books.

Stiver, I. (1986) 'Beyond the Oedipus complex: mothers and daughters'. *Work in Progress*, *26*. Wellesley, MA: Stone Center for Developmental Services and Studies.

Surrey, J. (1984) 'Self in relation: a theory of women's development'. *Work in Progress*, *13*. Wellesley, MA: Stone Center for Developmental Services and Studies.

Chapter 14

Reframing daughtering and mothering
A paradigm shift in psychology

Carol Gilligan and Annie Rogers

A PARADIGM SHIFT

A paradigm shift in psychology has followed from listening to women's voices. A psychology premised on a view of human life as lived ultimately in separation has given way to a psychology that rests on a view of human life as lived essentially in relationship (Gilligan, 1977, 1982; Miller, 1976; see also Jordan, this volume). Within the old psychology, relationships were seen as a means to separation, and individuation or autonomy was taken to be the hallmark of development or psychological growth. The primary relationship seen as necessary for good development was the mother–child relationship. Mothers in essence held relationships within a framework where relationships were seen simultaneously as necessary and as dispensable. Consequently, mothers, urged both to hold on to and to let go of their children, were idealized and devalued at the same time.

Psychologically, Freud traced the idealization and denigration of women to men's unresolved Oedipal struggles or, more specifically, to men's inability to either hold on to or let go of their mothers (Freud, 1910, 1912, 1918). And since societies and culture have for the most part been created by men, and are thus rooted psychologically in men's experiences, men's feelings and thoughts about their mothers have tended to shape prevailing conceptions of mothers and mother–child relationships, including relationships between mothers and daughters. In separating views of the mother–daughter relationship from the activities of mothering and daughtering, we begin with the voices of girls and women as key to a new psychology, because these voices transform the meaning of love and the understanding of reality. Descriptions of relationships between mothers and daughters commonly evoke images of women with little girls. Even in descriptions of therapeutic relationships involving adult women, the mother–daughter transference is generally portrayed as a re-enactment of the relationship between a mother and a little girl or a baby. Recently, feminist psychologists including clinicians have questioned this portrayal of mother–daughter relationships, recalling earlier attention to adolescent girls and young women, and exploring relationships between adolescent daughters and their mothers (Apter, 1990; Breuer and Freud, 1970; Deutsch, 1944; Horney, 1926; Josselson, 1987, 1992; Rogers, in press; Thompson, 1964).

Our studies of women's psychological development have led us to see relationships between girls and women as deeply transformative. As girls approach adolescence, they often manifest a healthy resistance to losing voice and replacing authentic relationships with idealized relationships (Brown, 1989; Brown and Gilligan, in press; Gilligan, 1990, 1991; Rogers, in press). The clarity of girls' voices at this time in development resonates strongly with many women, leading women back into painful and difficult memories, and also to questions as to whether losses that seemed necessary are really inevitable. Developmentally, girls' healthy resistance to disconnection in adolescence tends to become a political resistance, or a struggle against inauthentic relationships and corruptions of authority and love. This political resistance is then under great pressure to become dissociated, and to turn into psychological resistance (Gilligan, 1990). Girls in adolescence both enact and narrate this dissociation. Women's responses to hearing girls speak of psychological moves which they may only dimly remember reframes the meaning of mothering and daughtering.

From listening to women and girls, we have found that relational development within patriarchal societies and cultures poses a relational impasse involving disconnection from women. This disconnection typically occurs in boys' lives in early childhood, and in girls' lives in adolescence. As girls reach adolescence, their healthy resistance or ordinary courage (Rogers, in press) often leads them into open conflict or struggle, and this fight for relationship reveals realities which are generally unspoken and unseen. In this way, daughters' voices touch mothers deeply, and raise difficult questions about mothering.

For women, joining girls' healthy resistance and recovering the courage to 'speak one's mind by telling all one's heart' (Rogers, in press) is often in tension with psychological and political pressures to subvert girls' voices and in essence maintain the status quo. This subversion, which constitutes a deeply felt loss in women's development, often leaves a residue of bitterness in its wake. And the loss of relationship is marked psychologically by the idealization and denigration of both mothers and mother–daughter relationships. Thus, accounts of mother–daughter relationships or relationships between therapists and their women patients which are idealized, or which carry a denigration of women, reflect this developmental loss. For this reason, the voices of girls in the time before adolescence become crucial in understanding relationships between mothers and daughters, and in reframing women's psychological development. Girls' voices become touchstones for women to re-open or challenge moves away from authentic relationships which they have made in the course of their own development. Listening to girls speak about relationships with their mothers changes the meaning of love and the understanding of reality. Girls' voices thus become the key to shifting the paradigm of psychology.

DILEMMAS OF RELATIONSHIP BETWEEN MOTHERS AND DAUGHTERS

In 1989, after a five-year study of girls' development showed that girls were enacting and describing dissociative processes in relationships as they moved from childhood to adolescence (Brown, 1989; Brown and Gilligan, in press; Gilligan, 1990, 1991; Rogers, in press), we decided to enter this time in girls' lives to see if we could sustain the strengths of their childhood. Our project initially involved a week-long Theater, Writing and Outing Club with eleven- and twelve-year-old girls, whom we followed for three years into early adolescence. In the course of this project, the girls' mothers requested to become involved both with us and their daughters. We also met weekly with a group of nine and ten-year-old girls who were racially and socio-economically more diverse,[2] and also followed this group of girls for three years. In the younger group we focused more on our relationships with the girls, and on the ways in which the girls affected us individually and changed our relationships with one another. In both of these projects we were joined by a third woman, Normi Noel, a theatre director, actor and voice teacher. As part of these projects, we interviewed each girl individually once a year. In this paper, we can only present highlights of this work.

We begin with girls' voices to show the intricacy of their understanding and the psychologically detailed nature of their portrayals of their mothers and their relationships with their mothers. Through the girls' descriptions of these relationships, we came to understand difficulties and challenges and impasses in women's lives. The themes that arose repeatedly in our work with pre-adolescent girls included the open expression of feelings in relationships, including angry feelings; continuing connection, attachment and dependency on mothers; and an insistence on direct speech in relationships, as well as a careful rendering of the consequences of direct speech. With the child's eye and ear for detail, the child's capacity for a frame-by-frame telling of human activity and relationship, girls spoke to us in very matter-of-fact ways about the realities of women's lives – the tiredness and depression of mothers; the readiness of mothers to give in or compromise themselves in the face of disagreement; the readiness of men to resort to force in these situations. Following girls over time into early adolescence led us to a period when they and their mothers began to withhold their real thoughts and feelings, to turn away from direct speaking, and in the first shock of this loss, to feel not only a loss of connection with their mothers, but a betrayal of their truths in these crucial relationships. At the same time, adolescent daughters' deepening emotions and increased cognitive capacities gave them a new ability to see keenly into the lives of their mothers, raising questions and challenges for their mothers about her choices as a woman often living in patriarchal households as well as in a patriarchal culture. In short, girls' preoccupation with true and false relationships at pre-adolescence shifts to a series of painful dilemmas about lies and truths, about love and the betrayal of love, between girls and women as girls enter adolescence.

In the following excerpts, we reveal these themes and the emergence of these dilemmas as reported to us by the girls we worked with over a three-year period.

Amy at eleven is interviewed by Carol, who asks about her relationship with her mother. In response to the question as to whether she and her mother disagree about things, Amy says:

'Oh yeah. What usually happens is we'll scream and yell at someone, I mean, at each other, then I'll go and walk away, and then later I'll say "I'm sorry", and she'll say, "That's fine". And then we'll feel better about everything.'

This open expression of strong, angry feelings is part and parcel of Amy's daily life. Her brother and sister, she explains, are 'really wild', especially at dinner time. And the familiarity of this scene is evident as Amy quotes her mother as saying, 'Oh, no, not this again'. Like a quick storm, anger breaks out and blows over. Disagreement, screaming and yelling, followed later by apology and reconciliation.

Asked '*Do you and your Mom depend on each other?*' Amy interrupts Carol to begin her answer:

'I definitely depend on my Mom. I don't know if she depends on me, but at sleepovers, I really don't know why this happens, but I always think of my Mom at sleepovers, 'cause I think she understands how I have trouble sleeping over and stuff. . . . And I depend on her so much because she's there when I have something I want to tell her or something I need to tell her. . . . She'll listen to me whatever I want to say.'

The ease of Amy's dependency on her mother resembles the ease in her expressions of anger. Closeness and love sit comfortably side-by-side with anger and disagreement – in part perhaps because Amy can in fact yell and scream at her mother without losing connection with her, and also can tell her mother 'whatever I want to say' without fear of losing the relationship.

This evidence of strong and clearly articulated connection is confirmed by Amy when Carol asks directly, '*Can you tell her how you feel and what you really think?*' Amy says,

'Um, yeah. I can because she really listens and she understands and she'll give me advice if I need advice, but sometimes I'll say things like: "Just don't tell me what to do. Just listen" '.

'*Are there some things that are hard for you to say?*'

'Um. I don't know. [5 second pause] There are some things that my friends would ask me not to tell, and I won't tell them unless I slip. . . . I'll ask them, "Can I just tell my Mom?" And they'll say, "Don't tell anyone". But there isn't very much that I can't tell her, you know.'

Amy's directness in relationships is striking; she speaks freely with her mother, finding it hard not to slip when she is holding friends' confidences, and she also speaks freely about herself.

Eve, also eleven, is asked by Annie, '*Are there some things you can say out loud to your Mom and other things that are harder to talk about?*' She says,

'Well, education-stuff [meaning what school she will go to] is pretty easy to talk about, but then, um, my Dad is kind of hard to talk about.'

'*It's kind of hard for you to talk to your mom about your dad?*'

'Yeah. Because, uh, it's so emotional and everything. See, I don't want her to be really sympathetic and everything . . . because then I feel like, oh, she gets all emotional and everything, and I just don't like it. So I don't, I try not to talk about it. . . . But we never get in really big fights, just little arguments. . . . But she can make me feel really guilty.'

'*What do you do when she makes you feel guilty?*'

'Well, I can't really give in, because then I'll feel even guiltier. . . . She said, "I don't like driving you all over the map for ballet." I told her, "You're the one who always complains about that." I have to say, so she won't make me feel guilty. . . . I have to catch things, and contradict her sometimes, I have to be really stubborn.'

'*Why does it feel important to you to be stubborn with your mom?*'

'Because she, she's not stubborn, she's persuasive. In to getting her way, like my brother is. My brother's not stubborn, and neither is my Mom. They won't like block you or say no.'

'*That's something you really like about yourself?*'

'Yeah, because I don't like to be persuaded, because it's kind of getting around things. . . . I know how it feels to be guilty, so I don't want to make other people feel that way. [Oh] And I just want to tell them how I am feeling, I just want to make sure that they know. Sometimes I don't know what my Mom wants me to do if she's persuasive.'

What Eve calls 'persuasive' on her mother's part are messages which are so indirect that sometimes she cannot decipher them. In contrast to Amy, Eve – who also at times speaks very directly to her mother ('You always complain about that') – feels that she has to be stubborn, and in that sense withhold herself and watch her mother care- fully. Amy's free-speaking with her Mom differs from Eve's sense of her mother's indirectness or persuasiveness. Eve's efforts to resist her mother's persuasiveness lead her initially to oppose her mother's choice of a school for her, even though Eve and her mother in fact prefer the same school for Eve. At eleven, Eve tracks this whole process.

The directness in speaking and the clarity about relationships, which we heard among girls at the edge of adolescence becomes complicated by voices which girls take in from their mothers, and which may reflect mothers' growing apprehension about what may happen to their daughters if they continue to speak and move freely in the world. Given her ability to articulate her feelings and thoughts, Amy – now twelve – provides an especially vivid illustration. Carol asks her,

'*What about a time when you wanted to say something but didn't say it?*'

'Probably when I'm mad at my sister, or something, because if I'm mad at her, and I say something that's going to be really mean, then my Mom will say, "Don't say that. She didn't do anything". And I'll just get in a big fight. So I'll think it to myself, and I'll wish that I could say things like that, but I won't.'

'*What would you have said, and what is a rude or mean thing to say?*'

'Just like "Leave", or "Go away", or something like that. When it's like she comes into my room and I'm trying to do homework or something, and my Mom's in there also, it's kind of hard to say that. So I usually don't. And then she'll probably leave. So I just wish I could ask her nicely instead of getting mad at her, but sometimes I just get mad.'

'*And say "leave".*'

'Yah.'

'*And then what happens? What happens when you say that?*'

'Then she'll go, "Fine"; she'll leave. And my Mom will say something like, "Amy, you didn't need to say that".'

'*And what do you think?*'

'I think that I probably should be able to say that, because everyone gets mad at everyone else, and if I'm not allowed to say that, I'm just going to keep on getting madder and madder and madder and madder and madder. And then I will just be madder all the time, and never ever, like, be nice to her.'

'*Do you say that to your mom or?*'

'No. Nah. I don't think she'd really understand. But I don't know why she wouldn't though.'

Amy's mother's efforts to teach Amy to hold back her impulse to say 'leave' to her little sister is protective both of Amy's sister and also of Amy in teaching her to express anger nicely and thus not offend other people. Yet Amy's psychological wisdom contrasts with her mother's intentions in pointing out that the effect of such protection in the end works against relationships. Feelings unexpressed build up to the point where they crowd out other feelings; if Amy cannot voice her anger without being mean or rude, then – as she astutely realizes – it will become increasingly difficult for her to be genuinely loving or nice.

Such dilemmas of relationship become common for mothers and daughters as girls reach adolescence, often calling the relationship deeply into question, including questions about what is really happening, and also what love means. Joan, who is thirteen, tells Annie about her relationship with her mother; they tease one another playfully, they trust one another, they agree that 'one of the most important things in our relationship is our trust', and they also lie to one another. Joan begins to experiment with dressing in ways that her mother calls 'too skimpy' and 'provocative', and although Joan really does not understand what these terms mean, she does begin to cover her clothing with sweaters at home, and then removes the sweaters when she gets to school. Annie asks,

'*But you wouldn't talk to her about that?*' Joan says,

'I mean I could, it's not something that I, I, I would feel like. I would be like, oh, no. Do I have to tell her about that? I would just rather not, you know. It's easier not to.'

In a writing exercise, Joan writes about her experience of her parents' giving her 'reason to discard [my] trust' in them:

'That trust is gone. It left the day my parents told me they were getting divorced, not that I didn't already know deep down, but I trusted too much to believe it.'

What becomes clear in retrospect is that while Joan was beginning to lie to her mother about what she was wearing, Joan's mother was not being honest with Joan about her problems in her marriage. Consequently, the discovery that her parents were going to divorce felt like a betrayal.

Our conversations with girls in the course of our project provided repeated examples of girls beginning to withhold their real thoughts and feelings from their mothers, and girls' realization that mothers also are withholding their real thoughts and feelings from them. This is the ultimate betrayal in that it breaks the kind of connection which girls want intensely with their mothers, and mothers want intensely with their daughters. The deepening emotions, as well as the increasing cognitive complexity of adolescence, make possible a different kind of relationship between mother and daughter, in part because the daughter is better able to feel and see into her mother's life. Girls' knowledge of relationships then raise difficult questions for women: what can women allow girls to know, what do women want to say to girls about their lives?

Some sense of what daughtering means to girls as they enter adolescence is evident in the conversations and letters which girls write in the course of an outing to a fine arts museum. Asked to converse with or write to one of the women in the paintings, Rachel says to one of the women: 'Hi, who are you?' The woman in the painting replies, 'I don't know'. Rachel continues, 'Why not?' The painting says, 'Because I wasn't painted as an individual'. Rachel asks, 'Who were you painted as?' And the woman answers, 'A mother'.

Nina, walking through the museum, lists the activities of women: 'holding baby, kissing men, being abducted, committing suicide, attacked by men, comforted by men, playing instruments, praying, wearing dresses, picking flowers, mothering, emotional, temptress, passive, crying'.

At the time the girls wrote these entries in their journals, they seemed to all appearances to be untroubled. This group of girls was experiencing extraordinary success in school, and seemed self-confident and in good relationship with others. In short, they seemed psychologically healthy, as if in some sense they were not affected by what they were taking in, as if in some sense they did not know what they were seeing and hearing, or did not draw out the implications of what they knew, or feel the feelings about women and mothers that were implied by what they had taken in.

MEANING LOVE AND KNOWING REALITY

In the second year of our weekly meetings with the girls who initially were nine and ten, they taught us two games. They insisted, really, that we play these games with them, in return for their willingness to do our writing and theatre exercises. The first game is 'Agony Tag'. One person is 'it' and begins voicing agony, moaning and screaming as she writhes on the floor toward others, who she tries to tag. Once tagged, others join her until everyone is in agony together – moaning and writhing on the floor. The second game is 'Killer'. One person designates the killer while everyone else closes their eyes. Then the game begins with everyone walking around in a circle, politely shaking hands and greeting one another with smiles. The killer, in shaking hands, using her trigger finger to tap gently on the other person's wrist. The rules of the game are that one cannot die instantly, but instead must greet another person before falling into a melodramatic death. The object of the game is to identify the killer – to discern beneath the surface of smiling faces and friendly voices which relationships are safe and which are fatal.

We reflected on these games which we were taught by ten and eleven-year-old girls, and were struck by the astuteness and aptness of their play. In agony tag, girls and women are with one another in giving voice to painful feelings; in killer, a lesson is taught in how to see beneath the surface of false relationships. Approaching the time when it becomes 'rude' or 'mean' to voice bad feelings, and where false relationships can become truly treacherous for young women, girls play at what they need to become practised in as women, and in the context of our weekly meetings, they drew us into these games with them. Girls desire women to be with them as they begin to see over the edge of their childhood, and take in what lies ahead for them as women in this world. Like Amy with her mother, they often wanted us simply to listen, not to advise. But by listening and taking in the resonances of girls' voices, we as women were stirred to remember ourselves as girls in the years just before adolescence. And to reframe our understanding of mothering and daughtering from this remembering.

In the second year of our work with the girls, who initially were eleven and twelve, the mothers asked to be involved. First they wanted to spend a day with us alone; then they wanted to spend a day with us and their daughters. There was a fear among the mothers that they would lose their daughters in adolescence: some remembered a break in their own connection with their mothers at this time. Some linked this break explicitly with sexuality, and a feeling of having to get out of their mother's house. One mother speaks of her discomfort in discovering evidence in her house of her daughter's sexual curiosity and knowledge.

The meaning of love between mothers and daughters, and also their knowing of reality, become the crux of trust and betrayal. It is much easier for mothers and other women to act on their love, and to accurately name 'reality' in relationships with little girls. The little girl's dependency renders her love a given for the woman, and also the little girl does not have the same emotional and cognitive capacity of the adolescent to see into and to name the realities of her mother's life.

In the years just before adolescence, girls often experience the giving way of relationships of their childhood, as mothers and other women tell them not to speak what they are feeling and thinking, and in some sense not to know what they know about the world. Girls who struggle to maintain their voices and resist taking themselves out of relationship, paradoxically for the sake of 'relationships', pose the deepest challenges to women, calling mothers in particular to reflect on what they experience as love and what they know to be true or real.

In the company of these daughters, women may be able to change the psychological and political social order by sustaining love and by naming reality in the face of powerful inducements to turn away from their daughters' most difficult questions. Mothering then means to mean love and to know reality with daughters. Daughtering means to hold mothers to this love and these truths. The ability of women to stay with one another in love and in reality is key to the transformation of society and culture, which is implicit in women's healthy psychological development. Within the confines of our project, the power of this joining was caught by poems that girls and women wrote together, alternating lines so that their feelings and thoughts interweave with one another. We end with excerpts from these poems:

> A white feather drifts, falls into
> a night filled with stars . . .
> My mother wanted to play
> agony tag with the chair.
> And she came to tell me . . .
> She wasn't so good at saying when she needed help
> So she worked all night
> And dreamed of pomegranates and thunder.
> And she came to tell me . . .
> Her daughter was a second self who knew too much
> I remember knowing someone who
> I dream about, laughing.
> And she came to tell me
> coming home, cold, I remember oatmeal in a steamy blue bowl
> and at night I dream of walking quietly through the snow
> with my mother, her eyes like friends
> and my daughter, full of laughter, craziness and energy.

NOTES

1 Through the formation of a Theater, Writing and Outing Club, bringing girls into connection with one another and with women at a critical time in their development, we created a context and activities designed to sustain girls' voices, their resistance and their courage into early adolescence.

2 See Gilligan, Rogers and Noel (1992) for a description of these two groups and of us, the women.

REFERENCES

Apter, T. (1990) *Altered lives: mothers and daughters during adolescence*. New York: St Martin's Press.

Breuer, J. and Freud, S. (1970) *Studies on hysteria*. New York: Basic Books. (Original work published 1895.)

Brown, L. (1989) *Narratives of relationship: the development of a care voice in girls ages 7 to 16*, unpublished doctoral dissertation, Harvard University, Graduate School of Education, Cambridge, MA.

Brown, L. and Gilligan, C. (in press) 'Meeting at the crossroads: women's psychology and girls' development'. *Feminism and Psychology*.

Deutsch, H. (1944) *Psychology of women, I*. New York: Grune & Stratton.

Freud, S. (1910) 'A special type of choice of object made by men'. In *Standard edition of the collected works of Sigmund Freud. 11*. London: Hogarth.

Freud, S. (1912) 'The universal tendency toward debasement in the sphere of love'. In *Standard edition of the collected works of Sigmund Freud. 11*. London: Hogarth.

Freud, S. (1918) 'The taboo of virginity'. In *Standard edition of the collected works of Sigmund Freud. 11*. London: Hogarth.

Gilligan, C. (1977) 'In a different voice: women's conceptions of self and of morality'. *Harvard Educational Review, 47*, 481–517.

Gilligan, C. (1982) *In a different voice: psychological theory and women's development*. Cambridge, MA: Harvard University Press.

Gilligan, C. (1990) 'Joining the resistance: psychology, politics, girls and women'. *Michigan Quarterly Review, 29*, 501–36.

Gilligan, C. (1991) 'Women's psychological development: implications for psychotherapy'. *Women and Therapy, 11*, 5–31.

Gilligan, C., Rogers, A. and Noel, N. (1992) 'Cartography of a lost time: women, girls and relationships', Paper presented at the Lilly Endowment Conference on youth and caring, Miami, FL.

Horney, K. (1926) 'The flight from womanhood'. *International Journal of Psychoanalysis, 7*, 324–39.

Jordan, J. (this volume) 'The relational self: a model of women's development'.

Josselson, R. (1987) *Finding herself: pathways to identity development in women*. San Francisco: Jossey-Bass.

Josselson, R. (1992) *The space between us: exploring the dimensions of human relationships*. San Francisco: Jossey-Bass.

Miller, J. (1976) *Toward a new psychology of women*. Boston: Beacon.

Rogers, A. (in press) 'Voice, play and a practice of ordinary courage in girls' and women's lives'. *Harvard Educational Review*.

Thompson, C. (1964) *Interpersonal psychoanalysis*. New York: Basic Books.

Chapter 15

The relational self
A model of women's development[1]

Judith Jordan

Clinical and developmental theories have generally emphasized the growth of an autonomous, individuated self. Increasing self-control, a sense of self as origin of action and intention, an increasing capacity to use abstract logic, and a movement toward self-sufficiency characterize the maturation of the ideal Western self. While most theorists have struggled with the issue of reification of the self, all have to some degree succumbed to the powerful pull to de-contextualize, abstract and spatialize this concept.

ESTABLISHED THEORY

Several biases have prominently shaped clinical–developmental theory about the self. Psychology as a discipline emulated Newtonian physics, seeking thus to be recognized as a bona fide 'hard' science rather than as an arm of philosophy, theology or other humanistic traditions. Newtonian physics posited discrete, separate entities existing in space and acting on each other in predictable and measurable ways. This easily led to a study of the self as a comparably bounded and contained 'molecular' entity, a notion most visibly supported by the existence of separate body-identities. It became very seductive to equate self with embodied person.

A further influence on theory-building about the self was provided by the social-political context in Western, democratic societies where the sanctity and freedom of the individual greatly overshadowed the compelling reality of the communal and deeply interdependent nature of human beings. In this societal paradigm, as represented particularly in the American culture, there is an imperative in socializing children to wean the 'helpless' and 'dependent' infant towards greater self-sufficiency and independence.

Major support for the 'separate self' model came from Freudian theory. Specifically, Freud's understanding of the psyche grew from a view of pathology in which the ego was seen as coming into being to protect the person from assaults both by internal impulses and external demands. Its relational function was obscured. Freud commented that, 'Protection against stimuli is an almost more important function for the living organism than reception of stimuli' (Freud, 1920:

27). Derivative psychoanalytic theories view the individual as growing from an undifferentiated, then embedded and symbiotic phase into an ultimately separate, individuated state (Mahler, Pine and Bergman, 1975).

Furthermore, Freudian theory stressed the power of innate instinctual forces and the development of increasing internal structure and freedom from dependence on others for gratification of needs. Relationships were seen as secondary to or deriving from the satisfaction of primary drives (e.g. hunger or sex). Intrapsychic development was seen as the ultimate area of interest; and 'self development' (or ego development) was seen as a process of internalization of resources from caretakers and others in order to create an increasingly unique, separate, self-sufficient structure: the self. Connotations of control, ownership of action, mastery over both impulses and outer reality abound in this model.

Pivotal to this individualistic picture of human beings is the pleasure principle (Freud, 1920; Jordan, 1987). Attainment of satisfaction, motivated by desire or need, is framed as the primary goal of behaviour and therefore shapes the self. In this tradition (both psychoanalytic and behaviourist) 'the self' is the personal history of gratifications and frustrations of desire and the projection of these into the future in the form of intention (Jordan, 1987). While disagreements with Freudian theory occurred as quickly as the theory was put forth (Sullivan, 1953; Erikson, 1963; Horney, 1926; Thompson, 1941), the dissenters never gained a hold on the cultural vision of 'Man' or on the imagination of clinical practitioners in the way that Freud's original ideas did.

The object relations theorists in Britain advanced our understanding of the centrality of relationships in human development. But they, unfortunately, were unable to free themselves of many of the core premises of Freudian psychology and continued to view the other person as 'object' to the subject, that is, defined by drive factors in the subject. Most recently in the clinical realm, Kohut has emphasized the ongoing need for relationships throughout life.

In a study both psychoanalytic and developmental, Daniel Stern has creatively delineated modes of 'being with the other'. Early patterns of differentiation and relatedness, in which mother and infant participate in a mutually regulated relationship, are traced in his work (Stern, 1986). Earlier, Trevarthan (1979) pointed to a 'primary intersubjectivity' in human development which is innate and unfolding.

A contextual/relational view of self also has much in common with the earlier work of the symbolic interactionists (Baldwin, 1897; Cooley, 1902; Mead, 1925) and resembles the existential approach in which the 'being-with-others' is stressed as fully as the concrete existence.

The change in emphasis involved in a relational point of view is comparable to what other theorists have described as a movement to dialectical schemata (Basseches, 1980). Piaget's model of adaptation, with accommodation and assimilation in an ever-shifting process of equilibration, is helpful in conceptualizing the changing, active, ongoing and interactive quality of a relational model of development.

RELATIONAL BEING

In the past decade an important impetus for shifting to a different paradigm of 'the self' in developmental–clinical theory has come from feminist psychologists who have been increasingly vocal and articulate about their dissatisfaction with existing models of female development and the 'female self'. Although not always explicitly stated, the adequacy of old models for describing male development is also questioned. Miller (1976), Chodorow (1978) and Gilligan (1982) are the most notable of the new wave of women challenging existing conceptualizations of women's development and personal organization. All note the male (phallo-centric) bias in clinical–developmental theory. Miller's work takes a broad psychological–cultural approach to the problem; she explicitly notes, 'As we have inherited it, the notion of "a self" does not appear to fit women's experience' (Miller, 1984: 1). More recently she has been drawing on clinical work to broaden and deepen her alternative perspective of 'being in relation'. Gilligan's ideas about the nature of female development derived from her awareness that prevailing theories of moral development (Kohlberg, 1976) were not applicable to women but were being used in such a way that women consistently appeared as defective or deficient moral selves. As Gilligan notes:

> The disparity between women's experience and the representation of human development, noted throughout the psychological literature, has generally been seen to signify a problem in women's development. Instead, the failure of women to fit existing models of human growth may point to a problem in the representation, a limitation in the conception of human condition, an omission of certain truths about life.
>
> (Gilligan, 1982: 1–2)

An important truth being omitted was the power of the ethic of caretaking and relationship in women's lives. Chodorow re-examined object relations theory and found that traditional theory failed to acknowledge the importance of the early and longer lasting bond between the girl and her mother. This bond leads to a different experience of boundaries and identity than that which the boy, as objectified other, experiences with mother.

What all of these theorists allude to, and seek to begin to correct, in psychological theory reflects an old tradition, captured in Aristotle's statement that: 'the female is a female by virtue of a certain lack of qualities; we should regard the female nature as afflicted with a natural defectiveness' (Sanday, 1988: 58). Very specifically, all of these theorists note the failure of previous theories of 'human development' to appreciate the relational nature of women's sense of themselves. Miller and Gilligan also explicitly or implicitly posit a more contextual, relational paradigm for the study of all self experience.

One perspective of the 'interacting sense of self', self-in-relation or relational self, is currently being developed at the Stone Center at Wellesley College (Miller, 1984; Jordan *et al.*, 1991). It builds on work by Miller (1976) and Gilligan (1982).

New relational theory of self, perhaps like the 'new physics' of quantum theory and uncertainty, emphasizes the contextual, approximate, responsive and process factors in experience. In short, it emphasizes relationship and connection. Rather than a primary perspective based on the formed and contained self, this model stresses the importance of the intersubjective, relationally emergent nature of human experience. While there is still a 'felt sense of self' which is acknowledged by this point of view, it is a 'self inseparable from a dynamic interaction' (Miller, 1984: 4), an 'interacting sense of self', (Miller, 1984). From this intersubjective perspective, the movement of relating, of mutual initiative and responsiveness are the ongoing central organizing dynamics in women's (but probably all people's) lives (Jordan, 1989). This goes beyond saying that women value relationships; we are suggesting that the deepest sense of one's being is continuously formed in connection with others and is inextricably tied to relational movement. The primary feature, rather than structure marked by separateness and autonomy, is increasing empathic responsiveness in the context of interpersonal mutuality.

EMPATHY

Empathy, the dynamic cognitive–affective process of joining with and understanding another's subjective experience, is central to this relational perspective (Jordan, 1984). Mutual empathy, characterized by the flow of empathic attunement between people, alters the traditional boundaries between subject and object and experientially alters the sense of separate self in a profound way. In true empathic exchange, each is both object and subject, mutually engaged in affecting and being affected, knowing and being known. In interpersonal language, in a mutually empathic relationship, each individual allows and assists the other in coming more fully into clarity, reality and relatedness; each shapes the other (Jordan, 1987).

Thus, in mutual empathic understanding the inner conviction of the 'separate self' is challenged. Descriptions of the empathic process refer to the 'sharing in and comprehending the momentary psychological state of another person' (Schafer, 1959: 345) or 'trial identification' (Fliess, 1942) that occurs during empathy. The boundaries as well as functional differences between subject and object, knower and known, cognitive and affective are altered in the process of empathy. As two people join in empathic subjectivity, the distinctions between 'subject' and 'object' blur; knower and known connect and join in mutual empathy. The other's subjective experience becomes as one's own; this is at the heart of 'relational being'. Action, creativity and intentionality occur within this context.

Empirical work on empathy demonstrates that in addition to cognitive awareness of another's inner subjective state, in empathic attunement, people resonate emotionally and physically with the other's experience (this mirroring physiological arousal is sometimes called vicarious affective arousal). Women typically demonstrate more emotional/physical resonance with others' affective arousal than do men (Hoffman, 1977). Also of note, is that one to two-day-old infants demonstrate distress cries to other infants' wails of distress; sex differences exist at that time as well, with girls showing more resonant distress (Simner, 1971; Sagi and Hoffman, 1976). The sex differences at this age are not easily explained and the greater import of this study is to suggest that intrinsic empathic responsiveness exists in all human beings. This is a simple, yet dramatic, example of the deep interconnectedness between people that 'separate self' theory overlooks. Not just at the level of goals, values and beliefs do women experience a sense of connected self but at the very concrete and compelling level of feelings and body experience. The study of the development of empathy, then, may provide a route to the delineation of relational development and intersubjective processes, slighted for so long in Western psychology.

THE QUESTION OF BOUNDARIES

In moving from a theory of separate self to a perspective of relational being, the question of how we experience and depict boundaries becomes very important. Our metaphors for 'being' are heavily spatialized. Thus the self is typically portrayed as existing in space, characterized by the 'possession' of various unique attributes (a particular organization of physical, cognitive, psychological and spiritual attributes), demarcated or bounded in some way (typified either by 'open boundaries' or 'closed boundaries') and interacting from a place of separation or containment with 'the world out there'. This is a profoundly decontextualized self. The emphasis on boundary functions as protecting and defining, rather than as meeting or communicating, reinforces especially the self as 'separate' entity rather than 'being' as a contextual, interactional process.

If self is conceived of as contextual and relational, with the capacity to form gratifying connections, with creative action becoming possible though connection, and a greater sense of clarity and confidence arising within relationship, others will be perceived as participating in relational growth in a particular way which contributes to the connected sense of self. In empathic resonance the person experiences, at a cognitive and physical level, the powerful sense of connection. Further, if mutuality prevails, not only will I be influenced, moved, changed by my context, and most importantly by my relational context, but I will also be shaping and participating in the development of others' 'selves'. This growth and movement is participatory and synergistic. This view of 'self with other' typifies much of the socialization towards caretaking and empowerment of others which occurs for females in Western cultures.

The way one conceptualizes one's 'place' in the world broadly affects interpretive, meaning-making, value-generating activity. If 'self' is conceived of as separate, alone, 'in control', personally achieving and mastering nature, others may tend to be perceived as potential competitors, dangerous intruders, or objects to be used for the self's enhancement. A system that defines the self as separate and hierarchically measurable is usually marked in Western cultures by power-based dominance patterns. In such systems the self-boundary serves as protection from the impinging surround and the need for connection with, relatedness to and contact with others is subjugated to the need to protect the separate self. Abstract logic is viewed as superior to more 'connected knowing' (Belenky *et al.*, 1986). Safety in a power-based society seems to demand solid boundaries; self disclosure is carefully monitored, lest knowledge about the inner experience be used against one. As caricatured in this way, this actually prescribes much of the socialization of Western males.

Hence, it should be no surprise that we find important differences between men's and women's experiences of boundaries. Women feel most themselves, most safe, most alive in connection, men . . . in separation (Pollack and Gilligan, 1982).

Chodorow gives one explanation for gender differences in the sense of identity *vis-à-vis* boundaries. She suggests that Western cultures allow a much longer pre-Oedipal period for the girl in which the immediate and close attachment and consequent identification with mother is uninterrupted for an extended time. The boy's experience is marked, on the other hand, by an abrupt interruption of the earliest identification with the mother and a shift of the identification to father when he discovers the 'defective', penis-less state of the mother and the superior power of the father. He is further treated as an object rather than as an identified-with subject by the mother. This difference in intrapsychic development, in Chodorow's opinion, leads to more 'permeable boundaries' in girls and a greater premium on separation and protection from other in boys. Lynn (1962) hypothesized that the nature of the identification process is quite different in boys and girls by virtue of the very different roles mothers and fathers traditionally play in raising children; i.e., mothers are present in an ongoing way while fathers are typically more absent. Thus, it is suggested, boys are left having to identify with an 'abstract role' rather than a specific, particular, interacting person. This dynamic, alone, would shed light on the greater contextuality of girls and the greater tendency toward abstracted and separate functioning of boys. I would also like to suggest that boys are actively socialized toward a power/dominance experience of selfhood, while girls are socialized toward a love/empathy mode of being in the world (Jordan, 1987). The former stresses discontinuity between self and other, decreased empathic resonance; the latter enhances the movement of mutual impact and growth. These two very different approaches to organizing 'self with other' experience also have far-reaching effects on every aspect of our lives, including the theories of self and science that we construct. Psychological theories of self, especially value-laden notions of the ideally functioning self, in turn broadly affect our experiences of ourselves. And they are saturated with gender bias.

BIAS IN SCIENCE AND LANGUAGE

Evelyn Fox Keller delineates what I think are the consequences of this bias in the realm of science, pointing out that there are two basic approaches in science: the Baconian model where knowledge leads to 'power over' nature and the Platonic approach where knowledge occurs through entering into the world of the studied

(Keller, 1985: 34). The former lauds the capacity to abstract and objectify, while the latter suggests a much more contextual orientation. The Baconian approach might be thought of as fitting the power/dominance mode which I suggest is the ruling ethic for Western male socialization. It leads to what Belenky *et al.* refer to as 'separate knowing'. In contrast, the Platonic model represents the empathic mode or 'connected knowing', encouraged in traditional female development.

In no science is the bias of the scientist about these issues more likely to affect the material she/he studies than in psychology. I would submit that we are at all times, even in the most rigorous empirical studies, trying to learn something about ourselves; at worst, we are trying to 'prove' something about or for ourselves. Our efforts at being objective are limited by our prejudices, needs and conditioning. The enterprise is fraught with contradiction. If we could accept this contradiction and acknowledge it, perhaps we could come a step closer to the complex flow of life. But I think psychology as an enterprise has suffered from a sense of shame about the limits on its 'objective powers' and therefore has become even more heavily invested in extolling the separation of subject and object, denying the subjective nature of its own being. This pressure can lead away from a study of human process as movement and mutual influence to celebration of the dualism implied in subject versus object and contributes heavily to the metaphor of 'separate self'. Belenky *et al.* point to the differences between knowledge and understanding, a difference which is familiar to clinicians. Knowledge 'implies separation from the object and mastery over it', while 'understanding involves intimacy and equality between self and object' (Belenky *et al.*, 1986: 101).

Unfortunately, the effort to transcend these biases often fails, particularly with language. Our language, so neatly split into discrete words, nouns and verbs, further makes discussion of this material almost impossible. The drift toward abstracted entities occurs again and again as I struggle with these ideas. Nevertheless, in shifting from a study of separate knowledge to connected knowing (Belenky *et al.*, 1986) or from 'self development' to 'relational development' (Jordan, 1989), we attempt to leave a language of structure and dualism for one of process. We look beyond the polarities of egoism versus altruism, self versus other.

Central to any discussion of self is the dilemma of process and structure. Our language does impose limits on our ability to delineate modes of being, to trace continuities of intention, memory, energy, and sensation; we quickly resort to reifications, making solid that which is fluid, changing and ongoing. One reason I prefer the term 'relational being' to 'relational self' or 'self-in-relation' is that it is purposely true to the process nature of experience. The ambiguity of the term 'being' (noun or verb, structure or process?) nicely captures the paradox of the process–structure interface. The experience of being 'real', central to the sense of self, then emerges in an ongoing relational context. The metaphor of 'voice' so often used to characterize the experience of self, is apt, for one's voice is vividly shaped by the quality of listening provided, whether with a real audience or an imagined one. Rather than seeing the individual as lacking personal integration if we posit a contextual, dialogic movement, however, we need to learn more about the constancies of these interpersonal interactions and the ways they shape our sense of ourselves. Study of relationality is needed to supplement intrapsychic investigation.

SUMMARY

From a relational perspective, human beings are seen as experiencing a primary need for connection and essential emotional joining. This need is served by empathy which in authentic relatedness is characterized by mutuality. Further, in relationships one comes to experience clarity about one's own experience and the other's, the capacity for creating meaningful action, an increased sense of vitality and capacity for further connection. Relational capabilities and processes exist from the time of birth and develop over the course of one's life.

In our culture there has been a split along gender lines between the ideal of a separate, autonomous, objective male self and a relational, connected and empathic female self. Notably, different values, motivational patterns, ways of knowing, moral systems, primary ways of organizing interpersonal experience and spheres of influence have been delineated by gender.

Scientific inquiry itself has been aimed toward 'objective truth', mastery over nature; as such it represents a masculine ideal. Despite the revelations of modern physics of the interpenetrability of all movement and structure, the myth, and possibly the arrogance, of this notion of impersonal, objective truth perseveres.

In psychology we must be very cautious with our language, for in naming, we give form. We shape areas of study; we eliminate others. What is needed is a move toward a psychology of relationship and exploration of intersubjective reality, expressed by a relational language which supports relational understanding. While we can most easily see the importance of this in the depiction of women's lives, the exploration of 'relational being' should not stop with women. A larger paradigm shift from the primacy of separate self to relational being must be considered in order to further our understanding of all human experience.

NOTES

1 Portions of this article have been published in: Jordan, J. (1991) 'The relational self: a new perspective of women's development''. In J. Strauss and G. Goethals (eds), *The self: interdisciplinary approaches*. New York: Springer Verlag.

REFERENCES

Baldwin, J. (1897) 'The self-conscious person'. In C. Gordon and K. Gergen (eds), *The self in social interaction* (1968) New York: John Wiley and Sons, Inc.

Basseches, M. (1980) 'Dialectical schemata: a framework for the empirical study of the development of dialectical thinking'. *Human Development, 23*, 400–21.

Belenky, M., Clinchy, B., Goldberger, N. and Mattuck, J. (1986) *Women's way of knowing: the development of self, voice, and mind*. New York: Basic Books.

Chodorow, N. (1978) *The reproduction of mothering. Psychoanalysis and the sociology of gender*. Berkeley: University of California Press.

Cooley, C.H. (1902) 'The social self: On the meanings of "I" '. In C. Gordon and K. Gergen (eds), *The self in social interaction* (1968). New York: John Wiley and Sons, Inc.

Erikson, E. (1963) *Childhood and society* (2nd edn). New York: Norton.

Fliess, R. (1942) 'The metapsychology of the analyst'. *Psychoanalytic Quarterly, 11*, 211–27.

Freud, S. (1920) 'Beyond the pleasure principle'. In *Standard edition of the collected works of Sigmund Freud. 18*. London: Hogarth.

Gilligan, C. (1982) *In a different voice*. Cambridge: Harvard University Press.

Hoffman, M. (1977) 'Sex differences in empathy and related behaviours'. *Psychological Bulletin, 84*, 712–22.

Horney, K. (1926) 'The flight from womanhood'. In H. Kelman (ed.), *Feminine Psychology* (1967). New York: Norton.

James, W. (1890) 'The self'. In C. Gordon and K. Gergen (eds), *The self in social interaction* (1968). New York: John Wiley and Sons, Inc.

Jordan, J. (1984) 'Empathy and self boundaries'. *Work in progress, 16*. Wellesley, MA: Stone Center for Developmental Services and Studies.

Jordan, J. (1987) 'Clarity in connection: empathic knowing, desire and sexuality'. *Work in progress, 29*. Wellesley, MA: Stone Center for Developmental Services and Studies.

Jordan, J. (1989) 'Relational development: therapeutic implications of empathy and shame'. *Work in progress, 39*. Wellesley, MA: Stone Center for Developmental Services and Studies.

Jordan, J. (in press) 'Relational development through empathy: therapeutic applications'. *Work in progress*. Wellesley, MA: Stone Center for Developmental Services and Studies.

Jordan, J., Kaplan, A., Miller, J.B., Stiver, I. and Surrey, J. (1991) *Women's growth in connection*. New York: Guilford.

Kaplan, A. (1984) 'The "self-in-relation": implications for depression in women'. *Work in Progress, 14*. Wellesley, MA: Stone Center for Developmental Services and Studies.

Keller, E. (1985) *Reflections on gender and science*. New Haven: Yale University Press.

Kohlberg, L. (1976) 'Moral stages and development: the cognitive developmental approach'. In T. Lickona (ed.), *Moral development and behaviour: theory, research and social issues*. New York: Holt, Rinehart and Winston.

Kohut, H. (1984) *How does analysis cure?* Chicago: University of Chicago Press.

Lynn, D. (1962) 'Sex role and parental identification'. *Child Development, 33*, 555–64.

Mahler, M.S., Pine, F. and Bergman, A. (1975) *The psychological birth of the human infant: symbiosis and individuation*. New York: Basic Books.

Mead, G.H. (1925) 'The genesis of the self'. In C. Gordon and K. Gergen (eds), *The self in social interaction* (1968). New York: John Wiley and Sons, Inc.

Miller, J.B. (1976) *Toward a new psychology of women*. Boston: Beacon Press.

Miller, J.B. (1984) 'The development of women's sense of self'. *Work in Progress, 12*. Wellesley, MA: Stone Center for Developmental Services and Studies.

Piaget, J. (1952) *The origins of intelligence in children*. New York: W.W. Norton.

Pollack, S. and Gilligan, C. (1982) 'Images of violence in thematic apperception test stories'. *Journal of Personality and Social Psychology, 42*, 159–67.

Sagi, A. and Hoffman, M. (1976) 'Empathic distress in newborns'. *Developmental Psychology, 12*, 175–6.

Sanday, P.R. (1988) 'The reproduction of patriarchy in feminist anthropology'. In M. Gergern (ed.), *Feminist thought and the structure of knowledge*. New York: New York Universities Press.

Schafer, R. (1959) 'Generative empathy in the treatment situation'. *Psychoanalytic Quarterly*, 28, 342–73.

Simner, M. (1971) 'Newborn's response to the cry of another infant'. *Developmental Psychology*, 5, 135–50.

Stern, D. (1986) *The interpersonal world of the infant*. New York: Basic Books.

Sullivan, H.S. (1953) *The interpersonal theory of psychiatry*. New York: Norton.

Thompson, C. (1941) 'Cultural processes in the psychology of women'. *Psychiatry*, 4, 331–9.

Tiryakian, E. (1968) 'The existential self and the person'. In C. Gordon and K. Gergen (eds), *The self in social interaction*. (1968). New York: John Wiley and Sons, Inc.

Trevarthan, C. (1979) 'Communication and co-operation in early infancy: a description of primary intersubjectivity'. In J.M. Bullower (ed.), *Before speech: the beginning of interpersonal communication*. New York: Cambridge University Press.

Chapter 16

Mothers and daughters revisited

Jane Flax

Women no doubt reproduce between them the peculiar, forgotten forms of close combat in which they engaged with their mothers. Complicity in the non-said, connivance in the unsayable, the wink of an eye, the tone of voice, the gesture, the colour, the smell: we live in such things, escapees from our identity cards and our names, loose in an ocean of detail, a data-bank of the unnameable. . . . In this weird feminine seesaw that swings 'me' out of the unnameable community of women into single combat with another woman, it is perturbing to say 'I'. . . . A piece of music whose so-called oriental civility is suddenly interrupted by acts of violence, murders, bloodbaths: isn't that what 'women's discourse' would be?

(Kristeva, 1985: 113–14)

PASSIONATE ATTACHMENTS

Recently one of my patients, a white, professional woman in her late twenties from a relatively wealthy and socially prominent family, arrived at her session in an agitated state. She told me the following story. The previous week she had dinner with a man from out of town whom she met on a business trip. After dinner (their first date), as they were walking away from the restaurant, he told her he had no place to stay in Washington and that it was too late to return home. She named several hotels in the immediate neighbourhood, but he pressured her to let him stay at her house. She demurred, saying it was not set up for overnight guests, and there was nowhere for him to sleep. He said he did not mind sleeping on the floor. They discussed this for about 10 minutes, and finally she agreed to let him stay with her. At her house they talked and watched TV for a while (both sitting on the bed). Early in the morning she was exhausted and said she wanted to go to sleep. She changed into a sweatshirt and pants and went under the covers to sleep. A short time later she awoke to find the man under the covers with her, his hand on her shoulder, sighing loudly. She took his hand away, but he returned it to her body, moving it down her thigh and continuing to sigh. Again she flung the hand off, but he returned it. Finally she yelled at him, 'what are you doing?', took a blanket, and went to sleep on the floor. He left early the next morning and later called her (although she did not return the call).

The patient was very upset. She felt the man took advantage of her, but she was also angry at herself for 'being nice' and avoiding conflict by letting him stay. She called her mother to discuss the incident, but before she finished telling her about the dinner, her mother (as the patient felt it) began to criticize her for not giving the man a chance. The mother claimed her daughter was too particular. There must be something wrong with her; she had dated so many men but had found no one she wanted to marry. When would the daughter settle down? The daughter then proceeded to tell the mother the rest of her story. The mother began to criticize her daughter again; this time for being incautious. How could she let a man she hardly knew into her house? What was she thinking of? How could her judgement be so poor?

The daughter felt furious and rejected by the mother; she could do nothing right, she would be condemned whether she gave the man a chance or not. Why couldn't her mother be sympathetic to her and her feelings of being intruded on and ashamed? Why couldn't her mother help her work out the regulation of distance, propriety and potential connections with men? What was her mother's agenda, other than wanting the daughter to be married? Why wasn't the daughter's professional success and power enough to please her? Was there something wrong with her, she asked me, in her handling of this situation, in her expectations of and response to her mother and in her relations with men?

The patient's questions confronted me with a dilemma. This story, I felt then, and even more on reflection, exemplifies many problematic aspects in the constitution of female subjectivity. These include sexuality, power, and relations between and fantasies about mothers and daughters. My patient hoped for several contradictory responses: empathy for her pain, anger and shame about the situation and her mother's replies; reassurance and restoration of her sense of self-worth and her capacity to love and be loved; permission to be a sexual being on her own terms; critical analysis of her behaviour and conflicts about the wishes evoked by her mother and her ambivalence about sexuality and relations with men.

The context of the questions for me included a three-year relationship with the patient in which we have discussed the lack of attunement between her parents and herself. This lack contributed to the patient's low sense of self-esteem and security. We have explored the competitiveness between her sister and herself for first place in the family and the patient's ambivalence about sexuality and aggression. I also have a feminist sensitivity to issues of power, gender and date rape and wish to avoid the culturally sanctioned tendency toward simplistic mother-blaming. With this patient, I have expressed my wish by trying to increase her empathy for the pressures on the mother and the mother's history of growing up with very traditional white middle-class expectations of women's place and marriage. In this mother's experience, tradition paid off with a marriage to a successful man, motherhood and a second career when the children were older. Yet I also have the psychoanalyst's suspicion of split off and denied feelings including envy, desire, ambivalence, ambition, investments in certain kinds of relationships and images of the self, maternity, and 'good' girls; and their effects on both mother and daughter.

I have also been influenced by our culture's fantasies of the good mother. My immediate response to the patient was to empathize with her pain about the lack of attunement in her mother's response. I connected it to the ongoing history of their relationship. My response to her question about what she wants from men was to highlight her need for a high level of emotional attunement in present relationships to repair the past. However, by focusing on this theme, I also avoided the daughter's rage which would have been evoked had I immediately suggested she look at her own behaviour and motives more critically.

What is gained and lost by focusing on relational (mother–daughter; therapist–patient) issues first? Does this perpetuate or reinforce certain feelings and wishes of the daughter? Did I, like the mother, shut off access to the daughter's knowledge or experience of her sexuality to preserve our dyadic relationship? Shouldn't I also encourage the autonomous expression of her sexuality and aggression? Am I encouraging her to shore up her identity as a blameless and attached daughter? By so readily assuming the role of the good mother, am I sustaining unrealistic and harmful fantasies of the perfectly attuned partner? How much frustration is necessary for the development of self-reflection and a realistic sense of agency?

In retrospect, I also wonder if I was doing the patient a disservice by withholding my questions about her ambivalence about sexuality, ambition, aggression and power. A feminist sensitivity to date rape and sexual politics is certainly warranted. The man had access to contacts extremely useful for the patient's business. Yet, aren't there some ambiguities necessarily conveyed in sharing a bed with someone? Don't women sometimes wish to exploit a certain seductiveness or sexual tension for their own purposes, despite or even because it can be used against them by men? Although women still suffer under male domination, can't sexual politics be played by both genders?

My feminist wish to have her understand (not blame) her mother and the historical forces operating on her when she expressed the hope of having her daughter married and the fear of the daughter's sexual vulnerability seems reasonable. Yet, did I foreclose exploration of or participate in replicating other, less admirable behaviours? For example, shouldn't we pay attention to mothers' roles in regulating the sexuality of their daughters? What about their envy in our youth oriented, heterosexist culture of the daughter's potential pleasures and attractiveness to men or of the existence of career options much less available to them twenty-five years ago? What about this daughter's envy of her mother's sexuality, of her powerful and absorbing attachment to the husband and her obvious pleasure in it; of her rage that the father and not she occupies central place in her mother's affections? Why does the daughter still turn to her mother to mediate her relations with men and resolve her quandaries about sexuality, guilt, aggression and autonomy? Why does she continue to hope her mother will change into a more satisfying partner for her?

WHOSE BODY IS IT ANYWAY?

My patient's story epitomizes the complex enmeshment of mothers and daughters in issues of subjectivity, embodiment and sexuality. Mothers, as Kristeva (1985) and Young (1990) point out, represent the impossible borders, the confounding of the dualities of Western culture. A pregnant woman is simultaneously nature and culture; self and other. A nursing mother is both food (biology) and care (nurturance); her substance is inner and outer. 'I'm in the milk and the milk's in me', sings a child in one of the stories I read to my son. The nursing mother's breast also transgresses the border between sexuality and maternity, between woman as the (man's) object of desire and as the mother of (his) children.

One strand of psychoanalytic thought, spun out of the work of Melanie Klein, stresses the centrality of the mother's body in the infant's fantasy life and development (Benjamin, 1988; Dinnerstein, 1976; Klein, 1975; Winnicott, 1975). Her body is literally our first home and often the first source of food as well. As infants, her smell, feel, voice and touch pervade our senses and provide a bounded sense of space within which security and continuity become possible. Yet this same being is also our tormentor. She is the source of denial and frustration as well as gratification. Maddeningly separate from us, she has resources we desire within her, to give or not as she chooses. The feeding breast comes and goes, sometimes out of sync with the rhythms of the child's hunger and need. Each of us lives inside our own skin and what is in mother is not necessarily accessible or available to the child. Thus for daughter or son, connection with mother is suffused with desire, aggression and ambivalence. Prebirth merger can never be restored. With each expression of desire or need we risk frustration, rejection or damage to the other. While the question, to whom does the mother's breast belong, is enigmatic, another is equally so. To whom does the nursling's mouth belong? It signals and experiences a need, yet its satisfaction resides in part in the body of an other. Hence the well-known overlap of food and love, of feeding and control, the manifold possibilities of 'eating disorders' and the disciplining of the body and its pleasures (Bordo, 1988; Bruch, 1978; Chernin, 1985; Moran, 1991; Orbach, 1986).

One of these pleasures we call 'sexuality' (Foucault, 1980; 1988a; 1988b). Unlike Freud, Foucault would claim these pleasures are never external to power (or civilization); power shapes their very 'nature' and their naming as such (Butler, 1990; Martin, 1988). What can appear as sexuality depends upon complex networks of disciplinary practices, of power circulating between (among others) mothers and children, men and women. Part of the painful interplay between mothers and daughters is the initial evoking of desire and then forbidding it. Mothers often participate in turning daughters into objects of desire for men, not for themselves and not for women or their children. As my patient's mother implied (and my patient, too, believes), something is wrong with a grown woman without a husband, a man with property in her person/sexuality. On the other hand, just as my patient did, many daughters turn to mothers for permission to be sexual and for information about how to do it properly. They still often learn that some (but not too much) sexual display and exchange is necessary to 'catch' a man.

THE VIRGIN MOTHER

What is missing from my patient's (and my) story? Feminists have provided powerful and persuasive accounts of the psychological, political and philosophical importance of mother–child relations and of their reverberations throughout our lives. This focus has encouraged feminists to analyse many of the patriarchal fantasies that underlie and engender the productions of Western culture (Brown, 1988; Harding and Hintikka, 1983; Pitkin, 1984; Spivack, 1989). We have also become more sensitive to the frequent displacement of fantasies from maternal to paternal sites, even within psychological theories (Flax, 1990: 73–88; Kahn, 1985) Our understanding of female subjectivity and human development is far richer and more complex.

Nonetheless, I have become increasingly disturbed by and suspicious of the maternal turn which has been so influential within feminist theory in the past 5 years. Deconstruction of the functions of maternal fantasies within feminist discourses has hardly begun (but see Abel, 1990; Chodorow and Contrattro, 1989; Klein, 1989; Stanton, 1989; Suleiman, 1985). In 1976, Dinnerstein suggested a myriad of possible paths to pursue. She brilliantly analyses the work fantasies about mothers do to relieve humans of a sense of responsibility and fallibility, of the limits of our powers, and the lack of coincidence between intent and outcomes. Yet, evidently even she underestimated the power, prevalence and persistence of these fantasies. They continue to reverberate throughout feminist discourses.

In the 1980s a curious dynamic emerges in feminist discourses: the more the maternal dimension of femininity is valorized (and homogenized), the more sexuality is disowned, deconstructed, projected outward or made an effect of the actions of others. Like all disowned material, these aspects of female subjectivity surface elsewhere; for example in the recent 'sexuality debates' among feminists (Freccero, 1990; de Lauretis, 1990; Valverde, 1989). Sexuality becomes a mark of the victimization of women (MacKinnon, 1982; 1983; 1987: 6–7) or diffused into symbiotic merger (Irigaray, 1985a; 1985b); agency is shifted to maternity, or nowhere (Ruddick, 1980; 1984; but see Ruddick 1987 for a partial reconsideration). Sexuality may be exploited, distorted and misshaped by patriarchal power and heterosexuality, but maternity is portrayed as a relatively free space for the constitution and expression of female virtue.

I am convinced this turn is neither accidental nor innocent. A series of questions has begun to trouble me. Why has the story of 'woman' become the story of mothers and daughters? Why have the conflicts, sacrifices and confinements of these relations receded or been obscured in a valorization of women's connectedness? Why have mothers become central agents in the constitution of subjectivity? What purposes are served by this framing of the story? What aspects of female subjectivity are repressed or denied in this retelling? Where are stories of paternal power and relations of domination among women? What else determines gender identity? What are the relationships between gender and female subjectivity? Do relations of gender make us what we are?

The construction of femininity within the circuit of mother/daughter provides a number of secondary gains. These include shielding the privilege of hetero-sexuality, reinforcing cultural prohibitions on women's aggression and wishes for separation, sustaining the split between sexuality and maternity, and obscuring the constituting effects of racism in white feminist discourses on these subjects.

Despite Rich's (1980) efforts, heterosexuality is protected and reinforced. Dominant images of maternity are desexualized. Sexuality recedes discretely into the background, it is nowhere to be found, for example, in Ruddick's (1980) des-cription of maternal practices. The conflation of woman/mother, however, carries with it a necessary horizon of heterosexuality, a lack of disturbance or questioning of how the mother got pregnant, an unquestioned assumption of a man/husband/father somewhere. In our current discourses, woman/mother often presumes or requires the simultaneous existence of two related dyads: child/mother; father/mother. Consider, for example, the curious term 'single' mother. How can a mother be single, since by definition she is a being in some relation to an other? Obviously she is 'single' because she 'lacks' a husband; she operates outside the normal rules of the Name of the Father. Maternity without paternity is a deviant form.

Desexualized maternity also implies a lack of desire directed at the child. In psychoanalytic accounts the child has desire for the mother, and much is made of the girl's enforced shift from maternal to paternal love object. Yet what of the mother's desire? How does it shift between child and (adult) lover? In our justified concern with child abuse, are we denying the erotic charge of maternity, the bodily intimacy and the pleasures of that kind of knowledge of an Other? Can the child not bear the idea that it exists as an object for the mother, as much as she exists for it? How does the daughter experience the father as a rival for the mother (not just the mother as a rival for him)? What images do daughters have of their mothers as sexual beings, of passionate attachments that exclude and may come before and outside of them? How do their mothers feel when daughters too develop their own erotic interests, outside the circuit of reproduction; when daughters do not intend to become mothers?

Female sexuality outside the circuit of reproduction (and hence relatedness) seems threatening to many women and men. Can men or women stand to be simply an object of women's desire, with sex as an end in itself, not suffered or entered into for its extrinsic reward (a baby, feeling close to you)? If women don't need babies, do they need men? This is part of the emotion stirred by abortion; that sex and motherhood are not intrinsically connected. 'What if your mother aborted you?' a bumper strip proclaims, revealing our terror not only of the maternal power over life and death, but also the (potential) power of women to refuse to be mothers, or to be in relation to others all the time.

What if your mother refuses her gaze, turns her attention elsewhere? Does not serve as your mirror, your nurturance, your ground of continuity of being or of the semiotic, fertile source of aesthetic meaning ungoverned by the Father's Law? If she is no longer outside, but inside, power, power not wielded as care, nurturance, preservative love, but as assertion, need or desire of her own? Or if she is off playing, with other women or men? Or in her own head? Can daughters stand to be cut off, outside the dyadic circuit? If their mothers don't need them to be women, do they need their mothers?

MOTHERS' WORK IS NEVER DONE: THE POLITICS OF MATERNAL FANTASIES

Daughters as well as sons have difficulties with and investments in managing the threatening content and unpredictable boundaries of embodiment, maternity, aggression and female sexuality. The daughter's conflicts, resentment and ambivalence about the mother's individuality, sexuality and power and the dyad's hostile feelings towards each other are often split off or repressed. Feelings such as envy, rage, and desire for control and suppression of difference are denied. Or these feelings are assigned predominance solely in the constitution and psychodynamics of masculine identities.

Such denial or displacement makes possible the simplistic claims that the gender-based continuity of identity between mother and daughter is relatively unproblematic or positive and that it wields a predominantly beneficial influence in the constitution of feminine subjectivity. Such continuity is especially important because it is said to provide a motive or ground for women's allegedly greater propensity for relatedness and connection. The powerful connections established through hate or envy are defined away as 'not genuine' forms of relatedness. The dangers, aggression and potential abuses of or within relationships are rarely acknowledged. Only after such repression has occurred can connection be represented as a relatively unproblematic good and as a basis for an alternative and implicitly superior subjectivity (Gilligan, 1982; Kittay and Meyers, 1987; Miller, 1976). Women are now to be praised for their greater immunity to 'bad' forms of individuality in which the non-relational aspects of the self are given priority over maintaining connections with an other. The costs and deformations of contemporary femininity, so powerfully named by early radical feminists such as Rubin (1975), recede from view in a celebration of the 'female' virtues of (a now sanitized) connection and care (Phelan, 1991).

The generative effects of relationships of power and domination are also rarely discussed, except in relation to masculinity. Feminists have barely begun to explore the mutually determining or constituting effects of maternity, sexuality, female subjectivity and one's racial and class identities (Abel, 1990; Smith, 1983; Williams, 1991). White feminists have paid too little attention to the ways race and class circulate through and stamp our discourses and choices of tropes, foregrounding certain images of femininity and marginalizing others. The predominance of abstract and non-situated maternal images serves to perpetuate white women's political innocence. We (white women) become complicit in the intersections of racism/sexism by not challenging the treatment of black mothers and by replicating purified images of white ones (nurturing, caring, empowering, ethical, etc.) (King, 1990; Spelman, 1988).

By denying our own pleasures and expressions of aggression, assertion and control, we represent ourselves as innocent victims outside circuits of power. As mothers, we are somehow universalized and freed from complicity in relations of domination; our participation in and marking by racism disappears. This desexualized and deracialized 'goodness' then becomes the basis of our ethical contribution to the public world. Desexualized white women can be 'purely' mothers, a status denied black women in captivity and then turned against them later (the black 'matriarch') (Collins, 1991; Davis, 1981; Dill, 1990; Lewis, 1990). Isn't it odd that white women are valorized for the very relation (nearly exclusive responsibility for the emotional care of their children) that is now declared to be the cause of innumerable ills in the black community?

This way of conceptualizing maternal practices also reinforces beliefs about sexuality and the dangers of the body/passion and mortality that are some of the most dubious aspects of contemporary white Western culture (Braidotti, 1989; Jagger and Bordo, 1989). Traditionally, white women are portrayed as pure/ superior, because unlike black women our sexuality is modest and constrained (Carby, 1985; Hall, 1983; Omolade, 1983; Simson, 1983). Racism serves both white men and women by locating active sexuality as alien to white women (especially higher-class ones; class operates similarly: the pure wife and the loose servant). How often is it acknowledged that white, middle-class women actively participate in the constitution and deployment of our sexuality; that we like sex (sometimes), even or purposely outside of a 'meaningful' relationship or the gaze of an (masculine or feminine) other? Absence of aggressive, self- generated, non-object related sexuality is a mark of her race/class. In contrast to the more wild and dangerous sexuality of black men and women, white women's sexuality can be more easily controlled and satisfied. White men can claim protection of its 'purity,' and this legitimates their control over other men (potential defilers).

Women's sexuality is inscribed as the property (or contested terrain) and effect of men. Men's identity is partially defined/expressed by their control over female sexuality. Property in women is an intrinsic aspect of the modern meanings of masculinity, hence the more women one has access to, the better man/person one is (Pateman, 1988). Unfortunately, this ideal of masculinity has a regulatory effect. As the characters in the recent Spike Lee movie, *Jungle Fever*, discuss, 'liberation' for black men is often taken to include control of 'his own' women and sexual access to white ones (see also Cleaver, 1968; Hooks, 1990; Walker, 1983: 278–331; Wallace, 1978). Unfortunately, this view has been too uncritically adopted by some feminists as well. Feminists such as MacKinnon treat it as an accurate description of pure fact rather than as a complex mix of wish and power, exercised in different ways and for many conscious and unconscious purposes by men and women.

GOD IS DEAD, LONG LIVE MOTHER?

> If it is true that an ethics for the modern age is no longer to be confused with
> morality, and if confronting the problem of ethics means not avoiding the
> embarrassing and inevitable issue of the law but instead bringing to the law
> flesh, language, and *jouissance*, then the reformulation of the ethical tradition
> requires the participation of women. Women imbued with the desire to
> reproduce (and to maintain stability); women ready to help our verbal species,
> afflicted as we are by the knowledge we are mortal, to bear up under the menace
> of death; mothers.
>
> (Kristeva, 1985: 117–18)

Maternal fantasies serve ontological as well as political purposes. Note the
slippage here, between women and mothers, reproduction and immortality; the
evasion of human finitude. If feminism succeeds in displacing the Name of the
Father, or God the Father and his traditional paternal functions, in whose Name
will it be done? Will we install a regnant Holy Mother, and thus protect/preserve
the possibility of innocence once more?

If women might say what they want of the maternal, it could be that we do not
want to confront its limits and ambiguities. Mothers and daughters are complicit
in evading our full, mutual disillusionment. Motherhood is a heterogeneous and
conflictual set of experiences, wishes, fantasies – some of which have nothing to
do with the child. Mothers may sometimes have an interest in preserving life
(Ruddick, 1980; 1984), but they cannot save the species or redeem our messy
worlds. Maternity is not an essence, nor does it exhaust categories of woman or the
feminine. Contemporary Western cultures glorify, denigrate and isolate this status.

Perhaps such thinking reveals the recurrence of certain infantile fantasies: only
I can satisfy the mother, she needs me (the child) to reach her unique being. Yet,
motherhood is not an exclusionary state, separate and clearly differentiated from
all others (Suleiman, 1985). Being a mother calls upon and evokes an
heterogeneous set of capacities and feelings within a multiple subjectivity. While
it might conflict with or require the temporary suspension of other capacities (as
do many other practices) it does not transport anyone into a unique form of being.
We go on hating, thinking, etc., as mothers and otherwise.

Daughterhood also is not the royal road to an understanding of woman,
subjectivity or gender, shaped as these are by heterogeneous forces whose relative
power is often undecidable in individual instances. It too is a status overdetermined
by race, class, geography, etc. (Lorde, 1984; Marshall, 1981). Daughterhood is not
the mirror image of motherhood; we will not exhaust its meanings by analysis of
maternity; nor is maternity its necessary end or destination. The daughter's desire
does not originate or terminate in her relation with her mother.

Stories about mother–daughter relations reveal the recurrent power of our
desire for a benign force or agent out there in the world looking out for us, attending
to our needs, and ensuring their satisfaction. These wishes form part of the
common ground upon which women and men form a community through

sustaining fantasies about (maternal) possibilities. Certain fantasies about mothers ward off profound anxieties and discontents from which our contemporary species often suffers. Such stories can only serve their functions by the simultaneous operation of denial, evasion and pushing other material to the margins, rendering contradictory aspects of maternity almost unspeakable. The existence of our wishes and the return of the repressed, with its undesired yet acted upon knowledge, situates maternity as an inevitable space of contention.

We long for knowable origins that connect to guaranteed ends (including the goodness of our purposes and agency), for a loving home (Martin and Mohanty, 1986); for a meaningful, purposive, orderly, continuous, stable, nurturing, friendly and comprehensible universe; for roots; for protection against the multiple contingencies that destabilize but enable us to live finite lives in humanly constituted worlds. We want to be caught and held securely in an idealized mother's gaze; we ask her to assure us that someone is really still there, to protect us and catch us when we fall. Finitude, evil, death: all can be transcended in the re-birth of the holy, innocent child/mother. We promise to be good daughters if mother won't abandon us. But whose voice can we really hear? An echo, a delusion, a fantasy of a childhood always already past and yet disabling us still.

REFERENCES

Abel, E. (1990) 'Race, class, and psychoanalysis? Opening questions'. In M. Hirsch and E.F. Keller (eds), Conflicts in feminism. New York: Routledge.
Benjamin, J. (1988) The bonds of love: psychoanalysis, feminism and the problem of domination. New York: Pantheon.
Bordo, S. (1988) 'Anorexia nervosa: psychopathology as the crystallization of culture'. In I. Diamond and L. Quinby (eds), Feminism & Foucault: reflections on resistance. Boston: Northeastern University Press.
Braidotti, R. (1989) 'The politics of ontological difference'. In T. Brennan (ed.), Between feminism & psychoanalysis. New York: Routledge.
Brown, W. (1988) Manhood and politics: a feminist reading in political theory. Totowa, NJ: Rowman & Littlefield.
Bruch, H. (1978) The golden cage: the enigma of anorexia nervosa. New York: Vintage.
Butler, J. (1990) Gender trouble: feminism and the subversion of identity. New York: Routledge.
Carby, H.V. (1985) 'On the threshold of women's era: lynching, empire, and sexuality in black feminist theory'. In H.L. Gates, Jr (ed.), 'Race', writing and difference. Chicago: University of Chicago Press.
Chernin, K. (1985) The hungry self: women, eating and identity. New York: Harper.
Chodorow, N. with Contratto, S. (1989) 'The fantasy of the perfect mother'. In N. Chodorow, Feminism and psychoanalytic theory. New Haven: Yale University Press.
Cleaver, E. (1968) Soul on ice. New York: Dell.
Collins, P.H. (1991) Black feminist thought. New York: Routledge.
Davis, A.Y. (1981) Women, race & class. New York: Random House.
de Lauretis, T. (1990) 'Upping the anti (sic) in feminist theory'. In M. Hirsch and E.F. Keller (eds), Conflicts in feminism. New York: Routledge.
Dill, B.T. (1990) 'The dialectics of black womanhood'. In M.R. Malson et al. (eds), Black women in America: social science perspectives. Chicago: University of Chicago Press.

Dinnerstein, D. (1976) *The mermaid and the minotaur: sexual arrangements and the human malaise*. New York: Harper & Row.

Flax, J. (1978) 'The conflict between nurturance and autonomy in mother–daughter relationships and in feminism'. *Feminist Studies*, 4, 171–89.

Flax, J. (1990) *Thinking fragments: Psychoanalysis, feminism and postmodernism in the contemporary West*. Berkeley: University of California Press.

Foucault, M. (1980) *The history of sexuality, Volume I: An introduction*. New York: Vintage.

Foucault, M. (1988a) 'The minimalist self'. In L.D. Kritzman (ed.), *Michel Foucault: politics, philosophy, culture*. New York: Routledge.

Foucault, M. (1988b) 'Power and sex'. In L.D. Kritzman (ed.), *Michel Foucault: politics, philosophy, culture*. New York: Routledge.

Freccero, C. (1990) 'Notes of a post-sex wars theorizer'. In M. Hirsch and E.F. Keller (eds), *Conflicts in feminism*. New York: Routledge.

Gilligan, C. (1982) *In a different voice: psychological theory and women's development*. Cambridge: Harvard University Press.

Hall, J.D. (1983) ' "The mind that burns in each body": women, rape, and racial violence'. In A. Snitow *et al.* (eds), *Powers of desire*. New York: Monthly Review Press.

Harding, S. and Hintikka, M. (eds) (1983) *Discovering reality: feminist perspectives on epistemology, metaphysics, methodology, and philosophy of science*. Boston: D. Reidel.

Hooks, B. (1990) *Yearning: race, gender, and cultural politics*. Boston: South End Press.

Irigaray, L. (1985a) 'This sex which is not one'. In L. Irigaray, *This sex which is not one*. Ithaca: Cornell University Press.

Irigaray, L. (1985b) 'When our lips speak together'. In L. Irigaray, *This sex which is not one*. Ithaca: Cornell University Press.

Jagger, A.M. and Bordo, S.R. (eds) (1989) *Gender/Body/Knowledge: feminist reconstructions of being and knowing*. Rutgers: Rutgers University Press.

Kahn, C. (1985) 'The hand that rocks the cradle: recent gender theories and their implications'. In S.N. Garner *et al.* (eds), *The (m)other tongue: essays in feminist psychoanalytic interpretation*. Ithaca: Cornell University Press.

King, D.K. (1990) 'Multiple jeopardy, multiple consciousness: the context of a black feminist ideology'. In M.R. Malson *et al.* (eds), *Black women in America: social science perspectives*. Chicago: University of Chicago Press.

Kittay, E.F. and Meyers, D.T. (eds) (1987) *Women and moral theory*. Totowa, NJ: Rowman & Littlefield.

Klein, M. (1975) *Love, guilt and reparation and other works 1921–1945*. New York: Delta.

Klein, H.M. (1989) 'Marxism, psychoanalysis, and mother nature'. *Feminist Studies*, 15, 255–78.

Kristeva, J. (1980) *Desire in language: a semiotic approach to literature and art*. New York: Columbia University Press.

Kristeva, J. (1985) 'Stabat Mater'. In S.R. Suleiman (ed.), *The female body in Western culture: contemporary perspectives*. Cambridge, Mass.: Harvard University Press.

Lewis, D. (1990) 'A response to inequality: black women, racism and sexism'. In M.R. Malson *et al.* (eds), *Black women in America: social science perspectives*. Chicago: University of Chicago Press.

Lorde, A. (1984) *Sister outsider*. Trumansburg, NY: Crossing Press.

MacKinnon, C. (1982) 'Feminism, marxism, method and the state: an agenda for theory'. *Signs*, 7, 515–44.

MacKinnon, C. (1983) 'Feminism, marxism, method and the state: toward feminist jurisprudence. *Signs*, 8, 635–58.

MacKinnon, C. (1987) *Feminism unmodified: discourse on life and law*. Cambridge, Mass.: Harvard University Press.

Marshall, P. (1981) *Brown girl, brownstones.* Old Westbury: Feminist Press.

Martin, B. (1988) 'Feminism, criticism, and Foucault'. In I. Diamond and L. Quinby (eds), *Feminism and Foucault: reflections on resistance.* Boston: Northeastern University Press.

Martin, B. and Mohanty, C.T. (1986) 'Feminist politics: what's home got to do with it?' In T. de Lauretis (ed.), *Feminist studies/critical studies.* Bloomington: Indiana University Press.

Miller, J.B. (1976) *Toward a new psychology of women.* Boston: Beacon.

Moran, P. (1991) 'Unholy meanings: maternity, creativity and orality in Katherine Mansfield'. *Feminist Studies, 17,* 105–26.

Omolade, B. (1983) 'Hearts of darkness'. In A. Snitow *et al.* (eds), *Powers of desire: the politics of sexuality.* New York: Monthly Review Press.

Orbach, S. (1986) *Hunger strike: the anorectic's struggle as a metaphor for our age.* New York: Avon.

Pateman, C. (1988) *The sexual contract.* Stanford: Stanford University Press.

Phelan, S. (1991) 'Feminism and individualism'. *Women and Politics, 10,* 1–18.

Pitkin, H.F. (1984) *Fortune is a woman: gender & politics in the thought of Niccolo Machiavelli.* Berkeley: University of California Press.

Rich, A. (1980) 'Compulsory heterosexuality and lesbian existence'. *Signs, 5,* 515–44.

Rubin, G. (1975) 'The traffic in women: notes on the "political economy" of sex'. In R.R. Reiter (ed.), *Toward an anthropology of women.* New York: Monthly Review Press.

Ruddick, S. (1980) 'Maternal thinking'. *Feminist Studies, 6,* 342–67.

Ruddick, S. (1984) 'Preservative love and military destruction: some reflections on mothering and peace'. In J. Treblicot (ed.), *Mothering: essays in feminist theory.* Totowa, NJ: Rowman & Allanheld.

Ruddick, S. (1987) 'Remarks on the sexual politics of reason'. In E.F. Kittay and D.T. Meyers (eds), *Women and moral theory.* Totowa, NJ: Rowman and Allanheld.

Simson, R. (1983) 'The Afro-American female: historical context of the construction of sexual identity'. In A. Snitow *et al.* (eds), *Powers of desire: the politics of sexuality.* New York: Monthly Review Press.

Smith, B. (1983) 'Introduction'. In B. Smith (ed.), *Home girls: a black feminist anthology.* New York: Kitchen Table Press.

Spelman, E. (1988) *Inessential woman: problems of exclusion in feminist thought.* Boston: Beacon Press.

Spivack, G.C. (1989) 'Feminism and deconstruction again: negotiating with unacknowledged masculinism'. In T. Brennan (ed.), *Between feminism & psychoanalysis.* New York: Routledge.

Stanton, D.C. (1989) 'Difference on trial: a critique of the maternal metaphor in Cixous, Irigaray, and Kristeva'. In J. Allen and I.M. Young (eds), *The thinking muse: feminism and modern French philosophy.* Bloomington: Indiana University Press.

Suleiman, S.R. (1985) 'Writing and motherhood'. In S.N. Garner *et al.* (eds), *The (m)other tongue: essays in feminist psychoanalytic interpretation.* Ithaca: Cornell University Press.

Valverde, M. (1989) 'Beyond gender dangers and private pleasures: theory and ethics in the sex debates. *Feminist Studies, 15,* 237–54.

Walker, A. (1983) *In search of our mother's gardens: womanist prose.* New York: Harcourt Brace Jovanovich.

Wallace, M. (1978) *Black macho & the myth of the super-woman.* New York: Dial.

Williams, P.J. (1991) *The alchemy of race and rights.* Cambridge: Harvard University Press.

Winnicott, D.W. (1975) *Through paediatrics to psycho-analysis.* New York: Basic Books.

Young, I.M. (1990) 'Breasted experience: the look and the feeling'. In I.M. Young, *Throwing like a girl and other essays in feminist philosophy and social theory.* Indianapolis: Indiana University Press.

Part IV
Review and prospects

Chapter 17

Beyond daughtering and mothering

Janneke van Mens-Verhulst

This book is intended to advance the theorizing on mothering and daughtering, and to add a motherly point of view to the already available daughterly and outsiders' views. No definitive solutions will emerge from the pages of this volume – are these actually possible? However, the taboo on female subjectivity has been removed, and an enriched view of the development of female subjectivity is offered. New directions for theorizing are revealed, including a revision of mother–daughter relationships and the contexts in which they are situated.

FEMALE SUBJECTIVITY

Daughters start to construct their female subjectivity in a state of infantile dependency. Therefore, there is no doubt that early carers, i.e. mothers, have great influence on their development. In addition, however, Flaake, De Waal and Gilligan stress the importance of adolescence for the development of female subjectivity. They describe the disciplining as well as the supporting functions that are assumed by adult women in 'mothering' or educating positions.

The idea that bodily awareness and sexuality of women need to be 'awakened' by a father is considered passé in this volume. Flax, for example, is rather outspoken in claiming a female drive for sexuality, independent of 'objects' such as fathers or mothers. Other authors, for example Flaake and Lykke, focus on the mother as the person positioned for channelling initial sexual perceptions and bodily images of girls. Female subjectivity is perceived as encompassing the female body and the sexual desires and erotic feelings of women. Daughters are also conceived as 'daughtering', i.e actively forming their female identity in interaction with older, and more powerful people, instead of receiving it passively.

Mothers, either real or symbolic, are involved in their own struggle to become acknowledged as a female subject. Their problems play a role at several levels. As can be learned from Leira, they must take a stand in relation to the symbolic position that is charged with cultural myths on authority and love, and embedded in social regulations and arrangements, such as marriage. In addition, as de Kanter shows, mothers must evolve their personal social position, composed of a defined range and degree of participation in societal structures. On top of that, they have to deal with the needs of real, living children who have to be nurtured, cared for and disciplined. In that capacity, they are directly confronted with childlike fantasies centred on omnipotence and powerlessness, as Sayers points out. It may be concluded then that 'mothering' implies not only caring and nurturing activities, but also requires specific efforts if the mother is to remain a subject, to grow as a subject and to maintain or conquer space for this personal development. The work of Krips and Orbach and Eichenbaum show that a great deal of therapeutic effort may be required to overcome the taboos on motherly subjectivity.

When the efforts required from mothers and daughters to become female subjects are compared, it is clear that daughters have to accomplish a double task. In constructing their own subjectivity, they must also learn to accept 'the woman' in the mother, and to acknowledge her subjectivity while separating or differentiating from her. Besides this, their separation from – and connection to according to the relational paradigm – the mother encompasses three levels: a symbolic or cultural level, a level of social structures and a personal level. Therefore, the heterogeneity and complexity of feelings involved here is not astonishing.

Psychotherapy surfaces as an extra opportunity to realize female subjectivity if the process of subject development has been frustrated or is threatened in some way. As it would be beyond the scope of this chapter to give a detailed summary of the similarities and dissimilarities between practices, a brief outline will have to suffice. Orbach and Eichenbaum typify their female clients as women who need to be 'remothered'. As a consequence, they characterize their own contribution as developing from a motherly 'object position' to a motherly 'subject position', thus offering their clients a 'sparring partner' for their developmental struggle. In contrast, Surrey portrays her female clients as women who experience relational knots and alienation from their relational being, and who must learn to 'grow into connection' in all their relationships, but often with their mothers especially. As a therapist, she offers them insight in the socio-cultural backgrounds of their alienation, and especially the estrangement from their mothers. She stimulates them to accept the limits of their relationships with their mothers, without sacrificing the validity of their needs for healthy connections.

MOTHER–DAUGHTER RELATIONSHIPS

Most psychological theories, but especially that of the psychonalytic narrative, portray the relationship between mother and daughter as symbiotic. As a consequence, the mother–child connection has to be opened up at some point in order to provide the daughter with the opportunity to establish a relationship with the social context, and become an autonomous subject. In the past, the 'father', whether real or symbolic, appeared the obvious candidate to fulfil the intervening function. His advantage was his anatomical dissimilarity and his 'external' position. Time of intervention was located in the Oedipal phase, i.e. third or fourth year of a girl's life.

In contrast, the symbiotic relationship is exposed here as a construction rather than a biological fact (see for example Groen). The alternatives offered differ in their revolutionary spirit. On the one hand, de Kanter submits that the social context functions as an intervening and splitting force in itself, and points out that mothers may be intercedents because they occupy a social position themselves. On the other hand, the adherents of the relational paradigm (Surrey, Jordan, Gilligan and Rogers) introduce an alternative for the model of a symbiotic relationship with 'naturally' closed boundaries that must be interrupted by external forces. Their model comprises dynamic boundaries: to some extent shifting and permeable.

In general, the mother–daughter relationship is reconstructed as a space in which daughters and mothers both (have to) struggle for their subjectivity, also in matters of the body, eroticism and sexuality. This struggle involves separation and attachment, differentiation and acknowledgement, mutual regulation, dependency and interdependency. In short, it is a process not only of establishing boundaries, but also of orchestrating their opening and closing. Obviously, the process covers the whole range of human feelings, positive as well as negative. Moreover, daughtering and mothering are understood as never-ending processes of 'growing' female subjectivity. Early childhood and adolescence have been recognized as very remarkable periods in this development, but clearly there are no logical or practical reasons for the assumption that the process stops there. Nor are there grounds to believe that the process always implies progress.

Most theories on mother–daughter relationships do not incorporate attention to generational shifts. The presumption seems to be that each relationship can be considered as a re-run of preceding mother–daughter relationships. This is an ahistorical approach, however, that may easily obscure the real and important differences between generations, and the change stemming from them. An inspiring model to avoid this pitfall, and to trace generational shifts in mother–daughter relationships is presented by Bjerrum Nielsen and Rudberg. They make a distinction between gendered subjectivity, gender identity and cultural/social opportunities. In their view, change is produced by the lack of contemporaneity between those three components, and the accompanying matching tensions (forms of uncontemporaneity) experienced by successive generations. Obviously, the model invites further elaboration, and exploration of socio-cultural contexts.

SOCIO-CULTURAL CONTEXTS

The concept of patriarchy fulfils an explanatory function in this theorizing on daughtering and mothering. However, 'patriarchy' as a phenomenon remains fairly abstract throughout this volume. Indications mentioned here are: classical psychoanalytic theories, fairy tales, images of women as good girls, assumptions on heterosexuality and motherhood as women's supreme state. Its negative consequences are characterized as the objectification of women and the impediments to a mutually satisfying relationship between daughters and mothers. In this volume, the functioning of patriarchy is localized primarily in individual contextual agents, particularly fathers, schoolteachers and therapists, whereas brothers, sons, male or female partners, sisters and grandmothers are almost absent. Societal agents, such as class, ethnic and racial communities, are rarely mentioned, and legal and religious communities are not mentioned at all. Indeed, one can ask if this selection is legitimate or sensible from both a scientific and a practical and professional point of view. Actually, theorizing on patriarchal contexts requires a more profound analysis (see e.g. Walby, 1990). One-dimensional reductions especially should be avoided.

Meanwhile, critical analyses of the role women play in perpetuating existing, 'patriarchal' social structure(s) and culture(s) have become available. For example, mothers regulate the physical and intellectual dependencies and independencies of their daughters in accordance with the norms of their class (Walkerdine, 1985). Moreover, female teachers encourage their female pupils to be passive, hard working, helpful and obedient, but at the same time pathologize the behaviour of these schoolgirls by contrasting it with the qualities of 'real' children – who should be active and enquiring (Walkerdine, 1986). In addition, Gilligan (1991) and Gilligan and Rogers (this volume) point out that adult women (mothers and substitute mothers, such as teachers) are complicit in silencing adolescent girls. Moreover, Western white middle-class women maintain an image of innocence, while tolerating an inferior and deviant image of working-class and black women (Flax, this volume; Groen, this volume; Walkerdine, 1985). As Flax observes, women themselves reinforce 'patriarchal' myths on motherhood and mother–daughter relationships, and she offers two hypotheses to explain this phenomenon. First, it spares them the mutual disillusionment that motherhood is a heterogeneous and conflicting set of experiences, wishes, fantasies – some of which have nothing to do with children. Furthermore, it helps them to maintain the goddess image women and men both need to conquer 'their anxieties and discontents from which our contemporary species often suffers'.

All in all, it must be concluded that female subjectivity is not all there is, and that it is definitely not only produced in mother–daughter relationships. First, female subjectivity may be seen as a – more or less important – part of the multiple subjectivity women (and men) develop. Second, this femaleness may be partly constructed in the mother–daughter relationships, but this is not the only relevant or influential context. It is also constructed in other relationships – between women, and between men and women. Therefore, the daughtering–mothering scope is too narrow an approach for understanding the development of female subjectivity, certainly in the long term.

A more differentiated and systematic approach to the wider, and also gendered, context must be recommended. Actually, it will not be enough to distinguish separate contextual dimensions. It will be necessary to relate these mutually and to construct cohorts of historical, economical, educational, legal, geographical, religious and ethnically defined conditions. As such, cohorts will be different for almost all countries, so their construction can only be accomplished by abstaining from pretensions to universality.

MOTHERING AND DAUGHTERING PATTERNS IN TRANSFORMATION

So far, it has become clear that stereotypes on mothering and daughtering are no longer valid – if they ever were. They may even become impediments; not only in the reality as experienced by women, but also in the efforts to think about change and transformation of old mother–daughter patterns.

The favoured option for 'liberated women' has been to leave the mother–daughter archetype behind and to construct new images and live new realities/conditions, based on egalitarian options. Yet, by trying to ignore societal arrangements or to change them, reality reveals itself. Not only the 'patriarchal' patterns in the domains of sexuality, violence, household, employment, state and culture appear to be sources of resistance to change, but also intrapsychic patterns in women – and men. These patterns even appear to reinforce each other, and to sustain the continuation of other racial and class inequalities. The question remains how to stimulate the defrosting of existing 'frozen' patterns. The analyses in this book reveal what myths, fantasies and desires are part of the intrapsychic patterns, and how they are projected on to mothers, thus putting an impossible burden upon them. They also offer insights into the social indispensability of the values mothers are made responsible for. As already pointed out in the general introduction, these issues bear pertinence not only to parenting situations, but also to teaching and management arrangements.

An alternative for the individual egalitarian option has been to experiment with reshuffling and alternating the roles of caring and being cared for. It implies a lot of personal and interpersonal struggling, mostly hidden from the outer world until the arrangements stop working, and the participants give up. While exploring their psychic flexibility in caring, the participants may become frustrated by the gradual revelation of missing temporal, economic and moral conditions. Altogether, the points raised in this volume help understanding of the current limitations of the egalitarian option. The acquired awareness of the magic meaning of motherhood may be deployed strategically, in public and private debates on caring responsibilities and activities.

In fact, what is at stake is a new synthesizing of caring responsibilities in society. In the proliferation of sexual division of labour, these responsibilities have apparently been divided too much, as if biology offers the final norm or directive. And yet, this socio-cultural project is not an unrealistic one. After all, Western culture has been characterized by the ambition to overcome biology and nature for at least five centuries. In addition, the disappearance of general frames of meaning attribution in our culture creates space for small-scale experiments, albeit more for men than for women. What is more, a lot of relevant individual experiments are already ongoing, as we noted earlier. However, they remain almost invisible within the mass of mainstream arrangements. According to chaos theory (Gleick, 1987; Prigogine and Stengers, 1984; van Dijkum and de Tombe, 1992), all those individual streams and struggles, movements and transformations may intensify in quantity, and by consequence in quality, and may ultimately break through the dominant structures and transform these into a new constellation of fresh arrangements. In this 'chaotic' scenario, the 'time' factor is an almost hidden but essential helper; but time should span several generations at least.

At the same time, a debate is ongoing on the boundaries of Western culture; its emphasis on values of rationality and objectivity, technical solutions and the socio-economical principles of capitalism. 'Mothers' seem to embody and transcend the boundaries of this culture. By their very existence, they undermine the modern myth of individual liberty and symbolize human liability to social and psychological 'taxation'. Therefore, women – as insiders – may have a special (daughterly and motherly) access to some of the processes involved. For example, to the question of what makes human life worth living – an issue unjustifiably exiled to the private domain (van Asperen, 1992). Women can choose, particularly in their professional qualities, to explore these processes and provide food for the cultural self-reflections that are ongoing. An example is embodied in this book, with its analyses of daughtering and mothering, and of the possibilities and impossibilities, obstacles and opportunities to go beyond traditional patterns.

REFERENCES

Asperen, T. van (1992) 'De mythe van het onbegrensde zelf'. *Humanist*, 14–19.
Brown, L.S. (1990) 'The meaning of a multicultural perspective for theory-building in feminist therapy'. *Women & Therapy*, 1–21.
Dijkum, C. van and de Tombe, D. (1992) *Gamma Chaos*. Bloemendaal, the Netherlands: Aramith.
Gilligan, C. (1991) 'Joining the resistance: psychology, politics, girls and women'. *Michigan Quarterly Review, XXIX*: 501–36.
Gleick, J. (1987) *Chaos: Making a New Science*. New York: Viking.
Phoenix, A. and Woollett, A. (1991) 'Motherhood: social construction, politics and psychology'. In A. Phoenix, A. Woollett and E. Lloyd (eds), *Motherhood: meanings, practices and ideologies*. London: Sage.
Prigogine, I. and Stengers, I. (1984) *Order out of chaos*. New York: Random House.
Walby, S. (1990) *Theorizing Patriarchy*. Oxford: Blackwell.
Walkerdine, V. (1985) 'On the regulation of speaking and silence: subjectivity, class and gender in contemporary schooling'. In C. Steedman, C. Urwin and V. Walkerdine (eds), *Language, gender and childhood*. London: Routledge.
Walkerdine, V. (1986) 'Post-structuralist theory and everyday social practices: the family and the school'. In S. Wilkinson (ed.), *Feminist social psychology: developing theory and practice*. Milton Keynes: Open University Press.
Woollett, A. and Phoenix, A. (1991) 'Psychological views of mothering'. In A. Phoenix, A. Woollett and E. Lloyd (eds), *Motherhood: meanings, practices and ideologies*. London: Sage.

Name index

Regt, A. de 36
Rich, A. 58–9, 100, 103–4
Rogers, A. 109, 125–34, 162
Rubin, G. 151
Rudberg, M. 5, 6, 44–53, 161
Ruddick, S. 150

Sayers, J. 60, 62–9, 160
Schmauch, U. 8–9
Schreurs, K. 3–6
Smith, J. 115
Stern, D. 8, 77, 119, 136
Stiver, I. 114
Stolorow, R.D. 77

Surrey, J. 109, 114–24, 160
Swaan, A. de 35–6, 39

Torok, M. 10
Trevarthan, C. 136

Waal, M. de 5–6, 35–43, 159
Waldeck, R. 9
Walkerdine, V. 30–1, 46–7, 49, 53
Winnicott, D.W. 73–4, 78
Woertman, L. 57–61

Young, I.M. 148

Ziehe, T. 49

Subject index